Look

Forward

to It

Also by Stephen Elliott

NOVELS

Happy Baby
What It Means to Love You
A Life Without Consequences
Jones Inn

EDITOR

Politically Inspired

Looking Forward to It

Or,

How I
Learned to
Stop Worrying
and
Love the American
Electoral Process

Stephen Elliott

PICADOR

NEW YORK

www.picadorusa.com

Picador® is a U.S. registered trademark and is used by St. Martin's Press under license from Pan Books Limited.

For information on Picador Reading Group Guides, as well as ordering, please contact the Trade Marketing department at St. Martin's Press.
Phone: 1-800-221-7945 extension 763
Fax: 212-677-7456
E-mail: trademarketing@stmartins.com

Library of Congress Cataloging-in-Publication Data

Elliott, Stephen, 1971–
    Looking forward to it, or, How I learned to stop worrying and love the American electoral process / by Stephen Elliott.—1st Picador ed.
        p. cm.
    ISBN 0-312-42415-9
    EAN 978-0312-42415-2
    1. Presidents—United States—Election—2004.   2. Presidential candidates—United States.   3. Political campaigns—United States.
4. United States—Politics and government—2001–   5. Elliott, Stephen, 1971—Travel—United States.   6. United States—Description and travel.
I. Title: Looking forward to it.   II. Title: How I learned to stop worrying and love the American electoral process.   III. Title.

E905.E45 2004
324.973'0931—dc22

                                                                2004053498

First Edition: October 2004

10   9   8   7   6   5   4   3   2   1

Contents

II. LET ALL KNOW WHO WOULD ENTER HERE

III. THE EARLY STATE

IOWA

Looking Forward to It

1. Looking Forward to It

> A nation is a group of people united by a mistaken view about the
> past and a hatred of their neighbors.
> —ERNEST RENAN

July 2–3

No Time for Explanations; Cedar Rapids, Iowa City, Washington; Daven-
port; Cedar Rapids, Car Politics

It's been a long, boring summer and it's only July. July 2003, to be
exact, nearly a year and a half before two people you would never
invite over to dinner, and probably wouldn't want to live in your
town, will come head to head in the 2004 presidential election.

The weather never changes in San Francisco, it's always sweater
weather, never cold enough for a coat, and for the past two months

I've been dating Wilhelmina, a demon woman down in San Leandro who eats at places like Applebee's and swears if I ever write anything about her I'll be sorry.[1] She's already cut me four times with a scalpel. When things started to go bad between us, after she nearly tore my rotator cuff at 10:30 on a Saturday morning, I told her I was running off to join the campaign trail early. She said I'd be back. She didn't even question why someone would get on the trail a year and a half before the election. Just a couple of weeks ago she had told me that I better not cheat on her, but then followed it by saying she knew I wouldn't anyway. She said I wanted her to be angry, but she wasn't going to indulge me in that.

I *could* write about politics from my studio in San Francisco, but San Francisco doesn't matter when it comes to the big game. Whatever washed over San Francisco forty years ago, back when they were running naked in Golden Gate Park and killing people at Rolling Stones concerts and getting Clean for Gene, has left a residue of gray political impotence, a city so far Left it has ceased to exist. *San Francisco liberals*, they call them. In political circles it's the worst thing someone can say. It means you don't matter, you're worthless, you're dog shit, get out of my way. The country doesn't care what San Francisco thinks. No, I need to go where the action is, the fertile plain, the glistening bio-diesel stalks of Iowa, the libertarian hills of New Hampshire.

I meet my photographer, Stefan, at Eastern Iowa Airport, and we pick up an Enterprise economy and beeline to the University of Iowa, home of the Hawkeyes. Howard Dean is scheduled to speak at seven P.M.

"Do you think he has a chance?" Stefan asks me. He's more of a realist than I am. We met in Israel, where I was spending time with rock-throwing children, putting together an article for a magazine nobody's ever heard of. Stefan was on the other side of the line taking pictures of settlers for *The Washington Post*. Stefan's smiling a little because he lives in Washington, D.C., and probably already knows how all of this is going to turn out. What he doesn't know is that I'm writing for a magazine that doesn't carry photographs.

"What do I know about winners," I tell him. "I haven't voted for a winner since I started voting, which wasn't as long ago as it should be."

When Howard Dean comes into the small room with the low ceiling on the third floor of Memorial Hall, the students who are still in school for the summer let out a mad cheer. The room is packed with close to two hundred supporters. Dean is a small man with a long torso and a square head. He walks in smiling and shaking hands. I shake his hand and tell him I'm going to be shadowing him for the next eight days. I say I'm writing for GQ, which is a lie, but I can't help it.[2] "Oh, good," he says. "I'm looking forward to it." I'm not sure what he means. Then he goes on to the next person. He seems a little uncomfortable, a little surprised, a little too short to be a professional quarterback. Why do I keep thinking of Doug Flutie? Throw the long ball, Doug!

This is the first time I hear Dean talk on his big topics: the budget (Republicans don't know how to handle money or balance the budget), universal health care (for people up to age twenty-three), services instead of tax cuts, foreign policy (we need a foreign policy that is consistent with American values), education (more), Dean Core (volunteers representing in blue "Dean" shirts while working for Habitat for Humanity). If you've ever followed a politician, you know how amazing it is that he's saying what he's saying. That is, when he says, "We need a foreign policy that is consistent with American values," most politicians stop there. But Dean continues. He says we shouldn't have invaded Iraq and we should be in Liberia. But most people don't listen that closely when politicians talk, so they're unlikely to notice the difference.

After the meeting, half of the people leave, but half of the people stay to have a Meetup. Every month across the country there are Meetups where groups of people get together and decide what they can do to help Howard Dean. It happens through meetup.com, completely independent of the campaign. His campaign is making meetup.com an enormous success. But whether Dean can harness the grassroots energy of the fifty-five thousand signed-up Dean supporters will probably be the difference between whether he gets to be the next George McGovern or the next Bill Bradley.

In a room in the back, Jeffrey Zeleny is interviewing Howard Dean. Sarah Leonard is guarding the door. Sarah Leonard, the Iowa communications director, is a long, tall drink of water. Stefan has brought a picture of her leaning over a table during the Gore campaign. She's got the big smile and unhealthy glow of a compulsive exerciser—the kind of person who orders a banana at an ice-cream stop (of which there will be plenty). We say hi early, but she turns away. And when Dean goes into a private room, Sarah shuts the door on me. But her fingers still wrap the edge, and if I pulled slightly, she'd let out a yell and that would get some attention. She closes the door all the way and sits down, leaning on the table in her shirtsleeves and long gray skirt, while Zeleny, national correspondent for the *Chicago Tribune,* his button-down shirt tucked, calmly prods the candidate with a three-hundred-dollar tape recorder between them. *Look at me, Sarah,* I think, *look at me.*

At a brick bar near the Iowa City Sheraton, Stefan and I meet with some of the kids volunteering on the campaign. They are enthusiastic and come from all over the country. They are young and good and not quite so freaky as some of the weirdos who showed up on the Nader trail. We buy them a bunch of pitchers ($3.50 per), and afterward Stefan and I head toward Washington, Iowa, a town of not many, where Dean will be meeting the breakfast crowd at Buc's Steakhouse at eight in the morning.

"On a scale of one to ten, how charismatic is Howard Dean?" I ask Stefan.

"Seven."

"That sounds about right." We drive on a little farther. "There's something wrong with him. He's stiff."

"I know," Stefan says. Stefan has photographed every Democratic candidate, so he knows something. "You meet Gephardt or Edwards or Kerry—these are guys who were popular in high school. But Dean, you know, he wasn't unpopular, but I don't think he was popular, either. He was probably middle." It's well past midnight, I'm driving, and I almost run into a chicken truck.

"What the fuck are you saying?" I say.

"I'm saying those guys are golden. They walk around, you watch them, they're all shiny. They have charisma. Dean doesn't seem like he deserves it. Like, if Dean won, he'd be surprised, because he doesn't really feel like it belongs to him."

I think for a minute about what Stefan has said. "You don't know anything," I tell him.

"You don't know anything," he mimics back.

"That Dean Core thing," I say. "It's not going to work. It's a pipe dream. Kids doing volunteer projects, wearing blue 'Dean' shirts. He's going to get suckered into building a townhouse for Charles Taylor."[3]

"Kucinich wants a Cabinet-level department of peace."

"Kucinich is a menace," I say. I briefly remember Nader and the lambasting I still get on a regular basis for my role in the Deep South during the 2000 presidential election. I drove a big van with an enormous sign plastered on both sides that read "Corporate Clean Up Crew." It looked like a box of Tide on wheels. I took my instructions from Washington and Nader signed my paychecks. I gave speeches on Nader's behalf in Athens, Shreveport, Platt, and Charlotte to bearded hippies and tree-huggers in see-through summer dresses who had just graduated college. Like most liberals, I have swung to the right since then, hardly even noticing the Kucinich speed bump on the road through Ohio. "Nobody in his right mind would vote for a vegan," I say.

"A pro-life vegan," Stefan says.

"Don't even get me started."

We bunk down in the Hawkeye Hotel. The sign in the bathroom reads "Ambath Corp. of Phoenix Arizona installed these bathtub liners but will not honor their warranty. There is a tub under the liner, it is safe and will not leak."[4] The room smells of cigars and other things. Some of us know that there is nothing in the world better than an American presidential campaign. To say it's better than sex wouldn't even be halfway to the truth. How many stalks of corn in this state; how many voters? I have a friend from this state, Chris Cooney, but he moved out to California with a stud finder and a drill to hang drywall for rich people in Marin County. Do the Iowa caucuses even matter? We should know that by what happened to Pat Buchanan in 1996 and John McCain in 2000. But what does matter? That's the key. That's what keeps people guessing. Nobody really knows how to win these things, and the rules get rewritten every four years. Presidential politics is the beauty of the grotesque and the passion of apathy. I'd do this for free. I practically am.

In the morning we get to Buc's Steakhouse early for smothered hashbrowns and biscuits and thin Middle-America coffee. Washington, Iowa, is a small Republican town with a few brick buildings built around the square. The locals call it "the other Washington." There are two rooms in the restaurant, smoking and non-. A group of old men hang out around a table in the front; they've been meeting here for an hour every morning for twenty-five years. Dean glad-hands the crowd. Asked about alternative energy, he responds that the Bush policy is not a policy at all and assures the restaurant that he's in favor of making gasoline from pig shit and corn, and the farmers give him a warm hand. It's what they really wanted to know. They don't care about saving the environment, they care about making money. But then Dean says something unexpected: what small-town Iowa needs is broadband, the days of the pig farmer will not return.

"I like him. And yet . . . ," I say on our way to the next event, a grammar school in Davenport. "He's at least five feet nine, but he seems so short."

"He's your height," Stefan says.

"There's that second before he answers a question. What's happening there? He's fighting an urge. He doesn't go off-the-cuff like McCain or Nader or Buchanan. He stops and thinks about it. I wish he was more charismatic. If he was more charismatic he could win."

"Yes," Stefan says. "There's a word for that. What's the word? *Turgid*."

"No, not turgid."

At the school, the children surround the candidate. "Monsters," I whisper. I don't like children, but I know in politics liking children is important. They all want to be on television, and they're jumping and waving their hands, and at one point the pile falls forward and the governor laughs and I think what a great family doctor he would make. Then they get in line to play basketball, and Dean joins the line. He looks happy. He looks like he likes children. But he doesn't shoot the ball very well. Then there's Q and A.

One of the kids asks Dean if he's ever done drugs. "Not in a long, long time," the governor responds.

Stefan and I follow the candidate from the school. He's supposed to be at a meeting downtown but makes an unannounced stop at Whitey's Ice Cream to meet with three Iowa politicos. Sarah Leonard tells me this ice-cream stop is strictly off-the-record, but I don't agree to that. The governor orders an Almond Joy milkshake. This is my first encounter with the governor's sweet tooth.

Digression

Stop; A Break in the Diary; The Secret That Everybody Knows; The Iowa Caucus and the New Hampshire Primary; Politics Without Consequences

It was 1972 when Iowa and New Hampshire worked out a deal by which Iowa would get the first caucus and New Hampshire would get the first primary. Until January 27, 2004, the date of the New Hampshire primary, the bulk of each candidate's time will be spent in these two states, the way it always is early in the presidential election cycle. On January 19, voters will caucus in Iowa. Unlike a primary, a caucus is a big time commitment. You can't just go into a booth and pull a lever, then go home to your warm television. Only a small percentage of Iowa voters participate in caucuses, giving no indication of what the larger pool will actually do come November. They drive through knee-high snow to meet in gymnasiums, pig farms, and fire stations. Within a half hour of the start time, people have to declare what candidate they are in favor of. The Republicans caucus with secret ballots. Democratic caucuses divide into groups, and if your man gets less than 15 percent, you can go with another candidate or you can go home. Undecideds are wooed publicly, their fellows calling out to them in a process I call "mooing." Mooing sounds like this: "Hey Jay Bob, honey pie, come over to Gephardt country and get yourself some good loving." To caucus is to take two hours out of your day, at least, and travel to some forlorn destination in deep winter snow and still not have your vote counted. Based on the percentages, each caucus sends a certain number of representatives to a county convention from which the results are phoned in to the Iowa Democratic headquarters. Because of the heavy demands of the caucus, only two types of people attend: the politically committed and the chronically lonely.

In years past, if you won Iowa you could be the front-runner for three weeks. But now the New Hampshire primary, whose first-in-country primary is written into the state constitution, comes only a week later. So any real money is likely to sit on the sidelines. The other states, jealous of the attention still lavished on Iowa and New Hampshire, have moved up their primaries to get a piece of the political pie. So now, within seven days of the New Hampshire primary, you have primaries in Arizona, Delaware, Missouri, New Mexico, Oklahoma, South Carolina, and Virginia. The question that's going to haunt a state-by-state candidate like Dean is how to get a fully functioning political apparatus full of rented strangers up and running in eight states simultaneously by February 3. The answer, of course, is money. And so far Dean's doing OK in that department. Four years ago George W. Bush rented enough strangers to effectively crush the straight-talking juggernaut that McCain launched successfully in New Hampshire. In the past six elections the challenging, non-incumbent presidential candidate has won the New Hampshire primary only once. Michael Dukakis got beaten that year in Iowa by Dick Gephardt. Iowa and New Hampshire are political myths perpetrated by people who woke up missing kidneys in hotel bathtubs filled with ice. No professional politician has ever agreed with me on this point. But they've got jobs to protect. And because of their commitment to Iowa and New Hampshire these two states stay relevant, even though they shouldn't be. Deep down they know Iowa and New Hampshire don't matter any more than a cup of sand in the desert.

July 4–6

Back to the Story I'm Supposed to Be Writing; A Missed Parade in Merrimack Where the Governor Handed Out Tongue Depressors; The Opening of an Office in Nashua, New Hampshire; House Parties in Munsonville, Atkinson, and Deerfield; Dean Headquarters, Burlington, Vermont

Howard Fineman writes a front-page article for Newsweek.com claiming that Dean may have peaked too soon. It's one of those things reporters say when they don't know what else to say, and when there isn't anything else to say. Journalists call it a "non-point." Fineman finishes his article with a list of similarities between Bush and Dean, starting with their height. Drawing parallels between Bush and Dean is absurd. True, they both went to private schools, but to say they both had a privileged upbringing is really missing something. In fact, it's intentionally misleading. But Fineman's been around for a while and knows how to turn fifty cents into a buck. I'm convinced that I'm not going to have enough in the seven days I had planned to make a decent article so I resolve to stay on the trail an extra five days and meet the other candidates to get a *feel* for the competition.

While comparing Bush with Dean doesn't make sense, the comparisons between Dean and the sad George McGovern are a lot more accurate. But Dean doesn't want to be called a liberal. Every time I ask someone in the campaign, they say he's a moderate. Even Kate O'Connor, the most honest person you will ever meet in politics, insists he is a moderate.[5] But the liberals clearly form his base. The fifty-five thousand supporters who signed up on meetup.com did so with no help from the campaign. It's the Nader Effect. The liberals got their ass handed to them when their support of Nader led directly to Bush's election and the clear-cutting of every major liberal victory of the past fifty years.[6] The liberals want a candidate who can beat Bush in order to correct the wrongs that still haunt their dreams. Which is why they're not flocking to Kucinich's campaign. Which is why, if Nader runs, he'll get a fraction of the vote he got last time, presuming one of his own followers doesn't slit his throat during a bathroom break on a Southwest flight between Dulles and Dallas. Dean is the liberal compromise. He's strongly in favor of gay rights, including gay civil unions; he's against the tax cut; and probably most important for the liberals, he's the antiwar candidate. He never supported the Iraq war. Unlike Edwards and Kerry, he's been against the war from the beginning. Edwards is still in favor of the war. Coming from state politics, Dean's never had to vote on one of the president's initiatives. On the other hand, Dean believes gun control is a state issue and has an A rating from the National Rifle Association. He insists over and over again that he is not against using military force, and he strongly backs a U.S. intervention in Liberia. He's fiscally very conservative. He doesn't support medical marijuana. The liberals, hat in hand, are accepting this, which is why in the Moveon.org primary Dean took 43 percent of the vote. It might not mean anything to win a vote on the Internet, but more people voted in that "virtual primary" than will vote in the Iowa caucus and New Hampshire primary combined. Dean's message to the liberals has been, *You can have me, but I won't have you. You can help but don't ask me for anything.* But Dean's a straight shooter. The liberals, like a broken union, are going to take what they can get. The rest of the Democrats are trying to decide which horse has wings.

I miss the parade in Merrimack, where Dean marches, as does Massachusetts Senator John Kerry. *The New York Times* quotes Joseph Lieberman saying of Dean, "I think the policy of opposing all tax cuts, opposing the war, et cetera, et cetera, is a ticket to nowhere for the Democratic Party." In Nashua, Dean repeats his platforms, but he's better than most politicians in that he shakes up the order a little bit, so you don't feel like you're hearing exactly the same speech you've heard before, though mostly you are. He punctuates every third sentence by saying, "We can do better than that." He also adds a couple of new points, calling Bush a racist for a quota comment regarding the University of Michigan. It's a stretch. After Dean's speech he treats his staffers to ice cream.

The governor loves sweets. When he sees a table piled with candy his eyes light up and he presses his fingers together. I will see this time and again through ten days on the campaign trail, illicit ice-cream stops, rolling his shirtsleeves to his elbows and reaching into a stack of glazed Krispy Kremes. His sweet tooth adds to his childlike quality, supported by his unelectable innocence, his smooth skin and boyish good looks, and makes me think of a bunny about to be eaten by wolves. Which is not to say I won't vote for him. I will, by absentee ballot, foreshadowing his doom.

But what's wrong with innocence, if that's the right word? What's wrong with honesty and a guy who lacks polish and sometimes puts his foot in his mouth? Why do people think Dean is unelectable? Why do I think Dean is unelectable?

At a house party in a sunny backyard in Atkinson, I hobnob with Alex Pelosi—the documentarian daughter of Representative Nancy Pelosi of California—and a freelance CNN crew from Atlanta.[7] In the excitement I almost miss Dean getting hit with a one-two liberal punch. In response to a question about Palestine and Israel, Dean answers that the terrorism has to stop. He also talks about how much better the Palestinians had it before the Second Intifada. "Who funds terror?" Dean asks. "Syrians, Iranians, Saudi Arabians." What he doesn't mention are Jewish settlements. He seems to think the intifada is a plan hatched by extremist Iranians against innocent Zionists at the expense of an unsuspecting Palestinian population. It's a clear right-wing aversion of the real issues. I ask the questioner if he's satisfied with Dean's response.

"A president couldn't bring up the Palestinians right now and hope to appeal to the average American," he responds. This makes me wonder why he even asked. He tells me he's half Muslim.

The second question involves the death penalty. Vermont doesn't have the death penalty, so I expect Dean to be against it, or at least in favor of a moratorium, à la George Ryan. Instead he says he is in favor of the death penalty in three situations: in cases of multiple homicides, in cases when children are killed, and in cases when police officers are killed. I'm slightly shocked by the absurdity and political expediency of his answer. On the one hand, it would take 90 percent of the people off death row. On the other hand, he'll be painted as being soft on crime anyway. It will be difficult for people to follow an argument about executing someone for stabbing a cop but not for raping and murdering dear old grandma. It's an attempt to find a middle where there isn't one, with an unintelligible argument that reminds me of Gore at his vote-losing worst. But here's the grim truth. Dean is honest, this is a rare lapse of political blather, and the campaign professionals have not yet moved in to put a tight lid on things. And they won't if he blows it on *Meet the Press* again.[8]

I fish a beer out of the tub, and when I look around I see that Pelosi and CNN and all the other opinion makers are gone. Dean is shaking hands and moving steadily to his car and a five-o'clock house party where he'll do it all over again. The only thing to do now is to get my head straight, journey up to the northern Vermont hills, and hide away with my old mentor, Lewis Rickel, a Vermonter and foremost expert on Vermont politics, currently waiting on a work permit for Australia. Apparently he's got a cozy shack on a lake in the woods without electricity or a toilet. I lived with Lewis in Chicago during the summer of 1995, the hottest summer on record.[9] The elderly were dying in droves in the brown nursing homes along Touhy Avenue. Lewis and I were like seals on the beach that summer. He introduced me to gambling and heroin. We had great times.

Digression

Three Days Disappear; A Naked Dip in Lake Eden; A Long Quote from Lewis Rickel on Vermont Politics; Bernie Sanders and the Rise of the Vermont Liberal Machine

"It's pre-1980, and Burlington is a sewer. Mayor Gordy Paquette is a machine Democrat similar to the senior Daley at the time of the Wet the Blacks campaign. Basically, Burlington was the kind of small city where most of the important decisions were made *after* the council meeting was over. Market Place was a one-way drag strip. On the corner where Main and Church come together was

Uptons, and we knew it as Corruptions. Video games and cigarette smoke was what you could get there.

"So, Bernie Sanders, pre-1980, a perennial candidate for governor. The guy always got 2 percent, 3 percent. It seemed like he would never win, and like the two-party system would always be in place. But he organized; he got students declared as residents of Burlington. Then he campaigned really hard with the students. He had a strong group of canvassers, known as the Sanderistas, and he won mayor of Burlington by ten votes.

"The city got better almost immediately. People energized. After-school day care. Things that were always considered too expensive, Bernie made them work. He got reelected over and over. His supporters were elected to city council.

"A big thing that happened to Burlington during this time was assuming a chunk of land by the waterfront owned by a railroad company. We used to go there and have fires; homeless people camped out there. The city had tried to cut deals with the railroad before and failed. Then this guy Franco, the city lawyer maybe, found a ruling from way back. The result was the city got the land for not even a dime. So now they had this beautiful waterfront they could develop. Make it accessible to the people.

"So, uh, Bernie ran for Congress, leaving behind a handpicked mayor, Peter Clavelle. And Bernie's been in Congress ever since. Essentially doing nothing, because he's an independent, so the Republicans and Democrats ignore him. Massive margins reelect him every year. They won't even run against him.

"The history of Bernie Sanders sets the stage for the defection of Jim Jeffords. Imagine if Jeffords had tried that in some bloodthirsty hamlet like Arkansas. People feel that Jeffords stood on conviction. Bernie Sanders made Vermonters more comfortable with liberals and independents. The ones that don't like it move to New Hampshire, and you've seen what a dump that place is.

"But Dean wasn't like Sanders. He came through the ranks. He was a legislator—I don't know if you would say machine Demo-

crat, but you know, part of that establishment. Bernie is a true liberal, an avowed Socialist. Dean's always been a Democrat. Dean
was elected to lieutenant governor: kind of a toothless job, at the
very best a stepping-stone to governor. Then, when Snelling died,
Dean took over, won five terms at two years apiece. He had the
good fortune to be governor during some of the best economic
times the country has ever known.

"In Vermont, Dean had a reputation for being a bit of a bulldog.
Likes to get shit done when it's supposed to get done. When action
was needed, he, well, you know, he got stuff done. And controver-
sial stuff: the environmental impact act, the distribution of money
from rich towns to poor towns.

"What you should know is that Bernie Sanders is the guy in
Vermont politics. He's the one who made grassroots happen. Dean
is not a grassroots candidate historically. He was a family doctor
who happened to be lieutenant governor when somebody croaked.
So, in terms of the presidency, given the fact that Dean is such an
outsider, who is basically unknown nationally, the best chance he
has is to work that Bernie magic. But I don't think he has that. Because Bernie, when you consider the Bernie magic . . . [w]as it
Plato who said you need a maximum of 1,500 hundred people in
a republic? A politician like Sanders doesn't come along too many
times and more often than not gets Trotskyed with an ice pick in
the head."

July 8–10

*The Other Candidates; Kerry Won't Return My Phone Calls; Journeys
with Wolves; More Butter More Syrup; The American Federation of Teachers; Concord, Boston, New York, Washington, D.C.*

I've been calling Senator Kerry's office for days and they won't return my calls. Rumor has it he's gone into hiding with the rem-
nants of the Gore 2000 campaign. A *Time* photographer finally

gets me through to his office, and I ask the receptionist if Kerry has any public events scheduled.

"I'll transfer you to the press secretary."

"Why don't you just tell me yourself? I just want to know if he's going to be giving any town hall–style meetings or anything like that."

"Hold, please, I'm transferring you to the press secretary." Twenty-four hours later I finally get his schedule. I'll have to meet him in Washington, D.C.

The common wisdom is that only a right-wing Democrat can beat a Republican. For evidence, people draw on Dukakis and Walter Mondale and point out that Jimmy Carter handed the country to a B-movie actor with late-stage Alzheimer's. The only Democrat to win two full terms since Franklin D. Roosevelt got there by killing welfare and locking up every pothead between Miami and Seattle. Call it the Clinton Lesson: you beat the Republicans by pretending to be one, even if you're not. But it didn't quite work that way in 2000, when eight years of peace and prosperity lost to retirement privatization, school vouchers, and gun rights. Then, in 2002, Democratic representatives and senators egged on by Gephardt campaigned for reelection on a platform of voting 80 percent with President Bush. The voters responded that if they were going to get 80 percent, why not make it 100?

On the way to see Senator Edwards at the Conant School in Concord, New Hampshire, I do a double take at a pair of blue-shirted youths in front of a bloodmobile with handwritten signs that read "Give Blood for Governor Dean. Dean Core."

Edwards's team has layered the streets in signs leading to the high school where the senator will hold a town-hall meeting. When I approach someone on the staff to ask what the turnout was like earlier, I'm referred immediately to the press secretary. This is the difference between the big-time campaigns and movements like Dean's, where Web bloggers give you their home phone numbers and encourage you to call if you have any questions. Only a handful of Edwards's staff are allowed to speak. I wonder if Dean will continue his bottom-up management style when things get hot in December, and I consider pitching an article to *Fortune* magazine about the different business-management styles of the campaigns.

When Edwards walks in I'm struck dumb. He's glowing. He reminds you of whoever that was that you once knew, the most charismatic guy you ever met. Wow! What a smile. And those teeth. And what fun he's having. He launches straight into a talk about his father, a mill worker. And how his father believed in American Values. He talks about a country where the son of a mill worker can run against the son of a president. "I want questions," he says. "I'd love to hear from you." But then he continues his talk. His shoulders soft and at ease, in the hot room he's dripping with relaxation. I want to kiss him, or perhaps just run a comb through his golden hair while he says over and over again in that easy Carolina drawl, "People like my father."

He talks about people needing medicine. CEOs making too much money. "Wealth disparity is wrong," he says. Talks about a free first year of public college for kids willing to work ten hours a week. "The work won't hurt 'em," he says, smiling. "I worked myself in college, loading trucks for UPS."

The room must be a hundred degrees, but nobody seems to notice. Under questioning Edwards responds with things like, "I've heard you, now hear me." Asked about the Patriot Act, which he voted for, he says the problem is not with the act itself, though it could be improved. "[But] we cannot allow people like John Ashcroft . . ." He takes on the easy targets and I wonder, if I had a slice of bread, if I wouldn't butter it with his sweat. It takes me nearly two hours to realize that he hasn't really said anything, except something about "tax cuts for the middle class . . . helping farmers . . . American Values, it's about dignity and respect . . . the kind of people that I grew up with don't have lobbyists." I've never seen so much sincerity; it emanates every time he squints and places a foot on a chair and looks into the questioner's eyes.

I have seen Howard Dean's end, and his name is John Edwards. What have I been doing marching with Dean for the past week when I could have been dancing with my eyes closed to Edwards's sweet Southern music? I think of the lady I met in Dean's office who had sold everything she owned and moved out from Utah to answer Dean's e-mail. Rest in peace, Governor Dean, I believed in you.

Edwards' press secretary is Jennifer Palmieri, and she was the deputy press secretary for eight years under President Clinton. "He's better than Clinton," she tells me. "He connects with people."

"He's incredibly smooth," I say.

Palmieri wrinkles her brow at this. I see a string of adjectives run across her forehead like a ticker tape. "No, not smooth. Confident. Empathetic. Clinton dazzled. Edwards isn't interested in dazzling. Amazing powers of empathy . . . [*spin spin spin*] . . . It comes across . . . [*spin spin spin*] . . . He has an understanding of what their lives are like . . . [*spin spin spin*] . . . He's the only one that can beat Bush."

I want to ask Palmieri if she believes herself, but of course she does. Every great salesperson is also a sucker. You have to believe entirely in your product if you're going to push it on anybody else. But I'm always amazed by the kind of energy and ambition professional politicos bring to their game. It's not about money, it's about something else. Washington, D.C., is like Hollywood for ugly people.[10]

Outside, it's a hot New Hampshire night. A couple of the kids from the campaign are holding signs, greeting people as they leave. "What do you do?" I ask one of them, a fat kid with a neo-Beatles haircut.

"I'm an intern."

"Oh yeah? What got you involved with the campaign?"

His eyes widen. "You're with the press, aren't you?"

"I suppose so," I tell him. "But we can talk off-the-record. I just want to get a *feel* for the culture of the campaign. I want to know what's driving you."

"I can't talk to you without the press secretary present."

"C'mon, I don't want to talk politics. I want to talk about you." He edges closer to the other sign holder, who smiles painfully. The two lean together, shoulder to shoulder, like they're ready to bite. "Take it easy now. I'm here to help," I tell them.

"What's going on out here?" It's Tait Sye, the press coordinator for Edwards New Hampshire.

"Nothing, man. I just thought we'd have a talk. I just thought I'd talk to these kids."

"Where are you from?"

"*GQ.*" Dammit, why do I do that?

"Well, we have rules, you know."

"Yeah, I do," I say, waving, wading out into the parking lot and the long row of red-and-white signs toward my economy rental car. A mosquito bites me right between the eyes, and I smear its bloodstained carcass across my forehead. "I know all about your rules."

After Concord there's an uneventful night in Boston and a couple of days in New York, where I start to go through detox. Detox on the road is when you start calling your friends and telling them you're lonely. You can only do that once per friend, and associates are off-limits unless you can think of something specific you need to tell them. When I can't take it anymore, I get on a double-fare high-speed train into the nation's capital.

Washington, D.C., is political crack, the place where heavy users go to get their fix, and this is where I plan to finish stuff. In any bar at night, you see young men and women in pressed suits sitting around circular tables, their various passes and credentials still swaying on their necks like jewelry. At six A.M. you might see a woman on a train, so beautiful that in any other city she wouldn't have to work, heading off to some campaign headquarters to put in a twelve-hour day as a marketing assistant. Connecticut Avenue and New Hampshire bump against Dupont Circle like coke straws. In 2000 I was one of the organizers here for the most ineffectual inauguration protest since Nixon's; they confined us to a patch of grass between Starbucks and a movie theater, two miles from where the real action was. This is my first foray back into politics since that humiliating day.

I meet Senator Kerry at the American Federation of Teachers conference. Papers have recently been calling him the frontrunner, and it's a huge crowd, and he speaks at length, touching on points that are important to teachers. He says, "There are no more important promises than the promises adults make to children." He mentions his sister, who is a schoolteacher, and the problems she's having. He mentions another teacher, voted teacher of the year and then laid off because of Bush's tax cuts. He hits the familiar topics that every Democrat is going to hit; he says that Bush gave away all of our money to rich people.

This is my impression of Kerry: he looks like a president. He's tall and stately. I think he's wearing a wig; in fact, I'd bet a dollar on it.[11] He speaks in this way that you figure Abe Lincoln probably spoke, his voice rising in timbre. He's a politician to the core. He makes his point by citing individual cases, which, because they are individual cases as opposed to heavy statistics, don't actually mean anything, but have been polled to be the only things the electorate understands. He does this thing where he points at you with just the tip of his thumb laying barely over the bridge of his index finger. Watch the big politicians: they all do this, the thumb-wrestling thing. I corner him after his speech.

"Stephen Elliott, *GQ*," I say. And this time I have credentials issued by the ATF to prove it. "When you say roll back Bush's tax cut, did you mean you would completely kill Bush's tax cut?"

"No," he replies. "Just for the wealthy."

"So what percent? Eighty-five percent?"

"We don't want to lose the credits for poor people," he says. And I wonder if I could ever vote for a person like him,[12] and I wonder about tax cuts during a down economy and a war whose price tag has risen to four billion dollars per month. But then, economics is like sports, which is like politics, and nobody really knows anything until it's over and then only in retrospect.

I follow him and his valet down a secret hallway in the hotel basement. They glance back to see me stalking them with my large Mead composition pad pressed into my palm. I don't look like I write for *GQ*. I'm wearing sandals, green cargo pants, a blue T-shirt that reads "Alameda Juvenile Department of Corrections," and a dangling peace-sign earring. Someone recently called my haircut "Michael Bolton + frizz."

Kerry and his valet step into an elevator with an armed guard. If I had courage, if I were a real journalist, I would jump in that elevator with them. But then what would we do? Slather up in lard and rub our cheeks into the mirrors? I could press the button and stop the elevator between floors, the guard's fist wrapped over the handle of his gun. "Tell me," I would say, and Kerry would let out a little laugh. A little I-don't-know-what-you're-talking-about kind of thing. And I would say, "You do know. You know. And I want to know." And he would get serious for a moment, his smile dropping toward his collarbones, and the valet and guard would relax and maybe share a smile or something while Kerry dipped into his pocket and extracted what looked like a silver pen with no tip. "OK. You're not going to remember anything after this," he'd say, like a father reprimanding a small child, gently twisting the cap, exposing a thin beam of purple light. That's when the big sadness would come. With knowledge comes sadness. It's always a sacrifice. "You'll understand everything you want to understand, but your past will completely disappear. Everything you thought you believed will be reevaluated in a matter of seconds and your personality will completely change. You'll lose that twitch."

"I've always twitched."

"You will be a completely different person. You need to know you don't have to do this. As of this moment you still have a choice. If you do this you'll never see your family again, but you'll have a lot more friends. Or you could press that button and we could all get off at the next floor and you could write this off as some strange, deniable incident that nobody would ever believe anyway."

"I don't have a family," I would say as the warm beam began its gentle, fuzzy roll across my eye sockets, the light stretching over my cornea.

July 11–12

What Was That All About; The National Organization for Women; Kucinich, Moseley Braun, Sharpton, Dean; A Shoulder to Cry On; You Say "Metaphor," I Say "Tangent"; A Violent E-mail from San Leandro

I haven't seen Dean since a well-meaning intern shut the door on me at headquarters in Burlington, Vermont, four days ago. Frankly, I miss him, a lot. I'm searching for closure. I'm way over budget with no chance of being reimbursed. Tonight is my final stop, a forum sponsored by the National Organization for Women (NOW). Dean will be there with three candidates on his left: Kucinich, Carol Moseley Braun, and Al Sharpton.

Crystal City, Virginia, where the forum will be held, is a suburb of Pentagon City, if you can fathom such a thing. Twenty-two minutes from the Capitol by Metro. The architecture is reminiscent of the Soviet Bloc style popularized during Stalin's second five-year plan. The buildings are like housing projects, except they're actually hotels and condos, and people pay to live here. The city is built atop an enormous underground shopping mall. The buildings scratch a sky that is sickly and gray with white noise from

the highways. Military men walk steadfastly in full-length camouflage and combat boots along black rubble paths. Children are kept
indoors.

When I called NOW's national press office, I told Rebecca
Forno I was writing for *The Believer*. She'd heard of it. "Isn't that
the new magazine? I love it. You're in." I've turned over a new leaf
and stopped lying about my credentials. It makes me think that
maybe it's important: if I'm going to go around following politicians, then I shouldn't be a liar myself. It's no wonder nobody trusts
the press. Or maybe it's just a matter of what you have to gain.
Don't sell yourself for less than you're worth, that kind of thing. At
any rate, I'll be back home soon, where the air's cleaner, and I'll
write this off as a summer vacation. We all get off on different
things.

Kucinich, Moseley Braun, and Dean sit at a long table across
from a row of panelists, and the room is crowded with close to five
hundred angry women.[13] They like Moseley Braun, whose comfortable campaign pitch seems to be that she's qualified and should
be given a chance. Dean and Moseley Braun are good friends, and
they hold hands a lot and whisper in each other's ears while the
others are talking, and I think that they are either having an affair
or he is offering her the vice president slot. Sharpton shows up late
and makes a joke about having a male driver, which gives the audience a good laugh. In his talk Sharpton says he wants three constitutional amendments, and one of them would be that every child
gets a quality education. As long as we're throwing amendments
around I'd like to add a fourth one that states it's not OK to accuse
your mentor of smearing himself with Martin Luther King Jr.'s
blood for political gain.[14] Dean hits his normal points but is noticeably less smooth than the other three candidates. He doesn't,
however, do the thumb thing that Kerry and Moseley Braun do,
and I love that about him.[15] And while not a great orator, he clearly
has a firmer grasp than some he's sharing a stage with.

Kucinich starts in a high voice that becomes steadily more resolute. This is my first meeting with Dean's closest challenger on the Left. Kucinich looks like the kid who ratted me out for smoking pot in the locked facility when I was fourteen. I had befriended him and encouraged other kids not to beat on him too much. I remember giving him dirty looks when we were all on lockdown, and he marched right up to me and squinted and said, "I'm not afraid of you." He was a little guy with spiky hair and was caught in the system after a botched suicide attempt. He didn't have any reason to be afraid of me. I looked around at my friends. "Do you know this person?" I asked. I wasn't very tough. I got out a couple of weeks later, knowing he was stuck in an institution full of thugs, none of whom respected a snitch, and maybe the next kid he went toe-to-toe with would be Larry or Terrance or Lonnie Pope, and they would break every bone in his body that night with the one lone staff member locked in the nurse's station, because that's the kind of kids they were.

None of that has anything to do with presidential politics except that every politician will remind you of someone you met in school once, and you might want to ask yourself why that is. Or you might not. When Kucinich addresses the crowd at the NOW convention, he pounds the table and cries out to his "brothers and sisters." He talks about slashing the Pentagon's budget, giving power back to the people, getting the private sector out of health care. Kucinich believes all of the things you want to believe but know aren't true. The power of love, that kind of stuff. Then the issue of Liberia comes up.

Dean pipes in quickly that he would send troops, because the situation threatens genocide. Sharpton says he is leaving on a fact-finding mission *tomorrow* with Cornel West. And Kucinich talks about helping, giving support to, an international coalition and, uh, what they want to do, we'll follow their lead. His feelings that America is morally deficient are sustainable, but if we are morally deficient, and we are, and if all people are created equal, which is probably true, then all people are morally deficient. There's no reason to think ECOWAS or Nigeria are any less god-awful than we are.

I find Kate O'Connor, Dean's travel companion, at the back of the room and tell her this is the last I'll be seeing of her.[16] She's the closest I've come to having a friend inside the campaign. I wish she were my stepmother, but you don't get to pick who your stepmother is. I tell her about the things I've seen in the other camps, the strange pagan rituals, bloodletting, women who sleep in full-length dresses, interns from foreign countries you can't find on any map. I urge her to keep the campaign open, to stay bottom-up instead of top-down. "You're from Vermont," I say. "You don't understand what goes on in these places, what these people are capable of. It's your only chance. And really, I don't think you have much of a chance." She assures me things won't change on the campaign, but things are a long way off yet.

What are we doing here? When the forum ends, O'Connor and Dean are quickly engulfed by the crowd. The seats disappear, and the audience circles together in a sea of faces and hands, many of them pumping signs in the air. Cameras and boom mikes hang over the swarm. It's a small, tight room. I climb over a table and peer across the monitors and screens now gone black. I note the men at the rear of the room locking audiovisual equipment into steel cases. I look to say good-bye to Dean and maybe ask him if he has an appropriate metaphor to end this on, but he's gone.

I'm heading west via Phoenix. It's nighttime already, and I've taken ten milligrams of Adderall and chased it down with four cups of coffee. It cost me $150 to upgrade to first class, and I keep squirming in the large seat. Ever since 9/11 I've been certain I'm going to die in a plane, and so each time I fly I write a short tale about the plane going down and record it in a document titled "Plane Crash Stories." The woman next to me has her headphones on and is watching Queen Latifah on the small screen, and I'm remembering my first political experience.

When I was in third grade I started a petition to give everyone eight years and older the right to vote. I'm not sure what I was angry about or what I was looking to be empowered against. I clearly didn't want to do anything for the second graders, a year below us, whom I probably saw as childish incompetents. My classmates wouldn't sign my petition, even when I pleaded with them. They said we were too young to vote. "That's what they want you to think," I replied. "You're like sheep."

I didn't know at the time that democracy didn't always work. Better than Communism, I suppose, but nowhere near as efficient as a good king. Anyway, what I knew was that we kids had less money and earlier curfews than another part of the population who exercised, it seemed, unearned power over us. Why should we follow their rules? What made them so smart? Did they really have our best interests in mind? The only one who would sign my petition was Mark Holtzman, a weird and unpopular kid who ate from the garbage cans and shot chocolate milk from his nostrils during lunch. Mark was a discipline case with a lenient single mother. Our teacher was Ms. S., a kind spinster with gray hair in a bun and short black shoes. Mark gave Ms. S. a hard time all year, and at the end of the year, after spring had taken hold and after Mark said something he shouldn't have (and I only wish I could remember what it was), Ms. S. leaped from behind her desk like an elderly, blue-veined squirrel. She grabbed Mark in her claws, punching him in the face. He burst into tears immediately. We watched in disbelief as she pulled him to the floor and laid into him with the pointy toe of her shoe as he tried to curl into a ball. She didn't stop for a long time. She beat that kid within an inch of his life.

II. Let All Know Who Would Enter Here

The Frothinghams described themselves as undecided, and remained so after a 10-minute chat with John Kerry in their driveway.

——Associated Press

December 7–10

Leaving Home; I Do My Best Writing During Rainstorms; New York City, Dartmouth, New Hampshire; A Planeload of Shit Opens on the Lieberman Bus; The Great Debate; Hitchhiking Portsmouth

It's not even seven A.M. and I'm trying to open my eyes on an Amtrak toward Durham, New Hampshire. The only thing worse than a hangover is a hangover on the day Al Gore decides to endorse Howard Dean. I throw the paper on the bench and try to focus on the sound of the wheels as they rattle over the rails and try to understand what I'm doing back here. It feels like someone is digging in my head with a spoon. I wonder if it's too late to go home. It is. I've already given up my apartment and my job and last night I made smarmy advances toward my publisher's associate editor.

That's what happened! Two in the morning, New York, bar's open until five. She's wearing blue jeans and a tight white T-shirt in the middle of the winter. If she had come to the editorial meeting dressed like that they could have had this book for free. Then a cab ride to the Flatiron building, the Williamsburg Bridge. A bicycle in the snow? She was long gone before I ever got back to Brooklyn. It was all bridges and ice after that and then the taxi blew a tire.

"What happened?" We pulled off the highway and rolled slowly into an empty gas station. The station looked as if no one had used it for years. The twisted steel carriage of some long-abandoned vehicle lay next to a solitary gas pump. I stood outside with the driver examining the wheel. It was snowing so heavily I couldn't even see the highway, but I could hear it.

"I don't have a jack," the driver said, shrugging his shoulders. "You'll have to pay the fare and get another taxi."

"What is this, some kind of hustle?" I pressed ten dollars into his palm and stalked off through the slush toward Atlantic Avenue, shouldering my pack and wondering how I'd be able to find a ride late at night in Brooklyn. The buildings towered over the streets, black windows punctuated with an occasional glow. The snow was like a giant curtain, and I made all sorts of resolutions below the streetlights before I arrived at the place where I was staying. I'm going to try not to drink too much for the remainder of the campaign.

And boy, what a hangover. Al Gore. Did he even have a health care plan in 2000? My socks are draped across the seatback, drying in a shaft of sunlight. I have vague memories of a debate four years ago in which Gore agreed with George Bush that killing Clinton's health care initiative was a good thing. I'm sure they parsed out their differences, but that's not how it came across. Everything Al Gore did in that campaign was wrong. *The New York Times* is trying to play up the endorsement as a mixed blessing. Which I guess it would have to be. Otherwise it would just be a blessing. *The Times* had a full page to fill and they did it admirably, I think. There are no pictures of people crying, just men in khakis and Joe Lieberman's strange smile, puggish nose, eyes creased into sad slits as if suppressing some wry joke.

I take a long drink of water and place the bottle on top of my pack. Financially this was a bad idea. But this could be the last important election of my generation, if I even have a generation. I'm thirty-two and I don't own a car or TV. I was twenty-eight years old when I voted for the first time. I dropped the ball and now it's come to this.

When I say this is the last important election of my generation, the generation I like to refer to as the Non-Voting Generation, what I really mean is it's the last important election to me. I won't care in 2008. And if George Bush wins I really won't care. I see a period of martial law supported by dopamine in the water supply, political narcolepsy. Come 2005, it could be the first time in history that martial law is imposed on a population and nobody notices. Anyway, if Bush wins, Hillary versus Jeb is not something I'm keen to see. I'm going to tune out soon, but not yet.

Joe Lieberman, John Kerry, Al Gore. I think it's been a long time since anybody has talked about the youth vote. In 2000 there wasn't one, unless you counted the people working for Ralph Nader, who, with less than 3 percent of the popular vote, hardly comprised a movement. Certainly no one under twenty-five voted for Gore.[1] And the young angry Republicans who voted for George Bush are best left to the anthropologists. But this year the youth vote is making a comeback. Not culturally perhaps. The music and pop lit is still very internal. But there are signs that the youth vote is going to wake up. Matt Gonzalez will almost win the San Francisco mayoral race based on it. And Howard Dean began his campaign around it. Why now?

I've given my air purifier to a crooked poker player and my Dzama drawing to my former neighbor, Dr. Oblivious. I don't live anywhere. Wilhelmina took me back after I left her for Howard Dean in July 2003, and we had about three good days together. She promised to carve her initials into me before I left, but the last two times we were supposed to meet she didn't show. By then I was already so warped by the upcoming campaign that I lost interest myself. The last thing I got from her was a note: "I'm not mad at you, but I can't be bothered." Sounds like the rest of our country, doesn't it?

Blame it on the Internet. Why change the world when you can play Yahoo! Euchre at home. But maybe this election will be different. Every election is, after all.

My friend, the filmmaker Peter Alton is fond of saying, "Those that leave themselves something to fall back on inevitably do." He also likes to say, "I take my coffee like I take my women, by force." But the second quote is neither here nor there. It's the kind of joke that can really get you in trouble in the wrong company, or if your timing's off. The important thing to me now is that I have nothing except the 2004 presidential election to keep me afloat. It's where I live, for better or worse, until the money runs out. At which time I'll climb on some defunct and bankrupt campaign bus, probably Dick Gephardt's, and set up camp.

What happened to John Kerry, the front-runner, and little Howard Dean kicking courageously at his ankles? And what about the good Jew Joseph Lieberman? Mazel Tov on your demise. The guy you stayed out of the race for just went on record as backing Howard Dean. Imagine how it must feel to be Lieberman right now, as if a plane overhead just cracked in half and dumped fifty tons of shit on your campaign bus. Especially when everyone you've surrounded yourself with for the last six months has been telling you that the only reason things are going so bad is because your campaign started late. And now, the reason you started late to begin with, out of loyalty to a man you considered your friend, has just blown a lit fart in your face. Does a person recover from that?

I call up Natasha Choi in D.C. during a train switch in Boston to get a measure on this thing from the nation's capital. As a powerful lawyer at a major firm, she can help me get a perspective on this situation.

"It's very cold on this coast," I say. "I think I might have made a mistake. Can I come and stay with you?"

"You can stay with me sometimes when you're in D.C. But not for more than two consecutive days. I need my space. What happened with that girl you were seeing, the mean one?"

"Wilhelmina. I'm in love with her. But she's difficult. Her parents don't like me because I'm not Italian. Also, she took the three hundred dollars I won in the poker tournament. She said I owed it to her. Not that I care, but I'm a little squeezed financially right now."

"I didn't know she was Italian."

"She's half Italian."

"What's the other half?"

"I don't know, she she won't tell me." I look up to the board and see that my train is delayed. "So, Al Gore?"

"I wonder what he's getting out of it," she says.

"Maybe he wants to be VP again."

Natasha laughs at my little joke, but I have more planned. I want to test my theory on her.

"*The New York Times* conjectured that Gore was backing Dean knowing Dean's a loser so he'll be able to run against Hillary in 2008 with the Progressive vote," Natasha says.

"What about this," I venture. "What if he backed Dean because he really believes in Dean? What if he regrets not courting the Progressives in 2000 and not running a more open, spontaneous campaign? What if he legitimately digs Dean and is backing him for no other reason than personal integrity?"

By the time Natasha stops laughing I've purchased a hamburger, fries, and a Coke from the kiosk.

"So let me get this straight," I say. "You would sooner believe that Al Gore is backing a candidate he secretly hopes will lose than you would believe Al Gore would make a decision free of political motivation."

Pause. "Yes. I believe that. Don't you?"

"It's too much for me," I tell her. "I need more hope than that."

But what did happen? If Al Gore has ulterior motives, what might they be? I refuse to buy into the conspiracy theories always being pushed forward by Will Safire, that the Democrats don't want to beat Bush in 2004. Of course they want to beat Bush. And who would make a bet that doesn't pay off for five years when in five years they might well have closed down the casino. If Bush wins in 2004 there is no reason to believe there'll even *be* an election in 2008, let alone that Hillary Clinton would have a chance of winning it. And who the hell cares about 2008 anyway? I don't even want to think about that—it gives me a headache.

I run into John Edwards' press secretary, Jennifer Palmieri, in the basement of Holloway Hall at the University of New Hampshire just before the debate is about to start. Outside it's cold as hell, but there's a snack tray set up here with coffee and brownies. "You're with *GQ*," she says.

"I'm with *Harper's* now," I reply.[2]

"It's down to Dean, Clark, and Edwards," she tells me, and I feel like we're picking up an old conversation, except last time we met Clark wasn't in the race, and maybe he still isn't. I'm going to need to meet the general soon, figure out where he's really at. *The Washington Post* has a quote from him talking to a counter woman at a Dunkin' Donuts—"*Do you make your donuts here?*" "*No.*" "*So how do they get here?*"

I talk with Jennifer for a while and at some point she narrows her eyes on me, like she's suddenly seen deep into my soul. "You're smarter than you look," she says, and I realize that before this election is over she will tell me lies and I will repeat them, because she is strong and I am weak, and now that she's found me out I won't have much of a chance against her.

I still don't have a place to stay tonight. There's a postdebate party for credentialed press sponsored by the New Hampshire Democratic Party. I'm going to head there later and see if I don't have something I can trade.

The problem with the debate is that, with Al Gore endorsing Howard Dean, there isn't a whole lot to debate, except who is willing to bow out so a single machine candidate can mount a legitimate challenge to Howard Dean. Most of the candidates are just pissed off by the whole thing. You can pretty much see it plastered over their curled smiles, just dying to get out, *"Fuck fat fucking Al shit fucking Gore."*

Kerry says the election isn't over until the votes are counted, which sounds good but simply isn't true. I can't blame John Kerry for being angry, though. He was supposed to win this thing. Sharpton says that nobody is going to tell the voters who they have to vote for, they will make up their own minds. But Sharpton isn't even running for president, not in the real sense. And saying that the voters will make up their own minds is really giving too much credit to the average American. Lieberman says he thinks his chances are *better* now that Gore is endorsing Dean. He says the money is pouring in and people are stopping him in airports. Edwards' basic response to every question is that he is an outsider.[3] Edwards' constant harping on his outsider image really starts to wear me down in a bad way. It doesn't match his hairstyle or his suit. It might be when John Kerry says, "I love John Edwards," that I lose faith completely. It's the most amazing confession of the debate, and I have to turn to Shir Haberman from the *Portsmouth Herald* to make sure I heard it right. "Did John Kerry just say he loves John Edwards?"

"Yes, he did that."

After that every time John Edwards says he's an outsider I hear John Kerry saying I love you:

> **John Edwards:** "I am very much an outsider."
>
> **John Kerry:** "I love you."
>
> **John Edwards:** "I'm an outsider. I have not spent my whole life in politics, like most of these folks."
>
> **John Kerry:** "I love you, man."
>
> **John Edwards:** "The question is, Who is in the best position to change what's going on in Washington? People who've spent a lot of time there, people who've spent most of their life in politics? Or somebody who comes from a different place, who's been fighting these people all his life? That's me, and that's why people should vote for John Edwards."
>
> **John Kerry:** "I soooo love you. I'm just completely into you. I don't know what to do about it."

There are two hundred reporters in that room watching a big-screen TV but I am probably the only one who changes his mind about John Edwards.

Meanwhile, Ted Koppel just keeps hammering on it: "Things are going very well for Howard Dean in the polls. Things are going very well for him in terms of raising money. What has Howard Dean done right? Who here thinks Howard Dean can beat George Bush? If you were Howard Dean, what would you eat for breakfast?"

Finally John Kerry says, "I'd tell you where you can put your polls." Dennis Kucinich tells Koppel to stop focusing on money and polls and start focusing on the issues. Later, in the spin room,[4] I think Kucinich should have made more of an effort to remove his makeup. But none of that matters to me at ten o'clock Wednesday morning.

I guess I just figured that someone in the press fraternity would offer me a floor to crash on in their deluxe hotel suite and a high-toned ride to the next big event. I mean, we're all on the same team, right? But the other press people didn't seem into hanging out with me at all. They could smell my panic. They kept turning their backs or stepping away, always eager to talk to someone else. Also, I don't have an expense account. Picador gave me a flat fee, and it's all coming out of my own pocket. The only chance for me to make any money on this thing is if I can spend less than that covering the election, which is no chance at all. Basically, I have enough to hang out for a month or two and then go hide in Hawaii where I figure I'll follow things on television and make up stories à la Jayson Blair. I'm a little stressed out about it to be honest, but I've always wanted to learn how to surf, ever since I read Kem Nunn's *The Dogs of Winter*.

So at ten in the morning I am hitchhiking down Highway 1 in Portsmouth trying to get to the bus station and to Boston where I know a girl who once sublet my apartment. I stayed with her last time I was in town, back in July, when this stuff was really interesting. She has phenomenal soap and towels.

Meanwhile, the roadside is all freezing wind and passing cars, not a single one even slowing for my raised thumb. Is it my sunglasses or Ford hat that tells these folks to pass me by? Anyway, the Ford hat was a Christmas present two years ago from Ben Peterson and his mom and it's the greatest hat I've ever owned in that it is impossible to lose. But nobody stops to pick me up and when I find a corner store they want to charge me a dollar for directions. Then they give me bad directions.

I try hanging out at the light and approaching stopped cars and asking if they wouldn't mind taking me to the Portsmouth bus station. They all shake their head politely or reply that they're not going in that direction, which is a fairly obvious lie, but that's America for you. I was fourteen years old the first time I hitchhiked. My friend John and I ran off to Los Angeles from Chicago. The plan was to become beach bums. We had been homeless for almost a year at that point, and John was wanted for breaking into a basement and then not showing up for court. You could say it ended disastrously when we were arrested on a highway outside of Caesars Palace and placed in the Las Vegas Juvenile Detention Center. We were on our way home; Los Angeles wasn't what we thought it would be. After three days they took me in handcuffs to the Greyhound station and put me on a Trailways with four dollars. I was lucky to be on a bus with one of Michael Jackson's horn players. His wife kept me fed for most of the three-day ride.

John wasn't released for weeks, and when he stepped off the bus in Chicago he was arrested immediately. Three months later the state took custody.

That was then. Of course we had good times, too. Also, here's a tip: next time you're hitchhiking, hang out in rest stops. Ask people at the urinals if they wouldn't mind a little company. For everything that's wrong with Texas, it's probably the best state in the union for catching a ride. Walking down a Portsmouth side street in the dead of winter won't net you anything except frozen feet.

Digression

What About Health Care?; Oops, I Broke a Sodomy Law; Seriously, Health Care

Every Democrat mentions health care in his stump speech but it doesn't get much play in the news. That's because it's so hard to figure out the differences in the plans, if there are any. And every Democratic candidate has pledged to expand health coverage in a major way, some more than others, with gazillionaire John Edwards in dead last but still a significant improvement over George Bush.

Once the primaries are over this could turn into a major issue. The Democrats will want it to. It certainly won't swing as many votes as gay marriage which a *New York Times* poll suggests 71 percent of people are against. A sure loser for Howard Dean who signed the first in nation gay civil union law. Dean has done his best to distance himself from the issue, saying that he's not in favor of gay marriage and that his hands were tied anyway since the court and the legislature of Vermont had mandated he sign it into law, which he did behind closed doors. Meanwhile, George Bush has gone on record as supporting a constitutional amendment recognizing marriage as a union between a man and a woman. Joe Lieberman said it wasn't necessary but did support the Defense of Marriage Act.[5] Lieberman is also in favor of a constitutional amendment codifying "In God We Trust" as part of the Pledge of Allegiance. Thinking about Lieberman is the only time I honestly feel good for working with Ralph Nader in 2000. At this time, Lieberman could be the next Democrat to drop out of the race, unless Gephardt gets hammered in Iowa. Regardless, since the marriage amendment could be blocked easily by eighteen legislative state houses, Bush is saying he's in favor of something he would never have to actually ratify. Which isn't to say he wouldn't. One need only look at stem cell research to see how far the Bush administration is willing to go for his religion. The war in Iraq may or may not have been Cheney's idea, but when Bush backed Santorum's assertion that homosexuals will burn in hell, that was straight from the heart.

Health care should matter more than that and it's a lot more complicated. Anyone with half a brain and nothing to lose is going to be in favor of gay marriage. But few people understand the differences in the Democrats' health care policies.

Howard Dean has put across a plan at a cost of $87 billion, which he plans to pay for by repealing the tax cut. Dean's plan focuses on covering most children and young adults under twenty-five and creating a national plan to offer more affordable coverage to small businesses and the self-employed. Under Dean's plan 12.5 million uninsured, low-income adults like me should get coverage through a public program run by the states.

John Edwards' plan would similarly cover 8.4 million adults through state programs, and 11.7 million children to age twenty. In Edwards' plan, parents are mandated to get coverage for their children. An interesting scenario: a pair of otherwise upstanding parents sitting in a jail cell while junior is at home laid out on the couch with a bad case of measles. Edwards' plan costs $55 billion and would be paid for by repealing tax cuts for the wealthy.

John Kerry's plan expands public coverage to most children up to age eighteen and many low-income adults. Specifically, 7.5 million low- and moderate-income children would get coverage through the expansion of existing programs run by the state. He says he has a built-in mechanism that would lower all insurance costs by 10 percent through a "federal government reinsurance pool." His plan costs $72 billion and would be paid for, like Edwards', by repealing tax cuts for the wealthy.

But the two most interesting plans are offered by Dick Gephardt and Dennis Kucinich. The centerpiece of Gephardt's plan is a 60 percent tax credit to employers for the cost of covering their workers. But employers are not mandated to provide coverage. Employees could not be required to pay more than 40 percent of the total premium costs. Employers would save $112 billion, and it is estimated that 65 percent of these savings would go to increase wages. But I doubt that. Or rather, I don't know, nobody knows. It's pure speculation from the bottom up. The only thing that isn't speculative is that employers and insurance companies would make a big fat pile of cash. Whether or not they'd share that money is anybody's guess. My father, who quit writing pornographic novels to become a landlord, explained property tax to me this way: "Of course I want them to lower my property taxes. But it doesn't have anything to do with what I charge in rent. I charge exactly as much as I can get away with, whatever people are willing to pay.

That way I make as much profit as I can." It seemed unfair to me at the time, and I was only eight years old. But looking back on it, I can't say I blame him. I've always been on the other side of that issue. I never pay my last month's rent.

Gephardt's program comes in at the staggering cost of $214 billion, according to Ken Thorpe at Emory University, and would be funded, like Dean's plan, by repealing the tax cut. Thorpe also contends that the plans proposed by Dean, Kerry, Gephardt, and Lieberman all should provide coverage for an additional thirty million people, give or take a million. According to George Bush's Web site, he plans on providing coverage for an extra six million by increasing the use of Medical Savings Accounts and tax credits. And if you believe that, you probably voted for him in 2000 and also think Saddam Hussein was responsible for 9/11.[6]

The big difference in Gephardt's plan is the funding for already insured people. By giving massive subsidies to corporations who already insure and by funding programs currently funded on the state and local level, the federal government would greatly expand its role. None of the other major candidates are suggesting this.

Kucinich's plan is the only really good one, but of course that's because he has no chance of winning. "I win when people vote for me," Kucinich says. He's the only politician who didn't learn from the beating that Bill Clinton took fighting the health insurance industry when the industry ran ads featuring Harry and Louise, a couple of senior citizens played by actors claiming that Clinton's health care plan would mean they would no longer be able to see their doctors. In 1994 Clinton lost the legislature due in no small part to Harry and Louise.[7]

Kucinich's plan would cost $1 trillion. The irony is that, when factoring in prescriptions, Medicare, employee costs, and deductibles, we actually spend that much on health care already. Kucinich wants to institute a single payer system run by the government similar to the one in Canada. Fans of privatization don't like this idea because it cuts out the employer and the insurance industry. But privatizers are loath to explain why Medicare is consistently more efficient than private insurers. With Bush's new Medicare bill, the system will probably collapse anyway. Switching to a public system would save a whopping 10 percent in administrative costs, more than enough to offset the expense of universal coverage.

The problem is Kucinich's plan would never get through Congress. People are going to be asked to vote between what should be possible and what is possible. David Redlawsk at the University of Iowa says most Democrats are offering an "incremental step, which is the American way." Another way of looking at it is to take what you can get and shut your stupid mouth. Still another way would be to accept that you're going to die one day, and it may be slow and painful, especially if you're poor. The only real conclusion is that if you vote for Lieberman you don't deserve insurance, though his plan looks about as good as anybody else's, with the strange omission of a detailed plan for how he intends to pay for it.[8] At least as of this writing.

December 12–16

John Kerry Days; Cedar Rapids; Iowa City; Davenport; Jerry's Restaurant; Vilsak Fails to Endorse; Ottumwa[9]; Fairfield; Des Moines; The Death Bus; Going Greyhound

I was having bad dreams and couldn't sleep thanks to something Jim Rainey from the *Los Angeles Times* told me last night.[10] I'm haunted by an image from the 1988 presidential election when front-runner Dick Gephardt famously ran out of money and lost the campaign to Michael Dukakis. The gist of the dream is this: It's 1988 and Congressman Richard Gephardt's campaign is on empty. He is told that if he campaigns in Michigan he'll get beaten badly. It is time to cut his losses. But Michigan is where Gephardt decides to make his last stand. He's creamed the way everyone predicted:

Jesse Jackson carries the state. Gephardt is slumped low in his chair, his legs stretched as far as they will go, his heels dug in the carpet, his white skin translucent, pink capillaries pumping slowly just below the surface. The aides are nowhere to be found, the famous Rolodex lies on the floor next to the bed as if thrown. His wife sits with him and the two are mute. Like a thunderbolt the door bursts open and there, larger than life, surrounded by a rainbow-colored halo, is Jesse Jackson. The big man practically floats across the carpet. Gephardt struggles up toward him. He will be a man one last time before taking a long vacation in eastern Russia. The two hug and Gephardt tries to pull away, pushing his hands against Jackson's chest. But Jesse won't let him. Gephardt pushes and Jackson holds, squeezing, limbs locked, firm. Slowly Gephardt gives, his arms lower to his sides, knees bend, chin falls. He melts into Jackson's sternum. Then the tears come, tears of loss and failure. They come fast and hard, a broken dam, they tumble out, soaking Jesse's coat.

Downtown Davenport is empty except for a café and a newsstand where I buy the newest issue of *Rolling Stone*. I want to read the interview where John Kerry says "fuck."

"What's with this place?" I ask the store clerk while she stands outside, smoking a cigarette.

"What do you mean?"

"It's Friday morning. Where is everybody? I thought this was downtown."

She blinks twice and flicks her cigarette into the gutter. "It's winter. They're in their cars."

I head back to my hotel room to listen to Beck's *Sea Change*. As Beck sings "Let the desert wind cool your aching head" I remember that, on early maps of America, Iowa was part of what was thought to be the great American desert. I've always liked Beck, he's kind of a millennial David Bowie, unafraid to experiment and unconcerned with being pegged and categorized. If you want to dance you can play *Midnight Vultures*. If you want to jump up and down there's *Odelay*. If you're feeling weird there's *Mutations*. And now, if you're depressed for no good reason, there's *Sea Change*.

I've been with John Kerry for two days going on four. When you're "embedded" in the campaign, they arrange your meals, transportation, rooms, airfare. I thought I could get away without paying, but they take your credit card and bill you directly. There's no way for me to get around the charges unless I tell MasterCard that I wasn't in Iowa and deny the whole thing. "Kerry who? Some bastard must have stolen my card. I'm just an instructor at Stanford University. I live in San Francisco." Except that I'm no longer an instructor and I don't live anywhere anymore, and there's no way I can continue to afford to be "on the bus." And I definitely can't be "on the plane." Partly because I've lost my driver's license but partly because when you travel with these guys they charge you first class and a half. At least that's what Nedra Pickler from the Associated Press told me. She expects the AP will spend fifty thousand dollars on her airfare next year.

So much for being "on the bus." The concierge just slid a bill for a hundred dollars under my door, and I'm tempted to chase him down the hall and shove it in his face and say, "I'm not even here." Dare him to prove otherwise.

But I am here, in downtown Davenport. Saddam Hussein has been captured and will likely be hauled out in chains wearing a diaper and bonnet, commanded to dance for the audience every time Bush gives a policy speech, while Bush sneers, "Who's the big bad dictator now?"[11] Kerry is downstairs giving a press conference on it, but I can't imagine being down there. Nobody on Kerry's campaign questioned my credentials; they were just happy to have me along. He's traveling through the state with thirty or so supporters. Some of his supporters are veterans from Boston. Others were rounded up from local offices. At least ten are staff, so really only twenty people aren't being paid. Though I could be wrong about that.

We went first to a hospital where Kerry spoke with nurses and then gave a speech to ninety people, unveiling his health care plan. Thirty of those ninety were from the bus, and some of the people worked in the hospital and had nothing better to do. I found a stack of chairs around the corner that they would have used if more people had shown. Then we went to a fireman's union hall where there was a table full of seven-layer salad, sandwiches, baked beans, and free beer.

"We're not supposed to eat from the buffet," Nedra told me. "You don't want to be compromised."

"I don't mind being compromised," I said, loading up my plate. "This whole election is about compromise."

The fund-raiser at four P.M. in Iowa City was probably the most depressing part of the day. Kerry was speaking on behalf of a state senator, and there were only twenty people prior to unloading the bus. They had meatballs and chicken wings. The youth vote stayed home to watch *The Simpsons*.

It's easy to see where Kerry gets derailed. He goes on about George Bush on national security, talks about the president flying into Iraq with a fake turkey, mentions Bush landing on an aircraft carrier that his advance men have decorated with a banner proclaiming "Mission Accomplished," and Kerry sounds great. But he never finishes anything without taking some dig at Howard Dean. You can feel the room get hot as he talks about Bush lying to him, tricking the senators into voting for a resolution to authorize force in Iraq, and not following through on a promise to include other nations, to exhaust the UN. We'd all be with him. And then Kerry would finish with, "And Howard Dean was also in favor of going to Iraq. He was in favor of a bill similar to the one I voted on." And the air goes out of the room. Nobody shows up to hear John Kerry talk about Howard Dean. They want to talk about George Bush. But John Kerry can't let go of it. On the bus when he said something, and then took it back, for a joke, he said he was being a Howard Dean. I even get an e-mail in the middle of the day titled

"The Daily Dean Report." It's from John Kerry's office, pointing out today's Dean double-talk. Can you imagine a daily e-mail about a challenger's campaign? I guess for the rest of the time Kerry is running I can expect these e-mails about Dean. It makes me want to shake him.

But you can see Kerry is stuck. There's no chance of his letting it go. It's totally freaking him out. He just can't believe that little bastard from the Emerald Forest is going to get the nomination. He was the front-runner, the chosen one, the man who was supposed to be president, or at least Democratic nominee. He was *presumptive*. And part of me thinks it's too bad, because I didn't think I would like the guy in person as much as I do. But liking a person is not the same as liking an organization or a message and definitely not the same as wanting someone to be president. Other members of the press told me he's taken the gloves off recently, which is what one does when one is fearful of getting slaughtered in New Hampshire by twenty-seven points. He campaigns from dusk till dawn, bets on the caucuses, hits up the old folks' homes. He puts his life on hold, grovels before voters, most of whom won't even make it to the caucus on January 19. He tells them about his prostate, about the doctor removing the cancer from his ass, and the crowd squirms uncomfortably. His message isn't resonating. He chokes up at an editorial board meeting while requesting an endorsement from *The Boston Globe,* his hometown newspaper. And he was supposed to be the front-runner. But he's not. And who wants to be president anyway? They all do, more than anything in the world.

The Real Deal Express, the Death Bus. Laura Capps spins endlessly for the press while we eat our dinners. According to Laura, everything's going great for Kerry. When I ask her why Kerry is always attacking Howard Dean, she makes a face at me like she doesn't know what I'm talking about. It's awful to look at, mean and angry. Like she'd rip your throat out for predicting anything less than a first-place finish in Iowa, followed by a surprise show-ing in New Hampshire, and then smooth sailing through the South and Southwest.

Sometimes John Kerry plays guitar at the front of the bus and the photographers move forward to take pictures. His daughter, Vanessa Kerry, who has dropped out of medical school to campaign for her dad, sits in the back of the bus and introduces herself to me.

"I'm really shy," she says. "But I thought I should introduce my-self to the press."

Perhaps that's not such a good idea, I think. There's something fake in her proclamation, something I can't quite put my finger on. Political events in Iowa are no different from traveling circuses. The candidate talks for a while, giving the same speech each time. Then he says he wants to hear questions from the audience, he's ready to stay all night because he "really needs your vote." A question-and-answer follows and at some preappointed time a staffer interrupts, "Please, senator, we really have to go." Then maybe the candidate says something like, "Don't interrupt me while I'm talking to these good people." But the crowd has got the message, the show is over. In Kerry's case, at the end of each performance his daughter intro-duces herself and pleads with the room to support her father. Maybe it's just politics, but it seems wrong coming off a twenty-seven-year-old blond-haired, innocent-looking student. Some-where along the way someone told her to look people in the eye and ask for their vote, but that doesn't work for everybody. I ask Vanessa how to stay healthy on the road. She tells me I need to wear a scarf. Her father, I notice, always wears a scarf.

There is the slow ride across the frozen plain, the windows slick with the Iowa winter trying to squeeze past the rubber. There's the flat neon of weigh stations and roadside diners. The candidate jokes with his traveling supporters. The overhead light off, just the thin band from the moon illuminating his open suit coat. They ask him about his service in Vietnam, what he eats for breakfast, how he keeps it up day in day out. None of them add, "When your campaign is dead as hell." He answers, he jokes, at one point he says it's the white powder that keeps him going, then adds, "I mean vitamins." And I think I wouldn't mind some of that white powder right now. He talks about meeting his wife at a fund-raiser for her first husband, who was also a senator, but who died. Kerry has the record. He fought in Vietnam, where he was a hero, then came back to oppose the war. He led the investigation into the Iran-Contra affair, led the movement to normalize relations with Vietnam, exposed the CIA's involvement in drug trafficking and its connections to Manuel Noriega. It seems he did all the right things, slowly and with diplomacy, and then he voted in favor of a resolution authorizing troops in Iraq. Kerry's position on this changes from day to day. Before Saddam's capture his basic message was that he had been tricked by George Bush. Then, when the tide started to turn, he stated that he was proud of his vote. It probably goes a long way toward explaining why he made the vote to begin with—relying on the opinion of the moment, failing to look too far into the future. It also explains his inability to build a passionate political base.

The Death Bus lumbers on through all of this, the driver's bony fingers curled around the steering wheel. Charon's somewhere off past the last farm, the boatkeeper waiting beyond the wheat fields. The land is flat and underpopulated, tractor trailers smoking in gas stations. And every town square looks the same, a city hall strung with bulbs. Every endpoint is endless. I wonder sometimes if I've gone anywhere and if these aren't the same senior citizens who were asking questions at the last stop. This may be the state's last caucus, unless they move the next one up to July 2007, and even then I have to believe at some point the political pros are going to wise up to the scam. It'll be all TV after that. No more retail politics, town-hall meetings and shaking hands with the locals. They'll beam in their missives via satellite from holding companies in Bermuda. Now staffers at the front of the bus consider their job options between platitudes while Kerry seeks to buy time by mortgaging his mansion. It wasn't supposed to work this way. This damn lonely state.

"You're not really working for a newspaper," Jim Rainey says to me as the bus pulls into the hotel parking lot. Jim's jaw and shoulders are square, his skin clear. He's the kind of guy who sits on an observation until the time is right.

"No. Not really."

"What are you doing on the campaign bus?" he asks.

"Well, Jim, I don't really know how to answer that question."

At the BP the only choice is Budweiser and Michelob. There is no lounge in the Motel 8 so we sit on the floor with a twelve-pack, offering free beer to any staffer who will give a good quote. I pass Vanessa Kerry against the second-floor railing introducing herself to another reporter. "I'm really shy," she says. "But I thought I should introduce myself to the press." It makes my skin crawl. Near midnight, Teresa Wells tries to spin it for us. The reporters from *The New York Times,* the AP, ABC, and MSNBC have all gone to bed. It's just me and Jim, we're from California. I split the last Budweiser with Teresa in Styrofoam cups.

"For the homeland," I say. "We have to protect our shores."

Teresa drains her cup. "That Al Gore endorsement was actually a good thing for us." But now we know each other a little bit so we laugh openly. It's hard to be objective when the staffers on the campaign are so damned nice. She worked for Bill Bradley in 2000. I ask her if she could maybe not bill me for the transportation and the meals.

December 18–21

Kucinich; Many, Many Stops in Iowa; Cleveland, Ohio, Baby; Lost Days in the Dean Van

I meet Dennis Kucinich at Cornell College outside of Iowa City. The peace walkers are there. One of them, an emaciated kid with a thin, light beard spreads his arms and gives a short speech about hope and stars and enlightenment. There are close to a hundred people. A woman screams from the balcony, "What are you going to do about the unfair way we treat immigrants in this nation? Also Indians? I'm half Indian myself . . ." She continues for five long minutes, explaining her own solution to these problems, and claps loudly as Kucinich repeats her platform with a little more restraint. There is definitely a moment when I think she is going to twist over the rail and fall to the ground. If I were up there, and I were a more violent person, I might push her over myself.

There is no other press traveling with Kucinich. ABC apparently pulled its full-time reporter after Kucinich made a mockery of Ted Koppel at the debate in Durham, New Hampshire.[12] I climb into the van with Kucinich and Paul, his deputy campaign manager and head of security. We're going to travel to Mt. Vernon, Moline, a factory on the edge of a cornfield where they're building vehicle-tracking systems, a library, and a bookstore. We'll finish at a house party where a young girl will play an accordion as sixty grown-ups sing the Dennis Kucinich Polka.

But I'm getting ahead of myself.

Kucinich knows how to go off the cuff with the timing of a spoken-word poet. It's great to listen to a politician who can really give a speech. And he's got nothing to lose because the mainstream establishment has already written him off. And probably with good reason. Why cover a candidate who won't win? Kucinich will tell you that's a self-fulfilling prophecy, and maybe it is, but it doesn't give him any more of a chance. Kucinich refers to the mainstream media as "the Great Mentioner." And you can tell it personally offends him that he's so ignored. I feel that way too when they don't review my novels. I don't even believe in bad reviews, but there's nothing worse than being ignored and if Dennis wants to take on *The New York Times,* I'm right there with him.[13] Those elitist bastards have never once given me so much as a mention, the only exception being an article in which I was quoted as an expert on search engine optimization.[14]

Kucinich's campaign office back in Davenport, Iowa, is two blocks from the riverboat casino.[15] The office is as small as you'd expect it to be, right next to a gigantic, undeveloped suite that resembles a concrete ice rink. The gathering is upstairs, in the building's cafeteria. I make a ham sandwich at the small spread on the edge of the room. Several tables are set up and Kucinich walks among them talking mostly about the war in Iraq. When he's done a man asks him what he intends to do about drug addiction. "Something I have personal experience with," he says, licking his lips. Kucinich takes a while answering and the junky regularly interrupts him with things like, "that's me," "you got that right," "OK." This is always a problem with Far Left candidates. The people who show up at their events are often crazy, lonely, and starved for attention. Drug addicts are common. As are shamans, witches, and congressional candidates. And what they really want to do is talk about their own issues. They see a spotlight and an opportunity to steal it. And because the lefties are so politically correct nobody says, "Hey, shut up, you crazy bastard." You can bet that wouldn't happen at a Bush rally, or an Edwards rally for that matter, where Jennifer Palimieri would throw a full body tackle on the junkie before the nightly news teams were ready to reposition their cameras. And everyone would pretend nothing happened.

If people were really to get down to the issues they would know that Dennis Kucinich is the only candidate—unless you take into account Carol Moseley Braun and Al Sharpton, something I'm not inclined to do[16]—who is in favor of universal health care, as opposed to universal health insurance. He's rabidly anti-privatization. He's also the only candidate suggesting we leave Iraq within ninety days, which makes me uneasy. I think if it came down to it, Saddam would have beaten the shit out of Kucinich. It would have looked like a scene from the *South Park* movie.

But on health care he's clearly right, and that's important. I mean, why give all this money to the insurance companies, whose profit margins increase every time they don't answer the phone? He's probably right on Iraq, too.

Late at night before the house party I experience a deep connection with Kucinich. I can't believe there are no other press covering him. They assign ten press people to watch John Kerry implode. Why ride in the back of the Death Bus when the front seat is open and waiting in the happy van? If you want to get to know a candidate this is the way to do it, with your knees touching. At first we were a little cold on each other. After all, I've called him a kook in print before, and I made fun of his veganism, which is ironic considering our moment of connection comes while talking about diets. I confess to Kucinich that I drink too much coffee and I've been eating a hamburger a day for the last week. He shakes his head, because he knows writers, and writers always push their emotions too far and their diets reflect that. He explains how he became a vegan, how he used to drink six cans of Pepsi a day, and how he originally became a vegan to impress a girl.

"That's what I do!" I say, overjoyed. "I do things to impress girls, too!"

At the second-to-last stop of the day, at a public library, one of his supporters shows up with a huge home-cooked vegan meal. Dennis insists on splitting with me. "Are you hungry?"

"No, that's OK." But he knows I'm lying. We eat side by side in the van. I'm tired and feeling a little emotional after listening to Kucinich talk about love and peace all day. I want to call Wilhelmina and tell her how much I miss her. Ask if she'll see me when I get back. The difficult thing about Wilhelmina is that the more I want to see her, the more likely she is to refuse.

"Your whole life can change in one moment," Kucinich says. "That's what people are looking for. They spend their whole lives searching for that." He hands me a bottle of water—I didn't realize how dehydrated I've been. The stars are so brilliant that even at fifty miles an hour it looks like the sky might explode. And suddenly I really think I will cry. "Envision the world as one. We need to think about reparations for all the innocent victims." I think I see a fog bank coming east from Nebraska but I know that's not even possible. I think, look at the telephone lines between Des Moines and Davenport. No way, man. Look at America, just look at it. Would you shed an American tear for the innocent victims? When the collateral damage is counted will it touch your patriotic heart? Will they pray for us, to save our souls, while we pray for them?

It's the best food I've ever had. When it's over I am in an entirely different place and Dennis is splitting his apple pie with me. We are friends. "You're more in touch with your humanity than the other journalists," he says. But he has no idea how in touch I am in that moment.

Then there's the house party and the polka. One woman suggests loudly, when asked about vice presidential candidates, "How about a black woman?" I wonder if she is talking about anyone in particular or suggesting a constitutional amendment. In the parking lot of the Holiday Inn we sit for twenty minutes while Dennis speaks with a Christian radio station. Man, it's cold outside. In the lobby we hug and have our picture taken together. I realize that I have really been compromised. I don't know how. But when that AP reporter told me not to eat from the Kerry buffet, that was nothing. That was just baked beans and bacon salad. Kucinich didn't even charge me transportation. He split his meal with me. I love the guy. Could he be president?

No, not even in my most deluded moments do I think he could win. Just before I go to sleep I ask myself, Why not love your fellow man, why not peace on earth? In the morning the sun has risen over the enormous Coral Ridge shopping mall, the biggest in Iowa. And the shoppers from Iowa City and Cedar Rapids are pulling in like ants returning to a hill. I ask myself the same question, Why not peace on earth? And the answer occurs to me immediately—because the other guy wants to rape your women and kill your children.

When considering Kucinich one has to also consider Cleveland. It's the only way to frame the debate. When I think about Cleveland, I think about the canal district and my third week of college. I was sober at the time. I took six years away from drugs and alcohol, from the age of sixteen to twenty-two, but in Cleveland I made an exception at the Crazy Horse II. We had driven all the way from the University of Illinois, and at first they wouldn't let us in because we didn't have identification and we weren't old enough to drink, but then we went back to the car and put on sweaters. We were young and the women were beautiful and we stuffed hundreds of dollars of precious college money into their undergarments. It was my first time in a strip club and I still remember a woman with platinum hair, silver stockings, and five-inch heels, which she took off to allow me to massage her feet. At four A.M., when it was all over and the Crazy Horse II was closing, we asked where a couple of young guys should go to have a good time and the strippers told us to go to Popeye's. But Popeye's turned out to be a gay club.

Dennis Kucinich threw away his political career to save Cleveland's electricity grid. The city was trying to privatize its electricity. It was all very corrupt, as you would expect. So Kucinich ran on the platform of killing the contracts. He was only thirty-one when he won the election and became mayor of Cleveland. But then the big boys stepped in. They said he had to privatize the electric system or they were going to cancel Cleveland's credit. A city with no credit. Political suicide. Everyone, including both parties, told him he had no choice. But he held his ground and the banks canceled Cleveland's credit so for the remainder of his term he had to run the city on a cash basis. The middle class was embarrassed. The big interests, the fat cats, put a million into ousting the boy mayor and exiling him to a political wasteland. After they got rid of Kucinich they let the issue drop—it had become too much of a hot potato. Cleveland held onto its electricity and Kucinich wouldn't be able to hold office again for fifteen years.

"Those were hard years," Dennis told me, and I knew he meant it, because all he wanted in life was to hold political office. "Those were lean times, I had to scrape to get by. . . . I taught some classes, did some consulting. . . . tough times . . . fifteen years in the void . . . You have to keep it together, man." Then he gave me the that-which-doesn't-kill-you-makes-you-stronger stuff. But his smile was bitter when he said it. In fact, it wasn't a smile at all.

Fifteen years after Kucinich served as mayor, people started talking about the success of Cleveland's municipal utility. Kucinich was vindicated. The young mayor had been right. According to *Cleveland* magazine, between 1985 and 1996 Kucinich's gambit saved taxpayers $185 billion. He was invited to run for office again and won a seat in Congress, which he has held for four terms and still holds today. That is why he has two Blackberries, one for campaign e-mail and one for congressional business.

So that's the thing. If you're going to understand Kucinich you first have to understand Cleveland.

Digression

Front-loading; Lewis from India; McAuliffe's Gambit; Jeb Bush Opens the Nation's First Religious Prison; Home in California

Lewis Rickel writes me from India: "The Indian mafia has no moral code. Women, children—all fair game. The corruption runs so deep it's hard to believe this is the home of Gandhi, or that the political system can ever be fixed. On the top levels, Mother India's lost her cherry to the new world economy at some expense. Enron cashed it up big here. Years after Union Carbide crushed Bhopal with its chemical monsoon (for which there has never been a conviction), in the roaring 90's Enron paid off a handful of officials to sign a long term deal for Enron-sponsored electricity at the cost of tens of billions of dollars to the people of India. Imagine a few corrupt state officials holding that much power. In America, that type of power is reserved for only the big dogs, VP Cheney and Halliburton.

"And here, top BJP ministers are caught on video accepting huge piles of rupees for granting contracting favors. These guys are rarely disciplined, more like shuffled around to new jobs after claiming entrapment. At least in the States they made Admiral Poindexter sit on the sidelines for a few years before re-installing him to influence. At the grassroots level it's really shocking. A man grazes his goat on his neighbor's land. They have words, argue. That night, the neighbor rounds up a small posse, locks the man and his family in their house, and burns them alive. Drastic conflict resolution. And the same man who burned the family wouldn't kick a mongrel dog which was eating his lunch." A little further on Lewis segues into Howard Dean's announcement in Burlington this May. "It was an exciting speech, the first time a major party candidate has done that in my lifetime. So why don't I have that loving feeling anymore? Why am I seeing Dean and Bush as twin rails of the same runaway train: the lines appear to cross if you look far, far into the distance." I know what he means. There's something very sad about your guy becoming the front-runner.

I hang out for two days with the Dean machine. It's well greased these days, money flowing in from all corners. I go to a couple of events where he addresses crowds in the hundreds, but the gatherings are all so boring that after a while I just sit out in the hallways of places like the Veterans Memorial Center and wait for it to end. Maybe Dean mentions Bill Clinton along with three other presidents in a speech at the Elks Club in Cedar Rapids. The next day *The New York Times* will run a front-page story "Howard Dean Reaches Out to Bill Clinton." That one phrase dropped casually in the center is the whole point of the speech but no one in the crowd knows that except the journalists who have been hearing the same speech four times a day for months. It's a strange way of communicating, almost a bartering system.

Back in San Francisco it's raining and the junkies walk the streets wrapped in plastic bags. I don't remember San Francisco ever being so cold. I spend some time with Wilhelmina shopping for presents in Union Square.

"Did you bring me something from New Hampshire?" she asks. We're in Banana Republic two days before Christmas and she's pulling out sweaters and placing them back on the rack. She's wearing a yellow turtleneck and red leather pants with a stripe up the side.

"I forgot. I'll get you something next time."

"I don't want something next time. I want something this time."

"I love you very much," I say.

"I know you do," she replies, holding a shirt up to the light as if it were a counterfeit dollar bill, then holding it against me and frowning. "I worry that you're not being hurt enough out there. You need to be hurt a little."

"I know."

On Christmas, before she boards a plane to meet her parents in Kansas, I present her with a mini-waterfall I got on sale at Walgreens and a door-hanging with three stuffed reindeer dolls. "I'd bring you with," she tells me, kissing my forehead, "but my mother despises you."

There are times when I think Wilhelmina and I might work, but those moments tend to pass quickly. We rarely see each other more than once in the same week and she once left me at her house while she went on a "quick date" with another man. She says I'm not capable of fulfilling all of her needs and it's hard to argue with her. I was engaged once, in my early twenties, and I know what I'm capable of. Still, when she sits on top of me and touches my face and calls me beautiful I feel better than I've ever felt in my life.

With Wilhelmina gone there's nothing left now but to enter a couple of poker tournaments and wait for the shit that's going to fly and the all-out panic that will immediately follow the New Year as we get set for the earliest primaries ever. The candidates don't campaign too heavily during the holidays.

But nobody's ever faced a problem like this before. Years of study in political science has taught the operatives the importance of winning Iowa and New Hampshire, followed by a strategy of taking one state at a time and then going for the big fish, California. This year California has moved up from May to March 3. The Iowa caucus and New Hampshire primary both take place in January for the first time. And they're followed only a week later by seven states, including South Carolina and Arizona, the bellwethers of the South and Southwest, respectively. Michigan will weigh in four days later with 153 delegates.[17]

Front-loading puts a heavy premium on cash and had a lot to do with George Bush's election in 2000. It takes big money to campaign in states without being there. January is going to be a month without rest and it's possible that the Democrats will have their nominee on February 3. They'll certainly have it on March 2, when ten states weigh in, including New York, California, and Massachusetts. There'll be 4,319 delegates to the Democratic convention in Boston (California, with 404, has more than 10 percent; New Hampshire, with 27, has less than 1 percent), meaning in theory that a candidate needs 2,160 delegates to lock it down on the first ballot.

Terry McAuliffe wants a candidate early so the Democratic machinery can turn its guns toward G.W. But this strategy might have backfired and the current wisdom is that it might not be possible for *any* of the candidates to beat Bush regardless. But current wisdom is a funny thing that changes quickly and is then forgotten. Because of front-loading, the primaries are already ugly and vicious. John Kerry's press releases continue to get more and more bizarre. The most recent—*Dean Flubs Another Foreign Policy Question, This Time on Israel*—blasts Dean for promising to empower moderate Muslims in the Islamic world.[18] Kerry seems like a nice enough guy. He leaves it to people like Laura Capps and press secretary Stephanie Cutter to smack you in the ribs with the brass knuckles. Lieberman states unequivocally that if Dean were president, Saddam would still be in power—which is probably true. Gephardt's former press secretary forms a shadowy organization called Americans for Jobs, Healthcare, and Progressive Values, and they run advertisements on television in New Hampshire with pictures of Osama bin Laden while the words *Howard Dean* and *Weak on Security* flash across the screen. The advertisements cause such a backlash that Gephardt is forced to deny any knowledge of them and several unions associated with Gephardt request their money back.

Of course, in terms of negative campaigns, these guys are rank amateurs and putting them in a face-off with the Bush administration would be the equivalent of entering a gunfight with a butter knife. And one of the reasons the debate has been moved forward is so that all the bad stuff comes out now. Maybe after March we'll see three months of quiet while the nominee huddles with his advisers, figuring out how to grab the "crucial center," and everything will seem OK as spring seeps into summer. Until one gray August morning when the crows fly toward the Galapagos and Howard Dean's body appears impaled upon an oil well south of Houston. A warning to all who would enter here.

III. The Early State

They have a word for politicians that say they're going to bring new voters to the polls. That word is loser.
—James Carville

January 5–6

Happy New Year; I Miss My Girlfriend; What Happens on Planes; A Warning from the Captain; The South Africa Problem

"I tried to upgrade," I tell the lady next to me. "But they didn't have any seats left up there." I'm sitting in the sixth row center, between her and some guy in a blue sweater reading *The Economist*. The plane was delayed for two hours due to mechanical problems, and the pilot is talking to us about weight-and-balance charts. He also mentions blizzards in different parts of the country and alerts us to a noise we can expect to hear when we're in flight, a buzzing near the wings common on the Airbus 820. And if anyone is upset, he reminds us that the crew's day has been pushed back a couple of hours as well, so they're not exactly happy, either.

"I would have upgraded in San Francisco," I continue. She's from South Africa and she's reading *Hornet Flight* by Ken Follett. "I wanted to, but I checked in electronically at one of those self-serve kiosks. The only option was to upgrade for the *whole* trip. That's $100 from San Francisco to Phoenix, which only takes an hour, then another $150 for the five-hour flight to Boston. I'm not doing so well financially."

She nods her head and turns the page. I wonder how she feels about *Disgrace* by James Coetzee, but asking a South African about Coetzee is like asking a Hells Angel about Hunter Thompson. You're likely to get strong opinions.

"Most of the time I fly ATA or Southwest. No upgrading on those airlines, that's for sure. I figured I'd upgrade in Phoenix but then it was too late. The flight was already full and they stuck me in the center row, as you can see, even though I'm a member of the frequent flyer program. But I'm not complaining."

"I can tell."

"Yeah." I nod my head. "Flying sure is scary." I want to continue the conversation, but I'm rambling and I don't like to bother people. If we were in Paris on a plane we might not have left at all. But at least we'd be in Paris. They'd probably give us free wine and Code Orange cookies. America West wants five dollars just to listen to the movie they shove right in your face. I'm heading to the College Convention in Manchester, New Hampshire, to get a bead on the youth vote, presuming the plane lands safely, presuming there is a youth vote.

I took a couple of weeks off for the holidays and it would seem like I didn't miss much. But it was a heavier holiday than most people understand. Kerry continued his negative campaigning which at this point is about all he's known for. Ask the man on the street to name one of Kerry's policies you'll see what I mean. Better yet, ask him if Kerry is for or against the war in Iraq. Same with Edwards. Ask people what they know about Edwards. If they say anything it'll be, "I know he's the son of a mill worker." But then it's only January and people will know more about these men soon enough. But how much more? *The Times* ran an article today on the two of them, Kerry and Edwards, about how they're competing for third and fourth in Iowa.[1]

Wilhelmina said I was a fool for going back. She said she was losing respect for me and intended to see other people while I was gone, but she's always seen other people. I was lying on the kitchen floor at the time with my hand on her foot. She doesn't like it when I sit on her furniture. She was reading a magazine and sitting at the table. I ran my fingers over her toes and touched her ankle.

On the surface it looks like the big news recently is Wesley Clark's refusal to run for vice president. It was early on the West Coast when he said it. I was at Andy Miller's, Sunday morning. Everyone else was still asleep. My friends don't follow this stuff very closely; most of them have jobs. The ones who don't have jobs are busy with other things. The apartment was cold so I was wrapped in two blankets and I felt very emotional when Clark told Tim Russert he wouldn't be Dean's running mate. There are times when I think a Dean/Clark ticket is the only thing standing between school prayer, private prisons, and mad cow on the free lunch menu. It won't be long before we need a note from the Justice Department to take almanacs out of the library. And I've been worried recently with the current deficit spending that when I'm old there won't be any Social Security or Medicare; I was kind of counting on that stuff. I was looking forward to a subsidized old age in my white nightgown and flannel slippers playing bridge all day. Then I think about Wilhelmina and she occupies my mind for a while. Then I think about the book I have coming out in February and what a dark, hopeless book it is. But that's life off the campaign trail: you can think about all kinds of different things on the same morning, and if something starts to bother you, you just change the channel in your head. But on the trail there's only politics. It's like talking to someone who is angry with you and has a knife against your eye; it occupies you completely.

But I skipped what I wanted to say, about why the holidays may have been heavier than anybody knows, myself included. The big news from the holidays may not be news at all. Not only that, it might just be a rumor, and it may or may not have anything to do with all the editorials published about NAFTA recently.

I caught a whisper of something. Somebody called me a few days ago from a blocked number but I recognized the voice. He said there could be a secret deal in the works. Howard Dean might be negotiating a VP nod to Richard Gephardt.

"Why are you telling me this?" I asked.

"Why do you think I'm telling you this?" he responded. He sounded the way a snake might sound, if snakes could talk.

"Do you always answer questions with questions?" I replied. He hissed into the phone line. I'm new to cellular phones and this was probably the call that was going to give me brain cancer. "Take it back, fucker."

He waited a moment before pronouncing very slowly, "It's . . . beyond . . . my . . . control." Then hung up.

None of it made sense, unless one takes into account the industrial unions. But the Taft-Hartley Act passed in 1947, over a Truman veto, and the unions have been in a steady decline since then. Today only 16 percent of American workers belong to a union. Heck, who would tell me anything? But what a bummer that would be, Dean/Gephardt, a complete sellout, enough to make me vote for Kucinich. Anyway, with the New Year the common wisdom is that the race will boil down to two men, Wesley Clark and Howard Dean.[2] The machine inside the machine is likely to come out for Clark, especially after the other day, when Dean stopped just short of calling Clinton's old pal, Democratic National Committee chairman Terry McAuliffe, a bitch. He apologized later, but the message was pretty clear: McAuliffe would be the first casualty in a Dean presidency. Al Gore and Bill Bradley notwithstanding, the machine wants what it wants. How does it work? Nobody knows. Or maybe you know for a little while but then the machine changes and starts working a different way. Maybe it's not a machine at all, rather something worse. But the real question is, How long will the other anti-Dean candidates hang on by their fingernails, siphoning support that would otherwise move to the general. If Lieberman meant what he said about his reasons for running he would have dropped out of the race and endorsed Clark or Kerry a while ago.

But it's hard to give up on something after putting a year of your life into it. Lieberman must look at the polls and feel the way I felt when I lost my last six hundred dollars in a game of poker in West Yellowstone on my way to see my fiancée in Seattle eight years ago. Doomed and stunned, but also shocked into disbelief. My fiancée and I were in our early twenties, and we were learning things from each other, like what you could get away with and what you couldn't.[3] It took us a full year to understand the effect of what had happened in Seattle and long after that for me to finally connect the dots from that place she was bartending and the powder spread in painful lines across the glass countertop, back to that poker game and a folded straight with two hundred dollars in the center pot. I plan to spend the next four days figuring out what the youth vote has to say about these things, see if I can't bankrupt a couple of Young Republicans at the card table so they can feel what I felt when I was their age.

"Call daddy," I'll tell them as I clean out their trust funds. "Tell him to FedEx your bootstraps."

Yes, yes, the Young Republicans. There'll be plenty of them. I sleep for a while, dreaming of steel tariffs, and when I wake up we're an hour outside of Boston and the captain is warning of an ice fog that has lowered over the Northeast. The South African has a coffee and two bags of peanuts on the tray table in front of her.

"Do you want your peanuts?" I ask her. She's made a lot of progress on her book.

"Yes," she says, not looking up, "I do."

"How about I take your farm," I say, staring at the little red packets. An ice fog?

"What?" she asks, laying down her book, looking stricken. "What did you just say?"

"Or maybe we should just privatize the peanuts. Let the market do its work, send them off to the highest bidder. I'm not sure you'd be allowed to bid. Last I checked, South Africa wasn't part of the coalition of the willing. I might have to occupy your tray table. Incoming, head to the bunker."

"Oh shut up," she says. "It doesn't have anything to do with me." She takes a five-rand coin out of her wallet and hands it to me. Nelson Mandela is embossed on the front of it. "Look at that. He's everybody's grandfather," she says. "He could have burned everything down if he wanted to, but he kept us together."

"That's nice," I tell her, running the silver coin over my knuckles. "Thanks for telling me that."

"It's OK. Things can work out." She takes one of her packets of peanuts and places it on the armrest.

"Thanks," I say. "Hey, remember when Joe Pesci made out with Sharon Stone in *Casino*? His mouth was wide open. He slobbered all over her cheek."

"Yes," she laughs. "How awful. I see you like your good with your bad."

I rip open the peanuts with my teeth, laughing as well.

January 7–11

The College Convention 2004; The Youth Vote; What Youth Vote?; Manchester; Concord; Wesley Clark's Vision Thing

In 1992 12.3 million votes were cast by people between the ages of eighteen and twenty-five. In 1996 that number dropped to 9.4 million. In 2000 it took a small turn upward to 9.9 million. Veronica De La Garza of the Youth Vote Coalition says nobody knows for sure the reason for the numbers. But she speculates 1992 had to do with a young candidate who played saxophone and appeared on MTV. If a million more voters between eighteen and twenty-five vote in 2004 than voted in 1992 they could elect just about anybody.

But the problem with youth is that it gets old and the young are fickle. Their passions pass and they age quickly. Will the kids who turn out to support Dean in January still be around come November? Will they even turn out in January?

The 2004 College Convention takes place at the Manchester Holiday Inn. I spend most of the first two days taking speed with the hotel-room door bolted shut. I only open it when the bellboy comes by with another packet of Folgers. I have a couch and a desk and towels as well as the basic toiletries. The convention is on the first floor, where they're doing major construction, and it is not what you would expect in early January, the year of an election. There aren't that many attendees, maybe eight hundred. Outside it's so cold that it burns. Ted Turner came in last night and asked where everybody was at.

Yeah, I thought to myself, where are we at?

He told a thin crowd we had to think about the environment. He said it was time to switch to Plan B, which was the name of a book written by a friend of his.

After Turner spoke, someone approached him and asked if she could ask a question. Turner responded, "No, you may not." He kept his chin forward and squinted. He didn't have time for people who asked if they could ask a question before asking it. He was in a hurry to go for dinner with General Eugene Habiger who had assured us earlier that we were living in the age of the dirty bomb. A dirty bomb, it's too awful to think about, though we probably should. There was a panel of experts and they felt that some kind of atomic radioactive weapon was likely to detonate in America in the next decade. "The cleanup would take years. Tens of thousands would be killed. If it happened in Lower Manhattan, Wall Street would be a ghost town. Right now it's one of many issues facing the voters. After, it will be the only issue."

"The odds are better than fifty percent," Graham Allison, a professor at Harvard, told us.

Kucinich came through and electrified the crowd. Asked about NAFTA and the WTO he said he would pull out of NAFTA and the WTO. It's one of the things I like about him; it's very easy to see what his positions are.

I hung out with Kucinich for a few minutes before the event. He gave me a hug and I gave him a copy of my book *Politically Inspired,* and then he told me what he thought of Wesley Clark, off the record. But what he said off the record wasn't really very interesting and it made me wonder why people do that. Dean's whole airplane is off the record, they're probably flying naked. Kucinich's security guard asked if there was anyone in the crowd I thought he should worry about and I told him to watch out for Dick Bosa, a New Hampshire resident and Republican candidate for president. Bosa's a large man and wears cowboy boots and a hat and trench coat.[5] He looks like he could play a role in a Clint Eastwood movie. Everything about Bosa is large, including his teeth. Bosa had told me earlier that this was about jobs and that if you don't see anyone you can vote for then you have an obligation to run yourself. He didn't run in 2000 because he supported McCain. He was part of a forum called They Also Ran, with space-cake candidate Willie Felix Carter and Fern Penna, who likes to refer to himself as the "tenth Democrat," as if he were the fifth Beatle, and assures everyone that he has offices in many European cities.[6] All of the minor candidates complained about their lack of press coverage.

"They're doing a blackout on me," Bosa told me before taking the stage. "I'm blacklisted in the New Hampshire press. I'm going to do something about it." Somehow he reminded me of my father, which might be why I felt he was a security threat. My father used to sunbathe in front of our house in cowboy boots and Speedos. He also wore underwear on his head so his head wouldn't burn.[7]

Bosa was a pretty scary character, not only because of his size but also the way he had of stage-managing everyone else, telling Harry Braun when to turn around and smile, grabbing people for photo opportunities. He had been mayor of somewhere once before, somewhere north, in this very state. When the moderator told Bosa he was out of time Bosa blew him a kiss. It was a very sinister kiss. It was a kiss that said *I'll pummel your face in, little man.* Later, in the bar, the moderator told me he had brought some major muscle with him and he was ready to deal with Bosa if he had to. "Did you see all those big guys at the table near the stage? I had already heard about him," he told me. "We were ready."

"Is he really a threat?" Kucinich's security asked me but I just shrugged my shoulders. What do I know? Was my father a threat? Once, perhaps. He used to come home with black eyes and the state took custody of me when I turned fourteen. Now he's just an eccentric old guy, kind of likable unless he loses his temper. He ran for office a couple of times himself. He wanted to be alderman, but never president. When Jane Byrne was elected mayor of Chicago in 1979 my father told me she had let him down in a very personal way.

All I know is that there's something very wrong with anyone who wants to be president and the really minor candidates—people like Harry Braun III, who takes the stage with strange drawings of underwater cities powered by giant solar power rigs sticking above the curling white waves like great sails—the candidates who have never been elected to anything or held any kind of office and have no supporters, they prove it best. In them one sees political drive stripped of any window dressing or message, just an image of the beast within. If I was to describe what that beast looked like I would say it looked like a small human, tiny enough to fit in someone's stomach, with translucent skin and pale blue veins. It might look something like Gollum from *The Lord of the Rings*.

Kucinich said he would work to rid the world of nuclear weapons, and the kids cheered. I felt bad for not cheering. I wanted to cheer for the idea of a world without nuclear weapons, especially after what we had been told earlier. But I think that kind of stuff requires a lot of trust. If you say to someone, I'll show you mine if you show me yours, then you drop your pants and they don't, then you're the only one naked, and people are laughing at you and it can get worse from there.[8] People are capable of horrible things.

After all of that I went drinking with some of the students. It was mostly poli-sci majors from throughout the country. There was a table full of Lyndon LaRouche goons. And Students for a Sensible Drug Policy has sponsored 150 attendees so the place has a real reefer vibe to it. At the bar there was a live band playing cover songs from the sixties. Bars in New Hampshire close at one A.M. Someone from a local school approached us and said she wouldn't vote for Kucinich because of the way he looks. She was wearing a scarf and hat and a shirt that didn't quite cover her belly. She had very thin legs.

"A guy that looks like that can't be president," she said. "That's the way things are."

"That's the way you are," I corrected her.

"Maybe I'm part of the problem," she said. I told her I would

bet anybody in the bar twenty dollars that she wasn't even registered to vote. One of the kids I was with whispered to me that he
would like to take her back to his hotel room.

"Remember," I told him. "You're representing your generation."

"I wasn't even supposed to be here," he told me. "Someone
from my school dropped out so they asked if I wanted to come up
here for four days, all expenses paid. So I said why not."

In the morning I slept through Carol Moseley Braun but made
it downstairs in time to catch Kerry's old act. He had twenty campaign workers riding the bus with him and they lined up at the entrance to the hall rattling noise sticks, screaming "Go, Kerry, Go!"
Then the candidate came down from the dressing room, plowing
through his supporters and into the bathroom where three guards
were immediately posted so that nobody else could take a dump at
the same time as the senator. It was a very strange scene. He was in
there for about twenty minutes while his supporters chanted at the
top of their lungs, "Go, Kerry, Go!" Could he hear them as he
squatted on the toilet? If that ever happened to me I think I would
really freeze up. One of the regular reporters on the bus said that
Kerry has a real bathroom problem. Apparently he has to go to the
bathroom all the time, and it takes up a major portion of his day. I
never noticed when I was traveling with him but I can't say I was
looking either. It got stranger still when Kerry's spokesperson
David Wade preceded Kerry out of the rest room.

Kerry doesn't say much that's new. He's vague in his policies
when he's answering a question. Pressed on marijauna, as all the
other candidates are, he responds that he's waiting for the results of
a new study and gets roundly booed.

But the real drama is Joe Lieberman and the man with the gun.[9]
The police are called and Lieberman comes in late and through a
side door. The man with the gun is also running for president and
he wears a wide hat and an American flag sweater-vest and a lasso
on his belt. The gun happens to be registered and it's the policy of
the Holiday Inn Manchester to allow people in the hotel with guns

as long as they have permits, which he does. The police didn't take it very seriously. The four cops stood in the doorway and the man stood smoking on the sidewalk just outside. But the Lieberman security team totally freaked out. There were four people doing security.

Lieberman has the presentation of a comedian and when nobody introduced him he introduced himself. "I'd like to welcome the next president of the United States." He continued to tell us that he would push forward more tax cuts for the middle class, which would be paid for by the richest 2 percent, which sounds fine. I'm all for taxing the rich. But what about the deficit? I don't like it when people talk about cutting taxes while we're occupying other countries and increasing military spending. It makes me itch. I don't like borrow-and-spend economics pushed by people likely to be dead before I am, if everything goes well. And if I'm dead before they are, well, that's a different matter, but you can't live that way.

Lieberman was brief and when asked about the law that prohibits college loans for drug felons he said he was against it, for the most part, though he hadn't exactly heard of that law. But he said he didn't like the sound of it. He thought if you had done the time you should not be discouraged from going to college. He didn't seem to have any problem with people doing the time. When Lieberman left I had to decide between going to hear Lyndon LaRouche or going back to my room to dance to the Outkast CD before taking a ride to a temple in Concord with Rick Friedman to watch Lieberman compete with Edwards and Kucinich for the Jew vote. Rick's shot was the cover of *Newsweek* this week.

"I don't work for anybody," he likes to say. "You want to see my pictures you gotta pay my expenses. I have a pretty good life."

Before the synagogue Rick and I stopped to see a Clark rally. It was my first time with the general. He sounded great and his advance team had done a good job. They played a movie first and then the general came out in a sweater and answered questions. He had studied the issues. But I'm not ready to talk about Clark yet. I still think I'm missing something. I like him enough, but there's something to be looked into here, and I'm not sure what it is. When asked why he voted for Nixon and Reagan he asked the questioner why he had asked that question, then said he voted for people he thought were strong on security. "It was the Cold War," he said. "I voted for Clinton in ninety-two."

In the morning, Edwards came to speak to the College Convention. He brought with him thirty staffers carrying big signs, much like Kerry did. And before coming out they sang Edwards' songs led by a black staffer, the only black staffer in the group.

"Who is that guy?" I asked one of the sign holders, pointing toward the procession leader. He was such a good dancer that I thought maybe he wasn't a staffer at all, maybe he was an entertainer. I probably would have forgotten the thought altogether if the Edwards guy had answered my question straight.

"Polly," the sign holder said, eyeing me suspiciously. There was a real ugliness in his look. Just like the look I got from the first Edwards staffer I asked for a quote back in July.

"Polly what?" I asked, deciding I would push the issue a little further.

"I don't know," he said. "Why don't you go and ask him."

"Because he's on the stage leading twenty of you guys in a song-and-dance routine. It would be a little awkward for me to climb onto the stage right now. And also, I think you do know his name."

The sign holder turned away from me, so I asked another staffer, a redhead in a blue coat. "What's that guy's name?"

"I can't tell you," he said. "But I can take you to our press secretary. He can answer your question. The press guy is Tait."

"I know Tait."

Tait told me his name was Polly Rodney, and he was an outreach staffer for New Hampshire and graduate of Princeton University. It suddenly dawned on me that it didn't matter at all who this guy was, but I was worked up again by the difficulty of getting the most basic information out of anyone on the Edwards campaign. Jennifer Palmieri was sitting nearby in a pink striped shirt.

"What do you tell staffers about talking to the press?" I asked Palmieri.

"We don't tell them anything."

"Really?"

"They're loyal, well behaved. We don't have any blabbing out of the Edwards campaign."

"But you don't tell them not to talk to the press?"

"Nope."

I didn't have the guts to push too hard with Palmieri. In retrospect it's quite obvious she was lying to me, and probably not for the first time. I wonder what she would tell me if we went to a bar together and we had some time to kill? She would probably take some pills, some RU-21s straight off the Russian black market, so she would hardly get drunk at all. Then she'd drink me under the table and get me to make all kinds of promises and sign various papers pledging to support the Edwards candidacy every four years until one of us died. If anybody knows all of the secrets of this campaign it's Jennifer Palmieri, and she will never tell.

After Edwards there was Dean and Clark to close it out. Dean had the biggest crowd of the event and the youth vote jumped from their seats to applaud him several times. Asked if he accepted the Lord Jesus Christ as his savior and credited Jesus with his creation, Dean answered, "Yep." Asked in a follow-up if his lord created homosexuals, Dean answered, "Yep," again. It was a great moment. But mostly what he appealed to was the anger and disenfranchisement that many in the room felt toward the Bush administration and when Clark came in he did something completely different.

Clark spoke for nearly an hour about the promise of the people. He went into detail about the scientific advances of the last twenty years and the promise of science for the future. It was truly weird and quiet and I started to go to sleep and then I thought about leaving but I stuck around while Clark methodically took on education, medicine, and the proper use of military. He spoke of doing the right thing, creating something that would last a century. He didn't mention other candidates. He didn't even sound like he was running for anything. The last line of his speech was, "And today we can do this only if you and your generation are determined to do good and dare to be great." The kids went nuts.[10]

Holy shit, I thought to myself, walking to the parking garage to get my rental and return it to Boston airport and then take a cab from there to South Station and finally an eighty-four-dollar train ride into Penn Station. "What was that all about?"

IOWA

January 12–15

The Perfect Storm; Josh Bearman's Choice; A Red Grand Am with a CD Player; Iowa City; Waterloo; The History of the Iowa Caucus; Dave Nagle; Perfectly Played Aces at the Foxhead Tavern

A week and a day before the Iowans across the state meet in precinct caucuses to begin the process of selecting delegates for the party conventions in summer I meet Josh Bearman at the Eastern Iowa Airport. Josh is writing a piece for *The Believer* magazine, and we thought we would split expenses. We rent a red Grand Am with a CD player. The guy behind the counter asks us if we would like to upgrade to a Saturn SUV for an extra five dollars a day but I tell him no. I read an article that said people drive SUVs because they make you feel safe and nothing is more dangerous than feeling safe. When he asks if we would like insurance we decline that as well.

"You guys are writers? We have reporters coming through here all the time for caucuses next week. So what kind of magazine are you writing for? Is it a liberal magazine?" he asks us, handing over the keys and paperwork.

"I wouldn't say it's liberal. The people who run it are educated. So I guess in that way they're liberal."

He gives me a queer smile and doesn't say anything to me after that. The woman with him at the Alamo counter says she's for Kerry, but she's not going to caucus because it's really not that important to her. She says it's too hard and it takes too long—she has more important things to do.

"I think you made him uncomfortable," Josh says, putting his sunglasses on while steering the Grand Am onto the 380, heading into Iowa City. "With what you said about education."

"I hope not."

Less than a third of the people voting in the general election are expected to caucus on January 19. There's a Perfect Storm brewing. That's the name for the supporters arriving on buses and planes, being picked up at the airports and stations and driven to cabins in the woods that have been insulated for the cold Iowa winter. They're coming to work for the Howard Dean campaign, to get out the vote on Monday and make sure all Iowa residents committed to Dean make their caucus.[11] The Perfect Storm workers are flying in and driving from every state in the union on their own dime. The other candidates have supporters arriving as well but the numbers are not the same.

School is still out at the university and Iowa City is clean and quiet. The old buildings on the campus are mostly empty while across the rest of the state the candidates are working backdoor deals and trading positions for power. The kids in the Iowa City

Dean office are working furiously on the second floor of the deserted Capitol Mall. Dave Nagle is holding meetings and taking calls from his office in Waterloo. David Redlawsk, political science professor and Johnson County chair, is finishing a thirty-five-hour winter-break class on the Iowa caucuses.

"What if everybody wrote like you?" one of David's students asks me. We're in a room in the basement. Josh and I are discussing with the class what it means to be a political journalist, which is something I know nothing about.

"Well," I tell him. "I don't know if that would be a good thing."

"I usually write about video games," Josh says. "That's my area of expertise."

We talk for a while about the youth vote but the students in the class are clearly not very charged. There is one girl in the class who is working for Kerry. She's pretty, with dark hair and nice skin. "What do you think?" I ask her.

"We're not allowed to talk to the press," she replies.

"You should fail her," I tell David later in his office. "You should write it on her transcript—'any press is better than no press.'"

David laughs but doesn't agree. I ask David about the kids coming into the state to work the Dean campaign for the caucus weekend. I tell him four thousand of them are coming and ask what those kinds of numbers could do.

"Did you really hear four thousand?" David asks.

"That's what we heard," Josh tells him. Josh has his arms crossed and is still wearing his sunglasses. It dawns on me that Josh is a really weird guy.

"Well, all kinds of things. Don't underestimate the importance of knocking on doors. Also, what do you do if someone wants to caucus for you but they're busy? Maybe they have children and can't afford child care. The Dean campaign could assign a number of households who are committed to caucus, give each worker a set. The way to win an election is to organize. That means identifying your voters and getting them to the caucuses. If someone needs a ride, a worker could give him or her one. Child care, dog walking, lawn mowing."

"Not in this cold. There's no way they're mowing their lawns in January."

"True." David pauses for a moment. "It's hard even to estimate the political consequences of those kinds of numbers. I don't think that's ever happened before."

"David Redlawsk, good man," Dave Nagle says. Nagle is widely considered the father of the Iowa caucus. A former congressman who has fought to keep Iowa first in the nation for the past twenty years. When someone decides to run in Iowa, Nagle is one of the first people to contact. He gives his advice to all Democrats who seek it. When candidates come to the state he goes on the road with them for a couple of days. Then he writes them a memo. He wrote a memo to the Clark people after watching the general. He told them not to run in Iowa, he said their candidate wasn't ready.

Nagle's law office is on the seventh floor of a building in downtown Waterloo. You get there by taking the Avenue of the Saints, the connection between St. Paul and St. Louis, built with $350 million of federal money originally earmarked for Illinois but bartered between Dave Nagle and Norm Minetta. Nagle has a small law office and a computer that runs on Windows 3.1. Across the room stands a coffee machine and a blue Maxwell House canister and five volumes of the Code of Iowa. On the wall is a picture of a dog tied to a duck.

He's a big, friendly, trusting man who conveys real authority. "Don't photograph me when I smoke," he tells Josh. Josh has one of those enormous silver cameras from the 1970s and is wearing it around his neck like a barbell. I don't even know how he stands with that thing on.

"It says right here," Dave says, reaching into volume two of the Code of Iowa. "Forty-three dash four: 'Delegates to the county conventions of the political parties and party committee members shall be elected at precinct caucuses held not later than the fourth Monday in February in each even-numbered year. The date shall be at least eight days earlier than the scheduled date for any meeting, caucus or primary which constitutes the first determining stage of the presidential nominating process in any other state, territory, or any other group which has the authority to select delegates in the presidential nomination.'" David closes the book. "State law doesn't control the parties. But we always thought we should have a backup, to say that we don't have a choice, our law requires us to hold our process first. It's relatively unpersuasive, but I had the legislature when I was party chair adopt a statute that requires to hold its process eight days before the others. [laughs] Yeah, I stuck that in there.

"The thing about Iowa is that everybody knows the rules. When someone applies to work on a campaign the first thing they're asked is if they've ever done Iowa. That way you can't get backdoored. There's no surprises here.

"If you don't get fifteen percent you don't get to send a delegate to the county convention. So if your first choice doesn't make it you go to your second choice. But maybe old Ed is eighty years old and he's been a county delegate thirty years and he wants to support Kucinich. But Kucinich doesn't have fifteen percent of the precinct. Well, you can't exactly tell Ed he can't go so you send him anyway. Also, maybe Jane is on the concessions committee. You don't want to have a meeting without coffee and doughnuts, so Jane's got to go as well. Another thing that happens is maybe Mary and Marty don't like each other and Marty goes for Gephardt. Well, maybe that's enough for Mary to switch to Edwards. This happens at the county level. This is real politics. None of that walk-behind-a-curtain-and-pull-a-lever stuff."

Dave's wife, Deb, appears in the doorway and asks if we need anything.

"Do you have any food?" Josh asks. "I'm starving."

"We have some chocolates," she says.

"Bring in the whole bowl," Dave tells her, continuing his story.

"I was elected and went off to Congress in February of 1982. Then someone told me about 'the Vermont Problem.' I said, 'What the hell's the Vermont Problem?' Well, Vermont was going to hold statewide town-hall meetings on the Sunday before the New Hampshire primary. In response to that, New Hampshire said, 'We're moving up a week.' I said, 'We're moving too.' And the Democratic National Committee said, 'No, you're not.' I said, 'Yes, I am.'

"At that national convention, they approved a committee to study the rules again. That was called the Fowler Commission. Don Fowler chaired the commission. He and I were the only two people who went to every single commission meeting. I worked that thing to the ground. I mean, if you were a member of the Fowler Commission and I knew you were coming, I'd ambush you. If you were flying to Philadelphia, I'd fly to Philadelphia and arrange to be on the same plane with you. I was coming back from Boston one night, and I was talking to a guy and he got off the plane, so I got off the plane and we finished talking, and after he said good-bye and I said good-bye, I turned, looked around, and realized I had no idea where I was. I was in Pittsburgh. But in the end the Fowler Commission upheld us, and we've been first ever since."

"So that's how you have the caucuses," Josh says, peeling another piece of chocolate and then lifting his giant camera in front of his face.

Back in Iowa City Josh tells me about a group of people who play Ultima online. Ultima is an online world where people live in cyber-characters. In Ultima you can spend your time learning how to be a carpenter, and when a group of people has done that, sometimes a new character logs on and they surround the character and build a wall of furniture around him. But it's not like old video games where you could just kill your character and start over. You're stuck in a prison of bookshelves and chairs.

On our third day in Iowa I head for a game of poker at the Fox-head Tavern. I've been losing since I got to this state and am down nearly forty dollars to the Foxhead's poker elite. But this time is different. Before the game I eat an elk chop at the restaurant across the street. I feel virile. There's a new player and he's playing with a hat on and sunglasses in the dark bar. He's winning at first and at one point he even says, "Oh, I do love a check raise." But I make him right away for a fish and soon I'm cleaning up the table, forc-ing people into corners, making everyone pay to see the cards, con-trolling the action. I feel like one of those carpenters Josh was talking about in Ultima online, building furniture prisons around people. In a five-person game position is everything and you should always win when you're the dealer. Of course the deal ro-tates. In fifty cents/one dollar there's at least seventy-five cents in the pot posted by the small blind and the big blind. The bar is smoky and wet with the stink of tobacco. It makes my eyes hurt and I make that bar pay because once you realize what a table is go-ing to do you play accordingly. I save myself two dollars at the end folding two pair against a straight and walk into the Iowa street af-ter midnight with eight dollars more in my pocket than I had when I came in.

Digression

In Response to the President's War Against Homosexuals

Sometimes, when you're staying at the home of someone you've never met and there's only whole-bean coffee but no grinder, you have to improvise. You start by just boiling whole beans in a soup pot, but it takes an hour and the coffee comes out light and creamy-looking and slightly sour. It's almost noon already so you take the wet beans and lay them in a pan, slicing each one into thirds, careful not to slit your fingertips, and putting them back in the pot. Some of the beans shoot from your grasp and roll beneath the refrigerator. After another twenty minutes of boiling, you fish out the grinds and spoon them into a filter, which you place in the coffee machine and then pour the brown water over the mush. But you spill a lot of the water and so you maybe only end up with half a cup and there's a mess to clean, and your host will be home tomorrow, but you'll be gone by then, far gone. Still, half a cup is enough because once you have some caffeine you start to think more clearly. Maybe you've been missing your girlfriend, especially since she sent you a picture yesterday from some party she went to and in the picture she's wearing a body stocking under a latex bikini and a man is behind her in leather chaps with his ass showing, messing with the jukebox. *Remember, if the urge strikes you to show this to anybody,* she warns. *I've got pictures of you, too.* And your editor has you on some kind of sick deadline. And the politicians don't want to let you back on the bus because the bus is full. Sure, it was easy before, but that was then. This is the big time, buddy, and you and whatever third-rate organization you work for aren't worth the time of day. What's news to you, mister? A small drop in a big ocean, if you know what they mean. And maybe if they are going to let you on the bus you're going to have to find a way to get to Ottumwa, Iowa, and worse, a way to get back when they leave you stranded at a road stop the other side of Cedar Falls. And perhaps the night before you were drinking with someone from the Iowans for Clark campaign—a former actress who moved to Iowa to pursue a degree in creative nonfiction. Isn't that what you do, creative nonfiction? She's vegan with a triangular face. You tell her that vegan babies die quick. Children need milk. You say a vegan baby is a dead baby, no difference. She's worried she doesn't have the connections to be a writer—she's new to the game, and she loves Wesley Clark. She thinks he looks great in Speedos and also he's the only one who can beat Bush and she doesn't like Dean but she's not sure why, but still if he wins she'll hold her nose and vote just the same. And you stayed in the bar because you thought she had a car, but she didn't. In fact, you even asked before your ride left if she was going your way and she said she was but you didn't know she meant *walking*. So you walked to Muscatine at three in the morning and nearly froze. And if all of that is true, when you're done with that half cup you take some more beans and this time you wrap them in a towel because people in Iowa have small stacks of towels and rags on top of their refrigerators. Then you take the empty bottle of beer that belonged to your host and you begin to smash the beans. You smash them over and over again. You feel violent, but the violence feels healthy. Three more days and people will be in church, the day after that they'll argue over their candidates. George Bush is pushing for $1.5 billion to convince people to stay married and encouraging people to use condoms, as long as they already have AIDS. You like the banging the bottle makes. Even the slight possibility that the bottle will break and cut straight down your wrist, hooking then snapping a vein, turns you on. When it's over the beans are nearly dust and the blue rag is a deep brown. The neighbor is walking to his car and doesn't peer through the window this time. It doesn't look that cold outside, but you know it is. You pour the grounds as carefully as you know how into the coffee filter and you wait. Wait for the perfect cup.

January 15–17

Ottumwa; Oskaloo; Newton; Bad Blood on Press Bus #1

"Do you snore?" Josh asks me. We have a room at the AmericInn in Ottumwa. We're deep south in this flat state and past a handful of streetlights is the square darkness of the fields lying fallow for the winter, the frozen dirt as stiff and unforgiving as cement. Josh has unpacked all of his bags and placed everything on the dresser tops. Two of Dean's advance men drove us down here. We left the Grand Am in their parking lot in Des Moines. There's going to be a pancake breakfast in the morning.

"I don't think so," I tell him. "But I don't really know. It probably depends on how much I drink. My girlfriend never mentions it and she's not the type to spare my feelings."

"Because I can't sleep if someone is snoring. I'm a bad sleeper. I also need extra pillows, one for under my arm and one for between my legs."

"I can't sleep so well either sometimes," I tell him. "I have tinnitus. It used to really freak me out but I'm kind of used to it. I got it from a sinus infection."

It's nearly six P.M. and Howard Dean is talking inside. The door is propped open with a chair. It's the fourth event of the day. Beyond the highway I can see the yellow top of a McDonald's sign and something red having to do with gas. I'm at a community college and the lawns around the campus are littered with satellite dishes. This is a small rally in the middle of Iowa. I've traveled with Dean before and seen more people than this, but one never knows. With John Kerry in December we stopped in one town where only thirteen people showed up, and half of them were undecided. It seems like so many people here are on staff or with the press and the others go from stop to stop. There were fifteen cars behind press bus #2 when we pulled into the lot. How many of these people live here? After a year of this I wonder if Iowans aren't tired of hearing politicians speak.

Dean hits his usual planks: health care, education, wars based on lies, a Bush clean-air initiative that cuts down trees. This close to the caucus the candidates don't take questions. The big news is that John Kerry advocated abolishing the Department of Agriculture a few years ago. At least according to the Drudge Report. Iowa senator Tom Harkin alludes to it in his opening remarks before introducing the governor. And Iowa communications coordinator Sarah Leonard confirms it in the filing center. I prefer it when campaigns don't smear each other, but I guess it's the nature of the beast. Sarah's wearing a fifteen-foot scarf. She also informs us that the entire bus tour covers 631 Iowa miles.

The next two meetings are pool press only and Josh and I decide to take press bus #1 to Mason City. "This is like a half day," says Rebecca Rodriguez from the *San Antonio Express News*. "It's like the teacher is sick and they're letting us go home early."

Out the windows the fields are flat and endless, defying even the horizon. The speeches echo one another in my head until they no longer make sense. There are televisions on the bus and CNN says Dean is slipping. Everybody is saying it. Everybody has been saying it. Earlier I told Philip Gourevitch that I thought Dean would get 30 percent in Iowa.

"How do you know that?" he asked.

"I really liked your book," I told him.

"I mean, why do you think Dean will get thirty percent? I really want to know."[12]

"I guess I don't know why I think that," I told him, but I said it in one of those mushy ways that you say things when you've been caught commenting on something you don't have the authority to comment on. But I really did like his book on Rwanda.[13] It's one of my favorites.

The latest polls show John Kerry winning Iowa with 24 percent, but nobody trusts the polls this close to the day. Dean's campaign manager, Joe Trippi, tried to explain the polls to us last night. The Kerry camp has identified every name on the Democratic list committed to caucusing for Dean. The Democratic list costs sixty-five thousand dollars and, according to Trippi, the Kerry people robo-call the Dean supporters so many times they stop picking up the phone. That's how you explain the strange shift in the polls; the Dean people aren't answering their phones.

But it turns out not to be true. I ask the Dean supporters this

morning at the pancake breakfast and follow up in Oskaloo. Nobody's received more than one or two digital calls in a day. Joe
Trippi said seventeen, but most only receive one digital call a week.

"I'm not trying to rat-fuck anybody," Trippi said.

He was talking to John Harris from *The Washington Post,* and
when Harris left, Trippi turned away and I tapped him on the
shoulder. It was already past midnight in the Bar Ottumwa inside
the Hotel Ottumwa, only three hours after Josh and I had confessed our sleeping problems to one another. I said to Trippi, "How
long have you been on the campaign?"

"Since January 2003."

"Funny," I said. "I've never seen you before."

I didn't realize it was Joe Trippi at the time.[14] I thought what he
was saying was fascinating. I didn't realize he was lying to us. But
he wasn't really talking to me at all. I just happened to be there.
Maybe he was being hypothetical. But it didn't seem so. It was way
past midnight. Josh had already gone back to our hotel. The
AmericInn was almost two blocks away. But I had stuck around.

Anyway, the point is the difficulty of knowing anything. I bet a
senior Iowa staffer five dollars over/under 30 percent. She bet
against her own candidate.[15] I was in Des Moines early yesterday
and I saw the Perfect Storm office and the volunteers in their
bright orange hats, sleeping bags on the floor, one entire room
filled with nothing but trash. And I thought no other candidate
could do anything like that.

But the Perfect Storm people don't actually live in Iowa so they
can't vote. And Joe Trippi is rat-fucking John Kerry to John Harris.
Meanwhile, CNN has John Kerry in the lead but no one believes
it. And it seems as if no one believes anything. Which is fine except
that a reporter ought to be required to make a prediction instead of
repeating the same information that everybody else reports. One
magazine says Dean is angry and then someone else follows it and
soon the only question is, "Hey man, why are you so angry?" And
Wilhelmina is calling me, telling me, "Calm that man down!"

Why is Dean so angry? My first reaction is Why not? I'm angry too. I don't have health insurance. But then I start to think he's not as angry as people are saying. Less angry than he was in July and now he wears a sweater, which Deb Nagle thinks is a mistake. Deb likes men in suits. "Be a man," she tells me in Newtown, Iowa. But I wear earrings.

Still, what I'm working my way slowly toward is, What do these people know? Two buses full of reporters and every one of them could repeat Dean's stump speech verbatim. Somebody knows something. Probably the guy from *The Philadelphia Inquirer* has a pretty good clue. But it just seems to me that every journalist should be forced to make a prediction, to bet on it in fact. There are fifty-five journalists on and around these buses and it's easy to look back and say why something happened, but how many people made a million on the stock market crash? If it was all so obvious why not sell short? Didn't we all see it coming? If every journalist, especially the TV journalists, had to make a fifty-dollar bet on the outcome of each caucus and primary and then each article carried the results of our bets in our bylines or at the bottom of the screen, then people would know if they were reading a report from someone they could trust or if they were getting secondhand gossip filtered like a Chinese Whisper from the campaign bus to press bus #1 to press bus #2.

Doug Thornell, Dean's traveling press liaison, is so goddamn cool. Just as I'm feeling bad this morning he pulls a press credential over my neck and I feel like I've been knighted or something. My mood instantly changes.

What happened was Josh and I were late this morning so we got on press bus #1. It was the only one left at the second hotel, the Super 8, which was used for overflow when the Hartford Inn ran out of rooms. Press bus #1 turned out to be a major drag. It was different last night when they split us up between those who were staying out and those who were heading in. But press bus #1 is where the regulars go, the beat reporters permanently assigned to the campaign for all the major news outlets. When we pulled in front of the first hotel, the Hartford Inn, all the long-term press corps got on board. People have their seats and they get very upset when you sit there, even when you get up late.

"I think you're in my seat," one of the network reporters said to Josh. Josh has big eyes and if he isn't wearing sunglasses his eyes are so open that it looks like he has a thyroid condition. He looked at the reporter like a startled frog then glanced around the bus. Almost every seat was empty.

"There's a lot of empty seats," Josh said, licking his lips. "This is a five-minute ride."

"Yeah, but I really want to keep my seat," he said.

I thought bag call was at eight A.M., but it turned out to be at seven, which is how Josh and I ended up on the wrong bus to begin with, though I hadn't even realized there were assignments. "They might kick you off," Nedra Pickler from the Associated Press told me. "But you're a rebel."

"I guess so."

Josh got up and moved to the back. I finally decided I would get off but by then we'd pulled up at the first hotel next to press bus #2 and as I was trying to squeeze past, another reporter was trying to board the bus.[16] He looked angry. "I'm getting off the bus," I told him.

"You could wait for us to move first," he said. There really wasn't anywhere for him to move and it wasn't too crowded so squeezing past was the obvious thing. Also, nobody got hurt.

"Hey, shut up," I told him. "It's too early for you, man."

It was a small incident, indicative of nothing. But it freaked me out. I got on press bus #2 and threw my bag on the seat. I had a deadline but I decided to miss it. I'm not capable of working when I'm upset and I thought maybe I would see him again at the next stop and we'd get into a fistfight. But by the time I got to the pancake breakfast in Mason City I had calmed down a little bit, though not enough to give a speech. But it didn't matter because I wasn't giving a speech. Tom Harkin was giving a speech. The same one I heard yesterday, about Dean being the candidate who could build the party and beat the president, about this election being the most important in our lifetime. And then Howard Dean came on, gave essentially the same speech, and at the end told the same joke that he's been telling: "My wife and I were at a dinner party in Connecticut and this was after I had announced that I wouldn't be running for a sixth term as governor. A lady at the party asked what I would do now that I wasn't going to be governor anymore. I told her I was thinking about running for president and she started to laugh. That's what happens when you tell someone in Connecticut that you're thinking about running for president. But in Iowa when you tell someone you're thinking about running for president they don't laugh. Because they know they get to *decide* who runs for president."

Dave Nagle was on the stage with him, and Deb Nagle was in the hallway of the mall, which is paved with brick and linoleum, waiting to go back to Waterloo. The whole day brought back to me the incredible thing about running for president. How you have to be thick-skinned because people say awful things about you all the time. It doesn't pay to be sensitive in this world, picking fights, especially with people bigger than you. I tend to lose most fights and, when pushed hard enough, I almost always apologize. If I can't apologize, I leave town. If I was going to be dramatic I would say something along the lines of how once you go on the road, once you run away, it can take years to fully understand what you left behind. And you can't always get it back. Of course, the mind romanticizes the past and you didn't necessarily leave what you think you did.

But the thing is you don't have to apologize and you don't have to run away. You can stand your ground. You don't have to fight anyone and there's no point in taking revenge. If you're going to run for president you have to learn to get over things and move on. Myself, I've never gotten over anything.

I slide across the ice-filled parking lot to a coffee shop next to a movie theater. Back at the event I'm the only person with a decent cup of coffee. When the event is over, we pile back on our respective buses. This time I go straight to press bus #2.

January 19–21

Des Moines; Locust Street; Evenings at the Fort; What Would John Kerry Do?; The Yeeeaaahhh Heard Around the World

There's a bicycle on Locust that's been there for three days. A white ten-speed with full tires leaning against a tree. There's no lock on it and the handlebars are turned up and naked of tape. I pull the bike away from the tree and roll it back and forth. I consider touching the handlebars with my tongue. It's not stealing if it's been there for three days. Or maybe Iowans are just trusting. That's the kind of thing the candidates say, "Good people, plain speaking, hardworking, honest." But where would I go? I would need extra clothes, synthetic layers manufactured for subarctic windchill factors, designed to wick away sweat moments before it turns to ice. I could bicycle to Chicago where I grew up, where politicians are expected to be dishonest, where patronage is celebrated, where if you can't get a job at the water department it's because your father didn't do his job right and his precinct failed to bring in the vote. If I took the bicycle the wind would cut through me so quick it would slice me in half, and it's so cold out that my blood wouldn't even run.

So much has happened in the last three days and it's all coming down to tonight. Zephyr Teachout slept on my hotel-room floor the other night in an effort to save the Dean campaign money.[17] The streets of Des Moines are nervous. The Iowa caucuses are really a referendum on grassroots politics. I like grassroots movements, as long as they're pro-choice. The experts are all declining to speculate. The major newspapers are leading with headlines proclaiming the equivalent of, *Don't look to us, we don't know.*

It's as if the newspapers were suddenly trying to encourage people to come to their own conclusions, which is incredibly hypocritical. The stakes of guessing are too high. Joe Trippi is telling people Dean may come in fourth, he's talking 18 percent.[18] Nobody wants to say anything because everybody is afraid of being wrong, and the articles in the papers have all come down to an endless stream of horizontal reasoning, i.e., Dean's organization will be the key *if* he's going to perform well in the caucuses tonight. But it's a game of expectations and the only person sure to win is John Edwards because no matter how well he does it will be better than anybody thought.

I stopped by the rallies yesterday. Edwards has ratcheted his message so tight that he sounds like a Baptist preacher at a revival meeting. People hollered as he proclaimed he would "cut the lobbyists off at the knees." Two women fainted.[19] Hundreds waited in the room next door and there was no doubt that anybody who walked in undecided walked out rooting for Edwards.

After the rally I sat in the car with Josh in front of Jimmy John's Subs for a while. "That freaked me out," Josh said.

Kerry had the opposite effect. It didn't matter whether you like him or not, the event was a downer. It went on too long and people left before the senator even took the stage. There were twenty to thirty politicos on stage with him, as well as his wife and children, and the announcer sounded like someone from the WWF. "And now, your Polk County Democratic Leadership . . ." The message was totally off, at least for my taste. For starters, he made it sound like every Democrat in the state was endorsing him, which simply wasn't true. It's a matter of tone. Candidates often convey things without saying anything directly attributable. The day before Saddam was captured, for example, Kerry told an audience, "If you think if I was president we would be at war with Iraq then you shouldn't vote for me." What was that supposed to mean? What he was saying of course was that he was an antiwar candidate, even though he had voted for it. But the next day he changed his tune.

Last night the whole thing was a circus from start to finish, Gary Hart and Ted Kennedy up there. It was the big Democratic machine printing its wheels across the Iowa soil. Especially after all that stuff Kerry was saying in December when he criticized Al Gore for telling Iowans how to vote. Kerry's wife, Teresa Heinz, compared Iowa to Mozambique, but what does she know about people? She was born rich. Maybe she knows plenty, maybe I'm not being fair. I just didn't believe her. The event took place on state fairgrounds and the overflow was in a giant white tent with speakers. I was so bummed by the whole thing that I felt guilty for eating one of the corn dogs in the press area. If I'm not going to say something nice about somebody I shouldn't eat their food. And the fact is that the Kerry campaign has always been nice to me. The second fact is that even though I don't always like the way Kerry has campaigned in the caucus, based on his record in the Senate, he'd probably make a good president. At the minimum he wouldn't embark on wars of choice without postwar planning and blame everyone else for his bad decisions.

But that's just the way it's been. They tell their jokes on stage and everyone laughs as if hearing them for the first time. I woke up this morning and my inbox was filled with hate mail because I called Matt Drudge a scumbag in the *San Francisco Chronicle*. I guess I picked the fight and you shouldn't pick a fight if you're not willing to stick around. But Drudge put it up on his Web site so I'm getting all these notes from his supporters in the conservative press telling me what a dumb liberal I am. I've seen this before. You take ten guys with peace signs and one guy comes along swinging fists and breaks up the whole thing. I wanted to crawl back into bed, the Drudge supporters wanted to swing fists. That's why the Right wins—they're tougher.

Forgetting that, the best event last night was Chuck Berry playing for Dick Gephardt. It was all union members and the beer was flowing. Outside giant Teamster trucks circled the hotel like buzzards above a dying calf. I didn't stick around to see what Gephardt had to say because it was getting late and someone from the *Chicago Tribune* had told me that if I showed up at the Fort Des Moines early enough the newspaper would expense my dinner.

The people at the Gephardt event looked just like the people I grew up with. When I was eighteen and nine months away from starting college, I didn't come home on New Year's Eve. The group-home mom wouldn't let me back in the house so I moved in with my friends Benny and Jason, and their mom and her boyfriend, Josie. I lived in their basement for nine months while I finished high school, and during holiday breaks from college I would stay in their house.

It was a blue-collar family. Ma only made eight dollars an hour working for a Catholic charity but she cooked good meals from cheap ingredients and didn't ask me for rent though I gave her money sometimes. Benny and Jay eventually went into the heating and air-conditioning business, their sister Chrissy joined the pipe-fitters union. Josie and Ma sold the house and moved to the sub-urbs where Josie got a good job in a factory. Josie's favorite thing to say about me was, "Sure, he can go to college. But can he change an alternator?" I lived with them on Glendale in Edgewater which is the neighborhood just south of Rogers Park in Chicago. We were close to Clark Street and Senn High School, three blocks from the 24th District Police Station. There was a restaurant on Devon and Clark that was always changing its name, and we weren't far from Peterson or Thorndale and there were a lot of gangs around but they didn't tend to cause trouble on Ma's block. And something that's been obvious to me for a long time is that poor people are much more likely to give you a place to stay than rich people are.

I called Chrissy last night from the Gephardt event while Chuck Berry was still on stage and the trucks were still circling the building, laying on their horns. "Guess who's a Gephardt voter?" I asked her.

"Who?"

"You are," I said. "Your whole family is here, times forty."

"I was with Ben and Jay last night. You should hear the jokes they're telling."

"I don't want to know. If I printed their jokes I'd have the NAACP as well the NeoCons filling my box. But listen, you should send Benny and Jay to one of these things. They'd get a lot of work out of this place. They'd have a really good time."

After Chuck Berry was done he sat on the table in the hall and union guys in their thick jackets asked him to sign their flags, which he did. Then he fell off the table.

I got to Fort Des Moines via the intricate network of heated walkways running through the second story of downtown, but I was too late for dinner. There was still half a steak where Jeff Zeleny was sitting but I thought it would be tacky to eat it, especially since there was a napkin lying across the bone.[20] But the *Tribune* staff made good on their offer of free drinks. "I have money," I said, because I didn't want people to think I was a victim.

"You have money," Ellen Warren said, "but we have expense accounts."

"I don't really have any money," I said. "I'm getting screwed." Since the drinks were free I had too many, which for me doesn't take a lot. I had Mandrin and soda water, thinking that I wouldn't be hung over that way, and Ellen wrote me up in her *Tribune* column like I was some kind of sissy. She said I was drinking Midori something, which wasn't true, but I was happy for the publicity. I originally thought she was wearing leather pants which seemed pretty cool for a *Tribune* reporter. By the time I left the bar I didn't think they were leather anymore—they just *looked* like leather.

And then it was morning time, and the bicycle. I got up for a while but I couldn't make it so I went back to the hotel room. The caucus was going to start in less than two hours. It was a few degrees warmer today than the day before but not warm enough to take your hands out of your pockets. Josh left for the convention center and I stayed in bed until two. I had a headache and although I took six ibuprofen, it wouldn't go away. And all of the hate mail made me miserable.

Caucus night was a night for parties. Everybody in town was having a victory party except Dick Gephardt, who canceled his flight to New Hampshire and retired. Otherwise, it was a big celebration except people were a little sad at the Dean event in a giant ballroom on the outskirts of town. Which didn't mean it wasn't the best party—it was.

But that's not what I'm getting at. The bicycle is still against a tree on Locust Street. Except today it has tape on the handlebars. But I'm certain it's in the same place. Maybe I just imagined there wasn't tape on the handlebars yesterday. Maybe I imagined everything: the mothballed tractors, frozen cows, the Dean bus. The convention center where everyone filed their stories last night was nothing but pipe and wire by eight o'clock this morning. I wasn't at the convention center last night. I went to a caucus in Precinct 43 with Josh and Alex Pelosi.

This morning the city feels normal and for the first time in a few days I don't have any hate mail. The only journalists left are the ones who missed their flights. The hotel lobbies are empty except for a few bags, the campaign offices are stripped of anything that can be sold for more than a dollar at a flea market. Everything's been stuffed in boxes, wrapped in tape, and shipped overnight to New Hampshire. Except me. I have blisters on my feet I hadn't even noticed before. The only people in line at the coffee shop are the governor of Iowa and a reporter from *The Des Moines Register*. They can't leave.

I thought I would hang out for a day and try to relax but I'm already feeling the detox and itching to go east, except my girlfriend is west and I miss her. But she wouldn't want to see me as I am now, a depraved and obsessed political animal. Or maybe she would. She likes it when I cry. I always think it's going to freak her out but she encourages it. I'll tell her I'm sorry, I don't mean to do it, I don't know why I cry. And she'll look at me with a small, understanding smile and say, "It's OK. I don't mind." Anyway, when you're in the game, it's impossible to think of anything else, which in its own way is liberating. I woke up this morning strung tight as a drum, stone sober, a grid of Iowa lit like a computer screen across the back of my mind. I had a moment between sleep and sleeplessness when I could see every precinct and I knew every delegate's name and for the tiniest moment it was still January 19 and I was in every caucus in the state. It was like watching a house burn.

Viable, not viable. The crazy thing is that it takes 15 percent to get one delegate but it takes 50 percent to get two delegates.[21] Which is what happened in Precinct 43 when the three Kucinich supporters joined up with Edwards pushing Edwards across the bow. "Why are the Kucinich supporters going to Edwards?" I asked Josh.

"The deal is done," he said, crossing his arms and nodding his head. For the past week Josh has been hitting me with his idea of the Voltron candidate.[22] He says he likes a different thing about each candidate, that if you take them together they form the über Democrat. It's really annoying. We'll be in a bar or a filing center and Josh, who in direct defiance to everyone else in the world, now wears sunglasses *only* at night, will point to me with his bony finger and say, "Voltron." But the thing is, you can't vote for Voltron, and I don't think it's true anyway.

So the Iowa voters picked Kerry and Edwards, surprising everybody but making me look particularly bad. Which really shouldn't come as a surprise. My political predictions are always wrong, and I don't see any reason to change. Smart people don't predict, but I'm a gambler, I'm not wired that way. Before I went to the Dean party last night I stopped by the Kerry bash to get some free food and to pay my bet. There was steak, pork loin, and mashed potatoes. But the Dean bash was the place to be. At the Dean event you had to pay for your beer unless you came across the staff keg hidden behind the curtain. And in the filing area for the press instead of steak and potatoes there were cold cuts and macaroni salad. But the people were cool.

Back to the point I was making before I started talking about food. The Iowans picked Kerry and Edwards. The youth vote stayed home, doing what everybody always says they do, not voting, not participating. The youth vote failed on every level.[23] Meanwhile, the two winners last night both voted for the resolution authorizing force in Iraq, both voted for the Patriot Act, and neither wants to kill the Bush tax cut, they just want to make it more fair, which is to say, scale back the tax cut for the rich, which is nice of them considering how wealthy they both are. But if we don't balance the budget it's the youth vote that's going to pay the price.

James Carville and Al Franken were both at the Kerry event last night. The morning after the caucus, you feel like a junkie might waking on a slab of concrete. Everything is empty and hard and your muscles contract, your mouth bolts open but you can't scream. That might be a little heavy-handed but it explains the massive exodus last night as reporters and politicos streaked at illegal speeds to chartered planes lying in wait on the tarmac, looking to burn into Manchester before the first cold sweat, where the political madness is going to keep going strong for another week.

But I decided not to do that. And when I woke up this morning my main focus was on the Kucinich/Edwards thing. Why had the Kucinich supporters joined with Edwards? Kucinich's headquarters answered on the first ring and I said, "Hi, this is Stephen Elliott . . ." and before I got any further the guy on the line replied, "Hi, Stephen Elliott. How's it going man?" So I felt guilty for a second but then I asked him anyway.

"Yeah. So, uh, I heard . . . I mean, this is kind of crazy. What I'm about to say is completely ridiculous; you're going to laugh. But I heard you put the word out to your caucus-goers that if they were not viable they were supposed to join John Edwards."

"Well," he said. "It's both simple and complicated."

"Yeah," I said.

"You know you need fifteen percent to be viable." I almost interrupted to tell him that I know how the caucus works, I was at one last night. I've seen this stuff. But I let him keep going. "We made a deal with the Edwards people that if they weren't viable they would join us, and if we weren't viable we would join them."

I stopped on the cold street. It was a little warmer than it's been for the last few days but one could still get frostbite if one were to talk too long on a cell phone without gloves. The river was on my left and down the bike trail were the green lights of the Embassy Suites and the gold-domed statehouse. The cars cruised behind me on the 235 in an endless stream of white noise. To the north was Locust Street and the Marriott and above me running through the second floor of the buildings was the Des Moines skywalk.

Have you ever had one of those moments when your image of yourself just completely changes? Since working for Nader I thought I had grown cynical. I thought I was cynical and bitter but this morning I suddenly realized I was idealistic and naïve. I asked the Kucinich aide to repeat what he had just said, and he did, word for word. He waited for me to ask him another question but I didn't have any questions. It hurt.

Edwards, who took 32 percent and was viable in just about every caucus in the state, made a deal with Kucinich, who was polling 3 percent and was viable in almost no caucuses. They traded unviable delegates with each other. Except Kucinich had a bunch of unviables and Edwards had very few. Edwards got the farm, Kucinich got nothing. All the time Kucinich spent in Iowa was basically for Edwards. But it's worse than it sounds. Not only was the Kucinich campaign completely outmaneuvered, they were tricked into supporting the candidate most opposed to their own philosophy.[24] It would have made much more sense for the

Kucinich people to join the Dean camp but all of a sudden Kucinich decided to play politics.

For me that changed everything. I went to Lucky's Pub last night after the Dean and Kerry parties. Lucky's is located between the Dean office and the Edwards office. Dean workers were raising their glasses. "There's no Republicans in this bar," one of them said. They had their arms around each other. "It's all Democrats here." Then they started to chant. "No more Bush. no more Bush." But the chant soon gave way to "Go, Edwards, go. Go Edwards, go." And the Dean supporters screaming "No more Bush" were quickly drowned out. Idealism, you say. I say HA! I say I know what it means to lie and be lied to. You say idealism, I say they used to think Iowa was a desert but I look out the window and all I see is snow.

NEW HAMPSHIRE

January 21–26

Josh Freaks Out; Smoke and Intrigue from a Room Down the Hall; Team McSweeney's; Static Line Jump 3,500 Feet

The Econo Lodge building looks like a factory, sturdy red brick just down a slight hill on the other side of Highway 235. Two miles across the river is downtown and the Holiday Inn and the bars where all the action is. There are four campaign offices on Elm Street alone. But the rooms on Elm are all booked if they're not they're going for three hundred dollars a night which is too much to pay to stay anywhere in New Hampshire no matter what's going on.

The rooms at the Econo Lodge are large and there's a fridge and a microwave. It's a place meant for living by the week and as long as you can find the money those weeks will become months and maybe the months become years until one day you get caught doing something you shouldn't or you get on a bus and go far away. You leave your stuff in the Econo Lodge and the caretaker, a funny man not quite five feet tall with a serious smile and incredibly large hands, goes through your things and takes what he wants and leaves the rest on the street for the jackals. The thing about hotels is that you never have to make a commitment and you never have to say good-bye.

The hotel is only one highway stop from downtown but it feels further. Down the block in a strip mall is a 24-Hour Store but they stop selling alcohol at 11:30 at night, six P.M. on Sunday. The drunks hang out in front of the store, bundled in winter clothes. New Hampshire doesn't have an income tax. Not a lot of public services, nowhere to go. The smart junkies catch rides south, where it's warmer and a person can sleep outside without catching frostbite. If they can't make it that far they head to Vermont.

The Econo Lodge has a laundry, only seventy-five cents a load. There's a coffee machine in the lobby. The coffee is free. Just press a button, regular, 50/50, or decaf. Light, medium, or strong. There's a vending room in the Econo Lodge and last night when Josh and I checked in an old man stood against the snack machine, gripping the metal slats, rocking back and forth.

"Won't give me my potato chips," he muttered. His face was cut with deep lines, like he had spent years in places like this and the years had etched their names into his face.

Camera crews roam the halls. The whole town is booked tight. When we tell the clerk we need the room for two nights he looks at us very seriously then opens up a file cabinet and pulls out a pink and yellow pad. "You will have to pay for both nights in advance. There will not be any refunds."

"We could probably have had this room for a week for that kind of cash," I say to Josh up on the second floor. "I've been places like this, I know how these places work. You see that microwave? They save a lot of money that way."

"How so?"

"Hot-plate fires. Places like this used to burn down all the time."

In Dunkin' Donuts on Elm, different campaigns fight for the coffee vote. The Kucinich camp has moved into the wireless café. One of them says to me, "You down with Kucinich?" He seems to be the leader of the Wi-Fi for Dennis crowd and lays his phone down to shake my hand.

"I like him," I say. I don't know where to go after that. "He split his dinner with me."

The entire Iowa circus has transplanted itself to New Hampshire but all of the news is still Dean's caucus-night speech to his supporters at the Val Air Ballroom in West Des Moines. It's on every television on the strip. I was at this event with Josh and Philip Gourevitch. By eleven P.M. the filing center was deserted and it was just activists and beer. People were wondering where they were going next. There were a lot of good-byes, lots of making out. There were no TVs. There was some disappointment. Eighteen percent, a defeat, no doubt about it. But the buses had already left. Dean's speech was quick and then he was gone and the press bus left with him for a quick flight straight to Manchester. The rest of the press, thirty or forty, were eager to get to the Fort Des Moines, where the winner party was, where the liquor was top-shelf and free and the appetizers came with toothpicks.

Nobody in the room seemed to know what had happened. Thousands of campaign workers were chilling out, slightly bummed, but still kind of turned on by Dean's "Yeeahhh!" It was the other guys, the ones watching it on TV, who filled the wires with what the observers had missed. If you were there you didn't see it.

"How about that?" they said in Washington and New York.

"Strong stuff."

The media that was actually at the event didn't stick around. An hour after the biggest story of the week the press area was dead empty, nothing but thirty phone lines hanging from a corkboard ceiling. But the story was on television and call-in radio shows in the morning. And maybe it's Dean's own fault for not paying more attention to the media. His campaign has always been disdainful of journalists.[25] Nobody goes out of the way to accommodate the press, to make sure the cameras have a good shot. They never tell you they've missed you when you get back on the bus. And when Dean spoke on Monday night he was talking to the kids in the orange hats who had been knocking on doors for the weekend, the Perfect Storm. They had come from everywhere, but they hadn't helped. People didn't like to see unshaven kids at their door looking like dirty hippies holding clipboards. Nobody told the kids to get Clean for Dean.

The Kerry office did it differently. A handful of veterans on the phone, a target for each district, a war room lit with lights. When a precinct became viable a blue light went on and the word went out to shift efforts to the next precinct. Very organized, very slick. No dirty kids in orange hats.

Josh and I did it the other way around. We went first to the Kerry event, loaded up on some steak, and then split town to the ballroom to get a load of Dean. And even though Kerry was the winner there were still more people at Dean's event. None of the Dean supporters looked as crazy as Josh, who was wearing a one-piece silver astronaut suit and sunglasses. He looked like he was wrapped in tin foil.

"My friend Otis cooks salmon like that," I said.

"What are you talking about?"

"He lives on a farm south of San Francisco and sometimes he gets a big salmon and wraps it in tin foil and lays it across this giant burner he has. He'll invite a lot of people over and have a big party. You have to drive down into this valley. He lives at the bottom, in an Airstream. We'll play soccer and stuff and then eat the fish and then at night if it's clear the stars are like nothing you've ever seen. I always come back from there smelling like smoke."

"I don't understand," Josh said. He crossed his arms, the suit crinkling in bunches to his shoulders. "What's all this about a salmon?"

"That's enough. Don't talk to me," I told him. "You're killing my mojo."

But that was Iowa and this is New Hampshire. Josh couldn't find his spacesuit before our flight via Midway into Boston and then a rental car to Manchester. There's a debate tonight and the pundits say it's make-or-break time for the good doctor.[26] Gephardt's out of the race and his Teamsters are wheels-up across the Northeast. Kerry and Edwards are very much still in it, though nobody really thinks Edwards is running for president.[27] Josh and I have our room at the Econo Lodge and at two in the morning last night we snuck onto the seventh floor of the Holiday Inn and charged sixty dollars' worth of wireless Internet onto the tab of a major television station.

They don't want to let me in at the Edwards rally in Nashua because I don't have any identification. "Anybody could walk in with a notepad in his hand," the door guy says.

"That's true," I say. My face is dry. Several hundred people are being escorted into an extra room. I don't want to go with them. I want to go inside the main hall, where the bleachers have been stacked and a flag hung across the gymnasium. I don't want to go to whatever horrible place those other people are going. "I'm sorry."

Sorry goes a long way in this world. And I am sorry. Sorry for leaving my credentials three freezing blocks away. Sorry for telling 2.2 million Sunday TV viewers that Joe Lieberman doesn't have a chance.[28] But Joe Lieberman never had a chance. Joe wanted to protect our children from porn, but what about the rest of us? The Defense of Marriage Act is explicitly unconstitutional. And my credentials aren't real anyway just a series of press passes accumulated from events I didn't belong at. Every time I get another one I hang it on a binder clip that I wear on a string around my neck. Passes beget passes. Press passes are easy to get; they give them to anybody. I've got enough press passes to play pinochle. But that's going to end soon. The campaigns are going to tighten up.

"Ladies and gentleman, the senator is in the building!"

Chanting, thumping, clapping. This is the middle school and there'll be three times this many or more when Kerry shows up at the high school just down the road two hours from now. One thousand people will show up to see Wesley Clark in between. This is not John Edwards's state but it looks like he's going to make a respectable showing.

I took some polls of my own and found that 80 percent of the people at Edwards rallies are undecided, but 80 percent at Dean and Kerry rallies are decided on the guy they came to see. I don't know what that means but I know that it's true. I know that Joe Lieberman has taken an apartment in Manchester but that he'll finish with less than 10 percent of the vote anyway. And there are a lot of people in New Hampshire who have never heard of Al Sharpton.

Edwards comes to the platform amidst cheers, "Edwards, Edwards, Edwards!" Something about Edwards rallies resembles college football games.

John Edwards is easy to listen to. "Together you and I are going to change this country. We have so much work to do. . . . There are thirty-five million Americans living in poverty and it is wrong. You and I are going to do something about it." Edwards gets better and better—they all do. Edwards is so sincere that you would never know that he's said the same speech five times a day for months.

Toward the middle Edwards hits my favorite line, where he mentions civil rights and the pundits who told him not to talk about civil rights in the South and John Edwards says, "I'll tell you where we need to talk about it. We need to talk about it every-where."

"Oh yeah," I say to Josh, hanging out behind a bank of TV cameras. "You got that right."

"I thought you liked Dean," Josh says. This morning Josh got up, unplugged my phone, and went back to sleep. I was in that place between dreams and earth and thought to myself, Why'd he unplug my phone? Josh doesn't understand I'm not talking about Edwards. I'm just talking about who's talking *right now.*

Later, at the Democratic dinner, Dean thanks half the people in the room, using up three and a half of his seven minutes. I say to my friend Dave, who is just now getting on the campaign, "He's responding to criticism that he didn't thank the Iowans on the night he left the state." I love hearing a speech and knowing where it came from and taking a jittery pulse of a country with an un-elected president in a time of war. But I don't love the war. And the war is fading from the news but it's going to come back. It would only take one more attack on American soil to completely change the debate. Sometimes it really gets me down but today I feel better.

Politics is about holding people accountable for their record but also listening to what they're talking about, finding out what each candidate's big issues are. Separating the politics from the person, fusing the organization to the man. You never get it until you're on the inside and even then you don't get it. There're days like today when the roar is so quiet and clean it's like being inside a wave.

January 27

Primary Day; The New Pornography; Time Pilot; Ikari Warriors; Pengo; Front Line; Tutankhamen; Ghosts and Goblins; Qix; Bill Shaheen

The first coin-operated video game was called Computer Space. It had basic graphics and you went inside a strange box to play it. But the first breakthrough was Space Invaders, followed by Pac-Man, which was released at the same time as Gorf. I remember hanging out at the Howard Bowl across from the Big Bite with my friend Roger and when Gorf and Pac-Man came out I told Roger that Gorf was going to be a really big game. After all, it was four in one. I thought Gorf was groundbreaking.

The Howard Bowl was a dirty place near the bus terminal and just down the street from Howard Books, a yellow-lit twenty-four-hour adult bookstore where I would end up working while a junior in college. This was before the Internet cornered the market on porn. Girls would hang out in front of the store and ask the men going inside if they'd like a little company inside.

Apparently there were a lot of applications to work the graveyard shift and they gave us all a test that resembled the LSAT, twenty logic games composed of two sets of rules with a table of possible results, and a time limit. I scored the highest so they gave me the job. At the time I was living with a girl named Andrea. Her seventh-grade boyfriend's name was tattooed across her knuckles. But that's another story. In the mornings a truck full of illegal immigrants would come in and clean the booths where clients watched dirty movies. The consoles had fast-forward buttons but no rewind. There was a roll of toilet paper on the wall and a small garbage can near the door. I worked there two weeks and I've never forgotten the smell.

But I was talking about video games, and the Howard Bowl. The economic zenith of the video game industry was 1973 to 1984, when the industry crashed. In 1983 Atari made $3.2 billion. Video halls were packed with children fumbling their parents' quarters into slots. Kids without money would stand near the edges, trying to steal coins stacked across the player buttons when nobody was looking.

There were thousands of blue-collar workers attached to the industry then, keeping the games fixed, loading the games onto trucks, delivering them to arcades, convenience stores, pool rooms, and everywhere else.

In 1986 video games started appearing with a continue feature. If you had enough money and time you could play as long as you wanted. Even the worst players could get to levels they'd never even thought about before. The industry didn't realize the disastrous impact this was going to have, and the makers of the games probably didn't care. The continue feature killed the players' desire to improve and ended the status previously enjoyed by high scorers transferring the advantage to the kids with the most quarters, money over skill.

Economics aside, the golden age of video games ran from about 1975, with the release of Shark Jaws, to 1987. The year 1987 saw Double Dragon, the first game not to have any purpose. Before that it was all reflex, puzzle, and maze, at least according to Gary Vincent, the general manager of the Fun Spot, in Weirs Beach, New Hampshire.

"The industry took a turn then that we didn't choose to follow," he told me.

The Fun Spot makes its money now on bingo, poker machines, Skee-Ball, and miniature golf. But upstairs there are 225 classic games and pictures of the people who made the high scores are prominently displayed. They play music up there exclusively from the mid-seventies to late eighties, just to keep the mood right. The video games cost more in electricity than they take in and most go without being played for weeks at a time. The area operates essentially as a museum, a shrine to a cultural shift in entertainment that is still with us today.

Gary's been working at the Fun Spot since 1981. "I started in the business when I was nineteen. I remember when Poll Position came in 1982. Before that there were games like Turbo and Monaco GP. Very basic. We plugged Poll Position in and we were just staring at it. I remember saying, *This is real*. I would stay two, three hours after work playing it." We asked Gary if any politicians ever come in to get a game fix. He said the last time was in 1996, when he saw Phil Gramm and Lamar Alexander.

Gary broke down the evolution for us. When Dragon's Lair came out in 1983 people thought it was the beginning of a new industry. The laser disc was going to change everything. All of the trade magazines called it the wave of the future. At the Fun Spot they put a TV on top of Dragon's Lair so people in the back of the crowd could see what was going on. The first time someone saved the princess Gary thought there would be a riot.

"The place erupted," he said.

But there wasn't much to Dragon's Lair. It was like a Choose Your Own Adventure book. Left, left, down, down. Once you knew the patterns you just moved the stick, pressed the button, and watched the movie. No skill, no reason to go on. The crowds plateaued, then diminished, then nobody would play. It would just sit there. None of the laser disc games did anything after that. The pundits were wrong.

I prodded Gary with my own prejudices. The best reflex games, he told us, were Defender and Stargate, because of the sheer number of controls. "You get games like that with dual joysticks and six buttons, it complicates the game, makes it a little more intense. It's a matter of remembering what buttons do what while you're watching the screen."

Gary told me and Josh about Stratovox, the first video game with a voice box, and how that was quickly co-opted and put out of business by Berzerk.

"Right," Josh said. "Berzerk stole Statovox's message. It all makes sense."

"But the real thing was Pac-Man," Gary said. "Space Invaders was the kickoff but girls didn't like it. Pac-Man was the first game that was all-inclusive—it appealed to everybody. And it was so marketable. Pac-Man was the pinnacle. The game was in color. There were Pac-Man cups, plates, cartoons, T-shirts, bedsheets."

"I had those," Josh said.

Gary stopped talking for a minute, stared at Josh.

"I guess we all did," Gary said.

Gary gave us a cup full of tokens and Josh and I decided to start with Gunsmoke, a basic video game, circa mid-eighties. In Gunsmoke you have a joystick and three buttons used to shoot forward, forward left, or forward right. The character you play is a cowboy and you're fighting bandits with guns and scarves over their face and half-naked Indians throwing sticks of dynamite. If you run over the dynamite before it explodes you can pick it up.

"Why don't they give the Indians guns?" Josh said.

"It's not that kind of a game," I told him.

Even though it's been many years since I played these games I still beat Josh handily. It's the kind of game that I used to specialize in, straight reflex with multiple fire options. Meanwhile, you have to keep picking up things like rifles to shoot farther and boots for speed. If you find a horse inside a barrel it's like getting an extra life. Your gun only shoots so far so the important thing is to keep your focus on your own character and the bullets coming toward you. If you focus too much on the enemy, you'll get shot and you won't even see the bullet coming.

Josh proves better than me at other games, like Paper Route. Games that have more to do with patience and planning, where reflex follows knowledge.

By five P.M. we'd been playing for hours and our nerves were like piano wire. The polls were going to close at seven and we wanted to stop by John Kerry's party to get some food and then check out the damage control at the Dean camp. But first we decided we would play Qix. It's a complicated game with a simple interface, the best kind. I was winning at first. Intuitively I understood the importance of building small blocks up the center and then filling in huge areas with just a small line. But we couldn't stop playing and by the third game Josh was creaming me with his slow button. Once he pulled away in five games I was never able to take the lead again.

"How did you do that?"

"That's my slow strategy," Josh said, wrapping his blue scarf around his neck and zipping his jacket. "Adapt and learn."

The Kerry party was another downer, especially after spending the day at the greatest arcade in America. The guy at the door wanted to see my credentials so I showed him my laminate for the Kerry party in Iowa. "That was Iowa," he told me.

"Sure was," I said. "I was on your bus in December when there were only eight of us. You were happy to have me around. You didn't have fifty-five press people and two buses then. The Death Bus, man. I bet you weren't even working for the campaign."

"If you can show me an ID that proves you work for a major newspaper I'll let you in. Otherwise you have to go."

"Let me talk to Teresa," I said. I could see Bob Novak hunched over his computer at the third table back in the filing center. There was a rumor going around that Novak had punched a Dennis Kucinich supporter earlier in the day.

"I can't let you talk to Teresa," he told me. "And you have to leave."

The Dean party was where I really wanted to be anyway. We had just figured on getting some food from Kerry because he does stuff like that well. Kerry events are all shirts and ties and party bosses. Old people and veterans and go-getters slick with ambition hoping to shake the senator's hand and maybe ask for a job.

But the Dean event was hopping. There were no four thousand out-of state volunteers this time. No kids in orange hats. There was a VIP party behind a blue curtain and a gymnasium packed with local supporters. The results came across the wires and *The Union*

Leader immediately ran a front page declaring, "Kerry Buried Dean." But actually the results didn't break down that easily, and the *Union Leader* article had never been proofread, so it was filled with typos, and words were missing throughout. My own grammar is not particularly good but I've never written anything so riddled with error, starting with the headline.[29]

Dean took 26 percent and Kerry 38. Twenty-six percent is a reasonable showing. I could say it's like Qix, but it's not even as difficult. In Qix you need 75 percent and in politics you get to keep going after you get zapped. Unless you're Trent Lott, and you actually *are* a racist.[30] But that's different. The primaries don't operate like the general election. In the primary you keep your delegates, even if you don't win. There are a couple of states voting on Tuesday with more delegates than Iowa and New Hampshire combined.

The real losers on the night were Lieberman and General Clark, who had predicated his strategy on battling Dean.

Dean gave a great speech this time. Like Kerry, Dean is good at learning from his mistakes. It was a thoughtful speech and, as he so often does, he spoke primarily in terms of "you" instead of "I." He stayed calm but the crowd screamed and pumped their fists. Dean said, "We can give the fifty percent of Americans who have quit voting a reason to vote again, and we will."

By the time we got back to the Holiday Inn the Kerry set was taken down. The bar was full of journalists, the convention area was nearly empty. The laborers were carrying planks balanced on their shoulders and unscrewing hinges with tools and belt packs. Bill Shaheen the head of Kerry's New Hampshire office, was still there. His wife, Jean Shaheen, is Kerry's national campaign chairwoman. They weren't serving drinks anymore in the convention area but Bill convinced them to give us three Coors Lights. We sat on the radiator at the window.

Bill has the look of a serious political fixer on a national level. I asked him if he was going to continue with the campaign and he brushed off the question. He said he was going to return to his law practice. Then I asked him if he had maybe stolen some of Dean's message, if Dean had taught Kerry what was important to the voters right now, because I felt like Dean had framed the debate. Back in July Kerry wasn't criticizing the war or the Patriot Act. Bill started to agree and then changed tack. "Listen," he said. "They're all basically the same. They all want health care." I didn't point out that Kerry doesn't have a great record when it comes to pushing for health care in Congress. Then Bill talked about Edwards, and how Edwards was a great candidate but maybe his organization wasn't so good. "When someone says they want to help, you don't just say vote for me. You sit them down, you give them a phone. You make sure they bring ten people with them before they go to the poll."

"I know what you mean," I said. "The Edwards campaign won't even let me on the bus. I think they're wise to me."

Bill walked away for an interview with CNN England. The bar was closing and journalists were abandoning their rooms as a string of cars lined up outside to take people in packs of four to the Manchester airport.

"So that's New Hampshire?" Josh said.

"Live free or die," I told him.

"Where do you think they're going?" he asked, gesturing toward the exit.

"South Carolina, Arizona. I don't know."

"I don't know, either," he said. "I think I'm going to head home. Los Angeles, where the sun always shines."

He stared out across the parking lot, imagining Interstate 405, sick with smog, clogged with another two A.M. traffic jam. "There's got to be a way to keep going."

"There isn't. We all run out of money at some point. You'll end up like Gephardt. And even if you didn't, even if you had a house you could mortgage for seven million dollars it would still end at some point."

"I know."

"Don't," I told him. "It's never going to go away. It's not worth thinking about."

IV. The Long-Term Effects of Optimism

A positive attitude does not improve the chances of surviving cancer, and doctors who encourage patients to keep up hope may burden them, according to research results released Monday. Optimism made no difference in the fates of most of the 179 cancer patients whom Australian researchers followed over five years. Only eight people were still living by the time the study ended in 2001.
—ASSOCIATED PRESS

January 30–February 6

Newark; Delta; San Francisco; The Drug Question; Personal Stuff; Promises, Lies, and Screams

I was supposed to watch the Super Bowl with John Edwards in South Carolina but I missed my nonstop flight. The lady at the counter didn't know what I was talking about.

"I'm supposed to be in Myrtle Beach," I told her, sliding my reservation across the counter. "John Kerry just won by twelve points and John Edwards fought Wesley Clark to a statistical tie.

There's a blizzard in Boston and South Carolina is Edwards's last shot. It's a must-win state for him."

"We don't have you listed," she told me. "And we don't fly nonstop to Myrtle Beach."

I looked behind me. I could see a plain, frozen field speckled with tollbooths like fishing shacks and then the Marriott hotel in the distance and past the Marriott there was nothing. I was in Newark, ten dollars outside of New York. I couldn't decide if I was running out of time or if time had already run out. Al Sharpton was polling South Carolina at 15 percent and insisting that he was the *only* one who could bring his voters into the party. Wesley Clark was supposed to be in South Carolina as well but his strategy had changed. On January 28 his plane touched down only to refuel and then continued on to Oklahoma. I was losing my thread.

"Maybe you mean Hooters Airline," the lady at the Delta desk told me. I was wearing my white down jacket that's so dirty at this point it would more accurately be described as ash. The zipper is broken so it's very difficult to take off and it makes me look like a snowman at a gas station.

"I'd know if I was on Hooters," I told her.

Then I realized I was at the wrong airport. I was supposed to be at LaGuardia. Of course, why would anyone offer a nonstop flight from Newark into Myrtle Beach in the middle of winter? And why was I flying to Myrtle Beach when the Super Bowl party was in Charleston? And if the New England Patriots beat the Carolina Panthers, wouldn't that be the absolute worst election-year metaphor of all time?[1]

I turned away from the counter and balled my fists. There was the Marriott. It looked like Shackleton's *Endurance* caught in all that ice, the distances between the bergs immeasurable. It was obvious what I was supposed to do. I would just cancel my ticket and get another flight, a puddle jumper with a stopover in Atlanta. Except that it was already too late.

Not in the real sense (i.e., with 1 percent of the delegates accounted for, it's not too late for Howard Dean to make a come-back), but emotionally speaking. I'd been on the road twenty-six days with two changes of clothes and a computer. I had been in so many cities that I had lost track of time and place. Delta Airlines was charging me one hundred dollars for the mistake and Orbitz slapped on another thirty. They wouldn't give me my money back but said I could apply the balance to my next ticket as long as I didn't try to book the ticket over the Internet.

Speaking of the Internet, wasn't this supposed to be the Internet campaign? I was in the bar the other night with John Hlinko and Zephyr Teachout. John was the founder of draftwesleyclark.com, the Web site that convinced the general to run. It turned out that John was also my ex-fiancée's cousin, but that's another story.[2]

John had put his life on hold for six months while he organized and raised money, waiting to see if he could actually get the general into the race. By the time Clark finally entered, draftwesleyclark.com had sixty thousand members and had raised two million dollars. "It's the first time a candidate has ever been drafted by the people," John told me and went on to explain how Eisenhower had been drafted by other politicians. It really was an amazing feat. Zephyr, of course, is the person that made meetup.com a house-hold word. Between the two of them, Zephyr and John had changed politics forever, so what were they doing at my table?

The bar at the Center Holiday Inn was seven deep with journal-ists and not one of them came by to interrupt. On the one hand, I was semi-ex-related to John, and Zephyr had slept on my hotel-room floor. But this didn't explain everyone's lack of interest. It was the night before the New Hampshire primary and maybe everyone had already filed their stories, or maybe journalists are more interested in talking to one another. Worse, maybe they're only really interested in talking to the candidates, the rock stars of the process.

Meanwhile, Bush was still referring to weapons of mass destruc-tion in his speeches. The president was an idiot and a stone-cold liar, but I wasn't sure that anybody cared.[3] Bush was running as a wartime president but CNN was just as interested in a new diet that worked without exercise. I kept thinking that the sacrifices had to come from somewhere. I had been waking up paranoid and delusional, convinced that there wouldn't be an actual election in 2004. The lady at the ticket counter in Newark didn't know who John Kerry was, and maybe it was a coincidence or maybe it served me right for flying Delta. I was wet and strung out and tired of strangers. I hadn't played poker since New Year's Eve. The night before I had watched a debate between Christopher Hitchens and Mark Danner. Hitchens looked like someone had tried to drown him just minutes before he came on stage. He was supporting the war in Iraq; my heroes were letting me down.

I bought the cheapest ticket I could find from Newark to San Francisco and regretted it immediately. My veins squeezed shut. Where would I get my next political fix? Then the lady at the counter asked me, if John Kerry won five states on Tuesday, would it be over? She had been kidding about not knowing who John Kerry was. I laughed nervously and told her what mattered was Michigan and Wisconsin—we'd have to wait and see. I got on the plane from Newark two hours later. I had run out of places to go.

San Francisco was raining again and I called Wilhelmina to tell her I was home. She said she would be able to see me in three days.

"Oh," I replied.

"Are you pouting?" she asked.

"I guess I am."

"Well don't."

I spent my first night back in a drunken fog, hovering around bars within walking distance of her house. In San Francisco the buildings are colorful, even at night when the streets are black and wet. I felt like a stalker. I kept hoping she would walk into one of the bars, but knew that Wilhelmina never went to bars. She doesn't like to meet people and she doesn't like to drink. I left her a message every time I changed location so if she changed her mind she would know where to find me.

Of course, it was my fault. I had told her I would be home five days ago. The plan was to come back for two days and then go to Arizona, check out the difference between Flagstaff and the Grand Canyon, see if the Kerry camp could settle the desert like a sandstorm. Then Michigan; then Wisconsin, where Dean will roll the dice on a bounce two weeks before Super Tuesday. But this didn't happen. I tried to go to South Carolina and that didn't happen either. Now I was back in San Francisco unannounced and Wilhelmina wasn't ready for me. I was the one with the screwed-up schedule. But there was this election going on and I couldn't get enough of it. All the signs were pointing toward a John Kerry victory. The front-loaded timeline was going to screw everybody. Howard Dean had fired Joe Trippi and taken on a serious Washington insider, Roy Neel, to run his campaign. It turns out that Joe Trippi had given Dean some advice on January 19, the night of the Iowa caucus when Dean took only 18 percent, a serious drop from 30 percent just weeks before. Joe Trippi told Dean as he headed toward the stage, "When you've got nothing, you've got nothing left to lose." But Dean had a lot more to lose, starting with New Hampshire, where 26 percent was considered a massive loss. The Dean campaign had never got it together for the big time. In Iowa, Senator Tom Harkin couldn't believe Dean didn't have a concession speech ready; nobody had written one for him. Then the microphone was wrong. As usual, the television cameras were not positioned properly because the Dean campaign always paid more attention to their supporters than to the media. The result was the Yeeeaaah! heard around the world.

John Kerry has never made those kinds of mistakes. He's always had the best handlers money could buy. And nobody has ever expected Kerry to run as an outsider, so nobody gets mad when he turns out to be just another politician. Nobody really thinks John Kerry is going to deliver on health care, and if he keeps winning the way he's winning I'll have to spend a lot of time with him between now and November. And that's a hard thing to imagine. It's going to take lots of ephedrine, Ritalin, cocaine, and maybe some crystal meth. It's going to take more speed than I can currently afford but there might not be enough pills available when the press pack traveling with Kerry already occupies two giant buses, and it won't be long before they're hitching on a third. One of the reasons the press is rarely that hard on Kerry is because by the end of the day they're so tired they don't have the energy left to support their invective and the easiest thing to do in such a situation is just quote the speech and go to bed.

San Francisco is warm compared with the rest of the country, but colder than usual. I leave my old jacket on the sidewalk in front of Andy Miller's house and it lies there for days. The junkies and hookers step over it on their way to the 17th Street gas station and the one-dollar corn dogs and fried chicken breast always available near the lottery machine.

I buy a new jacket and two pairs of wool socks; I'm tired of being cold. The jacket is down with a six hundred-feather count, two sizes smaller than my usual. My clothes are baggy all of a sudden. I'd presumed that it was from wearing the same two shirts and pants for four weeks but at home I realize all of my other clothes are too large as well.

"You're shrinking," Wilhelmina tells me on February 3. "And you're going bald." We're watching the returns on her television set. There are seven states weighing in on the presidential candidates. I sit on the floor and she sits on the couch with her legs over my shoulders. She wears red and white tights striped like candy canes. I feel warm and safe and consider reciting the old Steve Martin skit, about small pills. How the police would pull you over and give you the balloon test. If you fit inside the balloon, they know you're small. But Wilhelmina wouldn't get it. So I watch quietly as John Kerry wins five states and John Edwards captures South Carolina.

WISCONSIN

February 8–11

Prologue as Epilogue; The Wisconsin Story; The Movie Metaphor; Howard Dean's Socks; Take What You Can Get; Drug Industry Whores

There are facts and truths and political truths but there's always another story and it's hard, oh so hard, to trust the media. The fact is that Howard Dean has stated he would drop out of the race for president if he did not win Wisconsin. That's the truth on the ground as the wheels of ATA Flight 936 kiss the pavement at Midway Airport late Sunday night. In response, hundreds of thousands of dollars are raised on the Dean for America Web site to fund Howard Dean's last stand. But what if Dean didn't say that? What if that was just an e-mail from Roy Neel, thinking aloud and then accidentally hitting the send button? And if Howard Dean denied it the next day? Would it be too late?

The roads north of Chicago are slick with ice. By three in the morning the only vehicles other than my own are tractor trailers jackknifed on the side of the tollway, their blinking lights blurred by the snow. The campaign has staked everything on a Wisconsin victory, whether it meant to or not. The former front-runner and presumptive candidate has yet to win a primary. The John Kerry machine has been leaving tire prints across the field and the race is not as close as it looks if you're just counting delegates. It takes 2,161 delegates to lock down the Democratic nomination for president. The numbers, nine days before the Wisconsin primary, have John Kerry with 320 compared to 136 for Howard Dean. But if

you look closer you'll see a different story. Most of Dean's delegates are super-delegates, political officials like mayors and sheriffs
who operate outside the primaries and caucuses, who gave their
support to Dean back when he was the hottest ticket in town. But
super-delegates often change their minds, and their votes are only
as good as what they expect in return. Of the pledged delegates,
the delegates elected in preference primaries and caucuses, Dean is
dead last. Several super-delegates have already switched to John
Kerry. The American Federation of State, County, and Municipal
Employees has pulled its support, saying they'll hold out for the
general election. This is a story about abandonment.

This is also a story written for people who already know the ending. Like in the movie *Casino,* which opens with a scene of Robert
De Niro exploding from his car in a small Las Vegas parking lot. Cut
back to the beginning: music, dice, money, and Sharon Stone.

But this is not about Las Vegas. This is about the American electoral process and the seventeenth state, a frozen voting bloc of
seventy-two pledged and fifteen unpledged delegates lodged between Chicago and Lake Superior. This is about an Indian tribe
that tried to open a casino in the state capital and ended up on the
same ballot as the presidential primary and lost. This is about what
money can't buy. Howard Dean spent close to fifty million dollars,
more than any Democrat before him, and never won a state.

Howard Dean kicks off his Real Choice, Real Change tour at the
Concourse Hotel in Madison at 9:45 on Monday morning. Several
hundred people sit in a ballroom on the second floor. There is a
world-weariness about the room as the supporters wait with blue
and white signs across their laps and the camera techs wrangle the
mike cords. These are not new voters, these are people who have
been Dean supporters since he forcefully posed his question to the
Democratic National Committee nearly a year ago: "Why aren't
Democrats standing up to Republicans on the war in Iraq?"

"What happened to you?" It's Toni Montgomery from the *Florida Observer*.[4]

"I slept in a rest stop," I tell him. "The chassis was on a snow-bank and I left the car running and the window cracked so I didn't die of carbon-monoxide poisoning."

"No, I mean where have you been."

"Oh. I went home for a couple of days to see my girlfriend. But it didn't work out too well."

Dean approaches the podium and thanks the local organizer. The crowd claps and Dean waits for them to finish.

"The lobbying disclosure system in this country is a joke. . . . Democrats who watched the popularity polls and cut bad deals with the White House are not the right people to stand up to George Bush this fall. . . . Bush wanted enormous tax giveaways for the richest people and corporations, creating enormous deficits that mortgage our children's future. The Washington Democrats went along. . . . George Bush embarked on a unilateral, preemptive, wrongheaded war in Iraq. He misled us about the facts. Washington Democrats looked at the polls and went along. Without asking the hard questions, they gave George W. Bush a blank check."

It's a great speech but a small crowd, and he sounds just like he used to when I got hooked on this trip back in July, like someone nobody has ever heard of speaking candidly, as if, yes, he has nothing to lose. The words don't flow from him and when he pauses it always looks like he's forgotten what he was going to say. There are more than five standing ovations.

Toni gives me the real scoop on background behind the riser. "Staff members are abandoning the campaign as if it were a burning building," he says, pulling out a packet of cigarettes and offering me one. "Go ahead." He pushes the pack toward me so I take a cigarette and put it behind my ear. "John Kerry's running the most vicious and mean-spirited campaign of any Democrat since Al Gore. Remember those late-night phone calls to Dean supporters in New Hampshire? That shit was Kerry straight down to the fingerprints on the receiver. Here's one last tip: remember the Lyndon LaRouche supporters showing up at Dean events throughout December waving Confederate flags? Check out the LaRouche/Kerry connection." Toni crosses his arms over his chest, the smoke hanging in his bangs like a mist.

I never know how much to believe with Toni, though the Lyndon LaRouche supporters were real—I saw them. They were dancing like mystics around a fire and wearing pointy white hats at the College Convention in Manchester. And the late-night phone calls in New Hampshire were well documented. But nobody knows where they came from and, with less and less coverage dedicated to Dean, no one is likely to make the effort to find out. The only thing people know for sure is that John Kerry and Richard Gephardt shared notes on Howard Dean in Iowa and former key operatives from both campaigns took part in a shady group called Americans for Jobs, Healthcare, and Progressive Values.[5]

After the event I run into Bill Margolin. He's eighty-one years old but looks closer to sixty-five. His wife passed away a year ago. He's still wearing his orange Perfect Storm hat that he got while canvassing for Dean in Iowa.[6]

Before retiring, Bill was an engineer in Detroit. "I had other hobbies. I love to sail. I was a musician. I played violin and my wife played viola. But I'm taking a year off of that." Bill is one of those cool old guys who are easy to like. He's very alive. He says he's never been involved in politics before but after Iowa he caught a flight to New Hampshire because he didn't want to miss a day. Then he rode with other volunteers to Michigan, and now here. "I knock on doors and make phone calls," he says, pulling on his gloves. He got the campaign to give him the software from Iowa so he could figure out how the canvassing operation works. He likes Dean the best but is willing to work with whichever Democrat captures the nomination. "We have to beat Bush," he says, and gives me a look that's part hope and part exasperation, as if what he's saying is obvious. Something in his look belies a faith in the basic goodness of humanity and for a moment I'm jealous. "We have to beat him," he continues. "The guy's an asshole and a cretin. He's running the country and he's a liar."

The downtown Hilton dominates the Milwaukee skyline, an enormous redbrick building in three sections with a giant middle and twenty-four floors of corridors stretching off its center like a gargoyle with its wings half closed. This is where the press will spend most nights, high above the Polish and black neighborhoods and far away from the political heart of Wisconsin's famously blue-collar city. The Dean national staff will stay here as well, working shortened days between the exercise room and tours of the beer factories. The hotel has a water park that you get to through a special elevator on the sixth floor.

Meanwhile, the Dean state staff is mostly in a series of shabby rooms above a coffee shop and a row of used bookstores in downtown Madison, near the capitol building. There's no getting past the sense of doom that now hangs over the campaign. Staffers speak openly of what went wrong and what their plans are for the future. They blame each other, they blame the media, and they blame the candidate. One thing that's clear at this point is that Iowa was the whole game. It's been said that you can't underestimate the effect Iowa has on New Hampshire, but everybody did. Wesley Clark criticized his own campaign for the decision not to compete in Iowa, a decision that, at least for a while, looked like a stroke of genius. But good instinct is something that can only be determined in retrospect. The truth is that Clark's whole campaign was predicated on John Kerry losing, at which point Clark, who had voted for Nixon and Reagan, would present himself as the last chance for Democrats who were worried that Dean would suffer a disastrous loss to George Bush in the fall. But when Kerry won, Clark became an unnecessary safety valve and he dropped out after humiliating third-place finishes in both Tennessee and Virginia.[7] Hindsight now says Dean's Iowa organization was fucked, their phone lists and databases a disorganized mess exacerbated by a massive data flush in December and the stress of handling four thousand mostly shaggy volunteers streaming in from all over the country to invade and annoy the Iowan citizenry. And people knew as early as September but nobody did anything about it, mostly out of a sense of loyalty and decency to the people who were there from the beginning. That kind of loyalty is something that filters down from the top and is unlikely to afflict a candidate like Kerry, who, not unlike Bush, is capable of doing anything to win. Dean's tightly run ship in New Hampshire was unable to overcome the Iowa disaster. With the primaries now moving at such a clip the Dean camp has the vantage point of an island looking at the back of a tidal wave; all of the houses are already destroyed, everything is soaked.

Dean now opens every speech exhorting the crowd not to listen to the media before rattling off a list of all the reasons John Kerry should be seen as a first-class scumbag. He reminds everybody that he was the one to start talking about the war in Iraq, the tax cuts, and the No Child Left Behind act. All of which is true but is hardly relevant since the other candidates co-opted his platform at the exact same time that Dean was toning down his act and running TV ads in Texas.

At dinner several journalists make tender jokes about Howard Dean's poor choice of wardrobe and the socks he was wearing, which had holes in them. We're at Sauces, an overpriced restaurant fifteen minutes from the hotel, with a strange, curvaceous interior and twenty-five-dollar entrées. All the major media—Fox, the AP, CNN, *The New York Times*—are here but in significantly smaller numbers, and the other outlets have pulled their coverage altogether. A reporter from *Newsweek* is in attendance but she's flying out tomorrow, pretty sure her story won't run in the magazine but might appear on the Web site. The AP has pulled their main reporter, Nedra Pickler, off the Dean bus, choosing to rely on coverage from its local staff and fly Ross Sneyd from Vermont for Dean's final stand. Nobody knows why I'm here, but nobody really cares.

Things are a lot more relaxed these days. I sit right across from the Fox executive who once asked me to vacate her seat in the back of press bus #1 before a six-hour leg toward Sioux City (not to be confused with the more volatile morning when Josh Bearman was asked to move for a fifteen-minute jaunt across town).[8] Those were the heady days before everything went so glaringly wrong. Though in retrospect, things had already gone wrong. There was a heavy pecking order back then and I was on the bottom of it, distrusted by staff and looked down on by the traveling press. But there are no stars on a sinking ship.

Somewhere in the wistful banter between the press and the staffers, one of the journalists says, "We never got him socks." Apparently, there was a plot among the traveling press to purchase four pairs of socks for Dean's fifty-fifth birthday. But that was November 17, Dean was the front-runner and the Democratic Party machinery was in a panic. Dean was saying that when he got to the capital, members of Congress would scurry "like a bunch of cockroaches" under a light. In all the commotion, as the turboprop whipped between D.C., Baltimore, and Manchester, the socks were forgotten. With so much money and momentum it seemed like things would keep going forever, or at least for another year, until the voters pulled the handle in the general election. But now the socks, which were never bought, are remembered as one more opportunity missed.[9]

The Hilton is hosting a convention of pharmaceutical workers. They hang out in suits with name tags taped to their jackets.

Hookers lounge near the poker machine waiting for easy money from traveling salesmen missing their wives. The young Dean staffers call the bar girls "cougars."

"You guys just don't know what it feels like to be on a losing campaign," says Jay Carson, Dean's spokesman, staring into his drink. Before Dean, Jay had worked in the capital for Tom Daschle and had contracted anthrax. The blue Dean pin is gone from his lapel, replaced with a red one that reads "Miller High Life."

"Actually, I do know what it feels like to be on a losing campaign," I say, referring to Nader's run in 2000. Nobody seems to think that's comparable, and a look of anger and blame stretches over some faces. But even that passes. No point in being angry now.

In a game of quarter ante/quarter bet, Jodi Wilgoren tells us about playing poker with Jim McManus in Chicago. She says she lost four hundred dollars in that game of poker with McManus, for which *The New York Times* reimbursed her one hundred.

Jodi's not a good player but she could be. She's got a sharp, impatient, analytical mind. If she played regularly she would destroy everybody. The game we play is slightly weird. Someone insists that whoever bets last has to lead the betting, negating the dealer's advantage immediately following the flop. Jay Carson stares at his cards too long, deciding what to do. A suggestion is made to play Seven Card Howard Dean, wherein you get the option of joining back in the hand after you muck your cards.[10] The problem with getting back in is that you're no longer eligible for the big pot; you only get to keep what you win from the point you return to the game. In other words, you have to start from scratch. A bad bet, but the only way to pull anything out of a low house on the river. Take what you can get.

And this is the problem the Dean campaign faces, a problem more insurmountable by the day: first he called Wisconsin a must-win state, but then backtracked from that to say he would continue on, no matter what. Meanwhile, the other candidates are getting coverage talking health care, education, an unjustified and poorly planned war, and tax giveaways. And nobody remembers that those were Dean's issues—that six months ago, the other candidates weren't criticizing the war and the Patriot Act and demanding better health care.[11] And maybe it doesn't matter. Maybe the message means more than the man and it was Howard Dean's job to bring that message and deliver it to someone electable. But voting for someone who is electable is a slippery slope. If you vote for someone who is electable and then he loses, then you have to go back and examine your vote and question your own judgments and motivations. If you don't like a candidate but vote for him because you want to vote for a winner, and he doesn't win, then someone has tricked you. You've given something away and gotten nothing in return.[12]

By this logic the people who really wasted their votes in 2000 are the ones who voted for Gore instead of Bradley and Nader because they thought that Gore was the best candidate to beat Bush. I remember that campaign and finding someone who really wanted Gore to be president was a real task. The people who supported Gore ended up with Bush in office anyway. Kerry's camp has played on this theme more successfully than anyone else in this election cycle. It was the main argument the Kerry campaign made through December and January, and it's probably the main reason he's about to secure the nomination. And they were probably right. Dean was probably not the best candidate to go against Bush and in the age of the dirty bomb it's possible we've run out of time. But if Kerry loses we'll have nothing left. It's a horrible lesson to take to heart, that you shouldn't vote for the person you actually want to be president, but rather vote against someone you don't. Nader's candidacy was the death knell of the third party. After what happened in 2000 it will be a generation before Americans stop thinking that way and insist on a president with integrity. And there's no reason to think there'll be anything worth salvaging at that point. We're now willing to forgive our politicians for all kinds of things in deference to the practicality of getting them elected. We've placed electability on a pedestal to be worshiped like a false god and surrounded it with the jewels of a stagnant voter base and their apathetic treasures.

In the last thirty-six years this issue may be the one that most defines the Democrats. It's the reason Hubert Humphrey was put up against Nixon in 1968 and the reason the party failed to get behind McGovern in 1972. It's a challenge of ideology versus practicality. The most practical Democratic president since Johnson would, by most standards, be Bill Clinton. He would also be the most successful. And that's unfortunate in so many ways. But who wouldn't want Bill Clinton back? In hindsight and by comparison he's a pillar of integrity and imagination, despite all the evidence to the contrary.

"Come on, Jay."

"I'm thinking."

The maximum bet in the poker game is seventy-five cents and a dollar on the final hand. With two fours in the flop I win a side bet with Jodi that neither of the two players are sitting on three of a kind. I find her faith in the honesty and skill of the other players startling.

February 12–13

An Angry Question-and-Answer; Sandra's Dance of Hope

On the sixth floor of a technical school in Milwaukee, Dean blasts Kerry in an unannounced press avail. He says that John Edwards is a better candidate. He says it would be a shame if the American people had to choose between the lesser of two evils. He's surrounded by cameras and tape recorders. Dean's anger is both vicious and justified. Under further questioning he says he will support any Democratic candidate but it's hard to imagine him really coming out for Kerry after saying, as he does in this appearance, that Kerry's "going to turn out like George Bush."

That's the message played in all the papers and TV, Howard Dean angrily denouncing John Kerry. Nobody pays any attention to what happens next, at the rally in Memorial Hall. Memorial Hall is on the campus of the University of Wisconsin and over a thousand students fill the seats. This is the news Dean wanted to get across, but didn't. Here are the new voters the campaign has been promising to bring to the polls since the summer, the ones whom Dean has promised to give a reason to vote again.

But nobody pays any attention. The big news for the day is a rumor downloaded from the Drudge Report that John Kerry had done filthy things with a bottle of Vaseline and an intern and the intern has been sent off to Africa to hide.[13] And that is all anyone in the press pool is thinking about. Dean won't comment on the issue and most of the newspapers still aren't writing about it, or not too much, because, without a smoking dress or some cryogenically frozen sperm, it's still just a rumor. But it's a rumor every paper wants to print—they're just waiting on a good reason.

In Memorial Hall Dean is introduced by his wife, Judy Dean, who stands awkwardly on the stage and says a couple of words about Howard being a good person who would make a good president. She had stayed out of the campaign until after Iowa. She looks around as if she is waiting for him to come out, but he doesn't. She begins to walk off; she goes left, then right, and then left again. Then music starts and the curtain lifts behind her and her husband is there with a bunch of supporters cheering and shaking signs. Howard hugs his wife tightly and for just a moment she buries her nose in his neck.

There are a lot of kids—the most I've seen since I first saw Howard Dean on the campus of the University of Iowa, but not enough to fill the balcony. And Dean gives the same speech he's been giving, with a little more emphasis on civil unions. When he's finished, the music kicks back in and the volunteers who were sitting next to me jump out of their seats and start dancing.

February 14–16

Into the Looking Glass Backward; Wausau! Wausau! Wausau!; The Orpheum; Everybody Hates the Media

Racine is south of Milwaukee on the lake halfway to Chicago. Chairs are set up around a podium with a stage in the middle. "This is a bad turnout," Mike Tate, Dean's Wisconsin state director, says to me. "But we planned this less than twenty-four hours ago."

"Maybe that's the problem," I say.

During the question-and-answer a supporter stands to tell Dean that she doesn't know where the polls get their data because *everybody* she's talked to is going to vote for the governor.[14] Dean nods politely, pretending he doesn't already know exactly how many votes he has as of yesterday, how many more he needs to get, where he has to go to get them, and what his chances are.

I can almost see past Dean's tight smile, to where his teeth meet his gums. This was the man who was almost the Democratic nominee for president and now he has to stand and listen to this junk. I want him to say, "Thanks a lot but you don't know anything. You won't be there to console me when you're proven wrong. Now sit down."

But he doesn't, and the thought brings me back to January 11, eight days before the Iowa caucuses, when the polls still had Dean with a strong lead and the landscape was endless all the way to Sioux City. That was the day Dean met Dale Ungerer. The event was in Oelwein and Dean had been campaigning nonstop. The press bus smelled of fish. Ungerer was sixty-six years old with skin like gravel. He looked the way Iowa looks, with its decreasing population and declining farms. He stood up during the question-and-answer period and told Dean to tone down "the garbage, the mean-mouthing [of George Bush]." He continued on for three minutes until Dean finally said, "Sit down. You've had your say and now I'm going to have my say." And that was probably the point at which Howard Dean lost the race. The trap had already been set. A whisper campaign had been under way for months about Dean's "famous" anger, and finally someone had coerced him into that net. Dale Ungerer was a registered Republican and was semifamous in that small county for building a thirty-two-foot corn cob made of gallon milk jugs. The Iowa voters didn't like it when Dean was impolite to one of their own.

But Dale Ungerer is an oversimplification. The word among Dean's own press and staff is that he'd been on self-destruct for months. Forget the organizational failures; many question if Howard Dean ever really wanted to be president, pointing to a series of misstatements that ranged from Osama to Saddam to Confederate flags. Of course Dean wanted to be president, but a person can want two conflicting things at the same time.

The writing is on the wall for Howard Dean, our journey together is ending. The sad truth is that I always thought he would be a great president, but he's not much of a politician. He wasn't perfect, he flip-flopped on Cuba, his views on the death penalty are absurd, and when he started talking about his personal relationship with Jesus Christ I went into a brief depression. But he has a level of integrity that's rare in candidates for the highest office. I remember the first time I heard him talk about the economy, and he said he would repeal *all* of the Bush tax cuts to balance the budget and with the money left over he would provide health care. The only other major candidate willing to repeal all of the tax cuts was Dick Gephardt but Dick's plans were much more expensive than Dean's, $224 billion for health care, compared with $87 billion.

So it's been a long journey that we'll both continue separately in some new capacity. In the final days he speaks about issues and voters coming together to change the party into something that can beat George Bush. The day before the Wisconsin primary I drive to Wausau, three hours north of Milwaukee. It's a flat and ugly drive until you get there, when tiny lumps of snow ringed with chairlifts struggle out of the distance to the north and west. Otherwise everything is white, the only variations are the exits, splotched as if with red paint by McDonald's and Arby's.

There's no reason for all three candidates to appear in Wausau the day before the primary, but they're all here regardless. Wausau has been devastated by factory closings and jobs being moved out of the country and every candidate talks about NAFTA and Bush's jobless recovery. Both Dean and Kerry have altered their positions on NAFTA and Edwards says he's the only candidate who's always been against it (but he wasn't in the Senate at the time, so he didn't have to vote on it). This morning it was announced that Steve Grossman, the chair of Dean's campaign, is leaving. Grossman worked Kerry's senate bid in 1996 and is a keen example of the political opportunism that tore apart the Dean campaign. When Dean appeared to be a lock for the nomination everybody was climbing aboard. Now he's taking their careers down with him. Grossman's resignation—or firing, depending on who you listen to—is the final nail in a coffin that was already closed.

The first rally in Wausau is for John Kerry. Risers are built six high but not in places that will block the cameras. Roughly 250 locals are squeezed together with plenty of space left over for the press behind the rope. An overflow room with a cable link is set up in the cafeteria and two hundred more watch on closed-circuit television. Kerry is questioned on his vote for NAFTA. He responds by pointing out that key side provisions are not being enforced. He says we need to review NAFTA. In response to a question about Colombia, he says we need to review our policy toward Latin America as well. As usual the rally is dotted with bright yellow shirts, representatives of the firefighters' union, the muscle behind Kerry's organization. Kerry has worked diligently in the Senate for first responders such as firemen. He also has one of the best records on the environment and was instrumental in the fight against oil drilling in Alaska.

These are my thoughts as I'm walking back to my rental car and my phone rings. It's Toni, back in Florida and now writing about celebrities in Miami Beach for the tabloids and working on his tan while watching the election on C-SPAN. "Did you notice how he licks his lips when he talks?" Toni says.

"Kerry?" I ask.

"Yeah. He does this thing where he opens his mouth and his tongue darts out to touch his lower lip."

"Maybe his lips are dry."

"Yeah," he says. "Dry lips. And his daughter's a doctor and he's never heard of Chap Stick."

I hang up on Toni and head to the Edwards event. Fewer than two hundred people show up for John Edwards and in the afternoon four hundred people pack the Labor Temple for Howard Dean. I place a losing twenty-dollar bet with the reporter from *The Washington Post* that Howard Dean will beat John Edwards by five percentage points. But I know I've made a mistake right away by his eager acceptance of my wager. After the Labor Temple I speed to Madison to catch Dean's last act before primary night, a rally at the Orpheum Theatre. There are roughly two thousand people there, including his staff and a ton of press. I'm late and take a seat on the floor in the aisle. Dean is conciliatory, thanking everyone for their support, emphasizing the importance of their vote, stating that he's going to back whoever the Democratic nominee may be. He mentions that the other candidates stole his message, but that's a good thing. He's glad they did.

Following the rally, I go out for a drink with Bill Margolin and eight or nine Dean volunteers. The bar has stopped serving food and closed its second floor. There's a lot of talk about the media conspiracy, about John Kerry owning fifty million in media stock. "Are you with the media?" someone asks me.

"Not really," I reply. I could just as easily have said, *Aren't we all?*

Many of them have been volunteering for Dean for months and tomorrow will be time to go home. It's a strange mix of anger, loneliness, and hope that drives a person to work on a presidential campaign, without pay, nine months before the general election. They talk about putting limits on what the media can and can't say. "They're not doing their job," one of them says. But I remember the Kerry bus when times were bad and how upset the Kerry people were, especially with *The Boston Globe*, which they thought was deliberately distorting the truth. Nobody's ever happy with the media. In Israel in 2001 I stood next to CNN outside the Jerusalem Sbarro, which a suicide bomber had turned into a twisted pile of beams and concrete with spider cracks along the foundation and wires hanging from the ceiling. One of the chefs was walking up and down the street in a daze, his white smock covered in blood. And Uzi Landau, the right-wing minister of the interior, spoke angrily about the media's biased coverage. He said Hamas and the Palestinian Authority were the same thing, a statement he surely knew was incorrect, even as metaphor. Some Hasidim were boycotting *The New York Times*.

The next day I was with a Palestinian general on a hill in Ramallah, overlooking what was once a police station. It was dusk and the edges of the sky were pink-purple, as if bruised. The Israelis had bombed the station to a pile of bricks and dust. The general spoke harshly of the false media covering the conflict, the lies propagated in *The New York Times*. "Four hundred people worked in that building," he said. "We were lucky to hear the planes coming and quickly evacuate."

I nearly laughed, except I was surrounded by men with guns and my taxi was waiting to take me back to the checkpoint. What the general said was nowhere near the truth. The Israeli authorities had warned them ahead of time to evacuate the building so they could bomb it. If the Israelis hadn't warned them everyone would have died. That was when I knew that everybody was lying, and that everybody hates the press.

But Bill doesn't jump on that bandwagon. He orders a Guinness and grips it tightly when the waitress comes by to clear the glasses. "Oh no you don't," he says, smiling like a child. If I could figure out what he does to stay so young and alive I would do it every day. He tells me that he started with Dean because he thought Dean was the only one who could beat Bush. And in the process he came to like Howard Dean very much. But he'll regroup, take a little time off, and then go to work for whoever the Democratic nominee is. Several other people echo his sentiment.

"It's going to be hard going out for Kerry," one of them says.

Bill tells me about his experiences in World War II. He worked in the signal core in the Pacific Theater. "I was almost four-F, because of my eyesight." I ask Bill if he wishes he had been political earlier. He says he doesn't think that way. "You've got to look ahead," he tells me. Bill has been sharing a room with two other Dean volunteers. He's the greatest old man I've ever met.

February 17

Howard Dean's End

The night of the primary Howard Dean comes in third with 18 percent of the vote and addresses a small crowd of loyal supporters. "I know some of you are disappointed. But I also want you to think for a moment of how far we have come. The truth is, change is tough. There is enormous institutional pressure in this country against change. There is enormous institutional pressure in Washington against change in the Democratic Party. . . . [But] you have already started to change the Democratic Party and we will not stop." It's a fine ending to a turbulent campaign, though not the ending many had wished for back when ten thousand people showed up to see Howard Dean in Seattle, during the Sleepless Summer tour.

The journalists from larger organizations like the *Los Angeles Times* and *Time* magazine have pitched in to get shirts made to remember their time together. The front of the shirts say "Establishment Media." On the back they say, "We Have The Power—Dean Press Corps 2004."

I hang out in the Concourse ballroom long after Howard Dean and his entourage leave on a charter to Vermont. I throw my press credentials in the garbage and grab a Miller Lite from the ice tub, but I'm not fooling anyone. "Where's your notepad?" somebody asks spitefully. Several volunteers approach to voice their complaints against the biased coverage their campaign received.

"You don't have to worry about that anymore," I promise them.

In the morning Howard Dean officially drops out of the race but urges his supporters not to vote for a third-party candidate, an obvious reference to Ralph Nader.[15] The newspapers are filled with Dean obituaries. It's easy to list the missteps and intrigues of the conflicted Dean organization. An A-list candidate with a C-list staff. Dean was insulated from his workers, iconoclastic. Joe Trippi, Howard Dean's second campaign manager, who was fired after New Hampshire, was brilliant but divisive. The most important thing was Howard Dean being Howard Dean. He ignored the advice and offers of help from the professionals who came on board. Some of the missteps are unforgivable, like his campaign's failure to find the episode of a Canadian TV show where Dean labeled the Iowa caucuses a tool for the special interests. Competing campaigns released it to the media and caught the governor off guard just days before the caucus. Tracking polls the next day showed Dean had lost twelve points.

Everything is so clear in retrospect. The things written about the campaign are mostly true, but there is something else that not too many people are talking about: I don't think people really wanted Howard Dean to win and I'm not sure he wanted to win himself. Worse possibly is that I'm not sure I wanted him to win, either. It was a protest vote from the beginning, a forceful message sent to the Democratic party that it needed to reach out to its base. When it looked like Dean was going to take the nomination all the hatred and fear left over from the race of 2000 came crushing forward like water through a broken dam. One Dean supporter who had switched over to Kerry put it this way, "Last summer we wanted to kick Bush's ass. But now we want to *beat* Bush's ass." The idea of putting an amateur up against a heavyweight like the Bush White House was too much to bear. The Democrats knew the Bush team wouldn't fight fair and they wanted someone ready to match that. Dean's integrity, forthrightness, and basic humanity was, in the end, the greatest liability of all.

But the Dean candidacy was more than just Dean—it was the most successful grassroots organization since George McGovern in 1972. The Dean campaign mobilized thousands of previously disinterested voters. The day before the Iowa caucuses, when Dean suffered his first and most disastrous loss, his offices in Des Moines were packed with thousands of unpaid staff. The nearby Edwards and Kerry offices were ghost towns by comparison. But the paid staffers on the Kerry campaign were far more effective and efficient than the volunteers who worked for Dean. And maybe the lack of organization within the Dean movement was a sign that a Dean White House would have been disorganized too. Are people really ready for a White House blog?

Then there was his lack of experience in foreign policy, which he admitted at one point was a "hole in [his] resume." Still, he had more experience than George Bush in 2000, but then who doesn't? And it's possible that his failure to serve in Vietnam would have poisoned his relationship with the military the way it did Bill Clinton's.

But what Dean brought to the table was an ability to think outside the box, to see when something was wrong even when popular opinion had not yet caught up. This can be shown in what worked in his campaign, i.e., opposition to the war, the tax cuts, and the No Child Left Behind education bill. But his honesty worked against him when he said that we're not safer with Saddam Hussein being captured, or when he advocated a fair trial for Osama bin Laden and stated that he wanted people with Confederate flags on their trucks to vote for him.

I started this story with a reference to the movie *Casino* and I'm not saying there's a link between politics and gambling (though there is). But what I left out was that, when the narrative caught up to the beginning, Robert De Niro was still alive and the movie continued for another half an hour. You thought you knew the ending, but you didn't.

February 17

An Alternative Ending; What If This Was a Choose-Your-Own-Adventure Book?; Bizarro Wisconsin

It warmed up a little bit today, cracking forty degrees in Green Bay. The ice has been melting for a while up here and people are no longer sitting alone in tiny shacks in the middle of the lakes waiting for a fish on a line. The time has passed for those solitary acts of quiet desperation, as Thoreau would say.

I've been waiting to see the fallout from John Kerry's decision to leave the race. His abrupt departure to Europe to marry an ex-intern has hung over the Wisconsin sky like a tarp on a sleeping elephant. And things only got weirder when Wesley Clark admitted to a stunned crowd that he's been a Republican all along. But that's politics. Most people don't even remember when Eddie Verdolyak left the Democratic Party in Chicago. These things happen.

Meanwhile, the Dean campaign continued its surge, following strong first-place finishes in New Hampshire and South Carolina. There was a time when it looked like the Dean for America train was going to fall off the rails and take Generation Dean and Dean

Core with it. But recently the campaign headquarters has taken on the feeling of a teapot about to whistle. So I was not surprised when they moved today's rally from a room at the University of Wisconsin to the Green Bay Town Hall. But I was a little stunned with the decision to relocate a second time into Lambeau Field.

The Green Bay Packers are the only community-owned, non-profit football team in the country and serve as a proud example for Socialists and anti-privatization activists everywhere. The Packers have a lifetime record of 832 wins, 608 losses, and they have won championships twelve times, more than any other team.

Any good advance guy will tell you that it's a balancing act trying to fill a room and generate excitement but at the same time not turning too many people away. Nothing's more depressing than a rally in a ballroom filled with empty chairs. The only way to understand it would be to imagine what would happen to Gucci or Prada if they started selling at T.J. Maxx. And by that measure the stadium was a failure. The stadium seats sixty thousand but only twenty-six thousand were in attendance. But the fact that twenty-six thousand supporters, including every black voter north of La Crosse, showed up for a political rally nine months before the general election does, when one stops to think about it, boggle the mind.

I almost don't get in myself. I had no intention of hanging out in the top bleachers to hear Howard Dean repeat the same speech I've heard a hundred times, but they don't want to let me into the press area. To make it worse, I know the guy working the door.

"Hey," I say. "You drove me down to Ottumwa from Des Moines. We're like this." I cross two fingers to demonstrate our intimacy.

He looks at me beneath his dark shades. His eyes are so bloodshot the red lines continue below his glasses down his cheek almost to his mouth. A winning campaign requires a lot of hours and advance men in particular tend to run very short on sleep. Still, we spent three hours in an SUV just days before, during what was considered a disastrous fifth-place finish in Iowa but in retrospect was really just an insignificant blip on a political radar screen. Nobody pays attention to what Iowa thinks. I was as wrong as everybody else about Iowa but I distinguished myself among the press corps by being the first to admit it.

I see the flash of recognition move quickly through the advance man's face, like a beetle below his skin, his hand holding steady to the end of the rope. Ah yes, Ottumwa. I still have my tags from Iowa and Arizona but there are over two hundred members of the media gyrating in a confusing mass behind me trying to get into the stadium. Pat Healy, who formerly covered John Kerry for *The Boston Globe,* is wearing a giant slab of cheese on his head and, unlike the other cheesehead hats, his is real. A massive block of provolone. It's painful to look at but I can't stop staring.

"You need a laminate," the guy tells me, and I know exactly what he means. Not some fake ticket to an old event, scammed and lied for, but a genuine Wisconsin press pass and an identification card with my picture on it from a major news agency. And the sad truth is that I am never going to get either of those things. There isn't much point in arguing with a guy who has based his life and dreams on a job with the White House security detail. He is well on his way.

I tuck my hands in my pockets and head to the main gate where I see Josh Bearman in a silk bowling shirt and bullet-proof vest leaning back on his elbows against the wall.

"What are you doing here?" I ask.

"Where else would I be?" he replies. He always answers questions with questions. "It dawned on me that I could be anywhere and do anything I wanted to do. I'm living up to my potential."

Josh and I do one of those man hugs where you shake hands and then lean in together and pat each other on the back. Then we funnel though Main Gate B with the rest of the late arrivers. Maybe it's better to see what they're seeing if we're going to write about it. And partly I'm glad we did. Though the buffet in the

Dean filing room tends to the four-star, I could just as easily eat a red brat and drink from a plastic cup shaped like a football helmet and hang out with Josh. Heck, I prefer it.

In order to give the appearance of a bigger crowd large sections of the stadium are closed off, leaving only the seats directly in front of the stage starting on the thirty-yard line and continuing up one hundred rows into the Wisconsin sky. Some of the seats are pretty far back from the stage, and to deal with this, the Dean campaign has rigged a giant video screen behind the Democratic presumptive nominee. I'm surprised to see so many kids in the audience and find myself thinking maybe I am actually part of something real.

"Voter symbiosis," Josh says, running a finger inside the collar of his vest. A steady drumming is already arching through the crowd. People tap their feet in a rhythmic and growing noise that at first sounded like a pulse but, as it grows, comes to resemble an earthquake both in intensity and unpredictability. It feels like the very foundations are going to come undone. I can feel the bolts shaking loose until the place erupts into a scream loud enough to power a small city as the governor takes the stage at a quick jog, waving at the crowd.

At a distance Dean looks even smaller. With Dean are cocampaign managers Roy Neel and Joe Trippi. Trippi is shirtless and painted green with a yellow GB painted across his stomach. He looks like Shrek. I admire Trippi's audacity and willingness to connect with people on a local level. Roy Neel is wearing a suit so some things never change. To the right of the stage is an advisory committee or a presidential cabinet, depending on how you look at things. Al Gore, Tom Harkin, John Edwards (who had dropped out to throw his support behind the governor after what can only be called a humiliating showing in Tennessee and Virginia), Jesse Jackson, Jesse Jackson Jr., Ralph Nader, and John McCain, who broke ranks with fellow Republicans.

The video relay goes up behind the governor, casting him larger than life, a fifty-foot president. And why not? It worked for Tom

Cruise. Then two sprays of fireworks go off and Dean appears on several large screens to the left and right of the field. It's like an Eric Clapton concert.

Dean hits most of his usual planks—health care, gay rights, balanced budgets, normalized trade relations with Cuba, and a constitutional amendment guaranteeing a woman's right to choose. Perhaps what impresses most is that he's sticking with the issues that propelled him to the top of the race to begin with, as opposed to desperately grabbing for some mythical center as so many failed politicians have done before him. It's especially impressive at this point, when he's the only candidate left and most people would have expected him to play it safe. Dean really didn't have to do anything.

The sun never sets in this state and I leave my sunglasses on and stare out to the cloudbanks in the distance. "I love this," I say to Josh, lifting my chin to take some sun on my neck. "Why would anybody do anything else?"

v. A Phoenix from the Landfill

He who fights with monsters might take care lest he thereby become a monster. And if you gaze for long into an abyss, the abyss gazes also into you.

—Friedrich Nietzsche

CALIFORNIA

February 26–28

Hollywood; The Famous People Issue; Angelyne; The Real California; David Poindexter; Arianna Huffington; Larry Flynt and the Violent Backlash of the American Dream

There's an orange adobe Thai restaurant on the corner of Hollywood and Western with a giant plaster hotdog on the roof. Across the way is a new shopping center with a Ralph's and a Starbucks.

The houses on the hills stare down on this tinsel valley, their own underbellies defaced with spray-paint tags blending into the haze. On the other side lies Disney's kingdom, shrouded in smog and filth. They call this golden hour, the time when the sun has not yet risen or set, where everything is lit with a perfect, diffuse light.[1] The cameramen in this town love golden hour, and this is where John Edwards and John Kerry have come to air their differences at the University of Southern California five days before the largest state in the union casts its mighty vote in the Democratic primary.

Josh Bearman and I sit in AstroBurger drinking coffee and eating french fries. I was late getting here. Parts of Hollywood have been closed down for the Oscars a week away. From where we're sitting the view of everything is blocked by an enormous billboard for Angelyne. Angelyne's been there for years, for as long as I can remember, at the end of streets and boulevards all across town. Her image is a vision of plastic surgery, determination, and wealth. Hair dyed rock-star blond, cheeks pinched toward the tip of her nose, looking playfully across the endless stream of cars. Angelyne stares down on us in her low-cut pink dress and peculiar face, her half-naked breasts bordering the smog. Beneath her image it says "Management," and then a phone number. I jot down her number on the hamburger wrapper.

"I'm getting sick of this political stuff," Josh says. "I can't keep it straight. Who's the governor now?"

"Schwarzenegger," I tell him. I look at the picture again, those enormous breasts that can't possibly be real pressed flat against the horizon. The billboard seems to say everything there is to say about this place: that the individual is more important than the state, that appearance is more important than character, and that if you have enough money you can buy the skyline. Who is Angelyne, really?

Last year Gray Davis was thrown out of the California governor's office after four years as the most tough-on-crime governor in the nation. He was just coming off a successful and incredibly corrupt reelection bid in which he handpicked his own challenger by funneling huge sums of money into Bill Simon's primary campaign against the more formidable Richard Riordan. If Simon had become governor it would have been the biggest tragedy to hit the state since the earthquake of 1971—a risk Davis was happy to take. When Davis was ousted in a referendum shortly after his reelection half the state ran for his office. Angelyne ran for governor as well. Her advertisements exhorted voters to be fabulous and showcased her blowing a kiss before zipping away in a tiny pink convertible. If you look her up you'll find a documentary film about the "Hollywood Icon." It's an interesting tactic, putting up billboards and declaring yourself famous. But then why not? Cut out the middleman as long as it works.[2]

"I've always wanted to meet her," I say to Josh. "She represents something very basic and important to me."[3]

"She's fake," Josh says. "Like a Barbie Doll."

"She's real," I reply. "Because she admits it. She's honest about that horrible little longing inside of us. She's as awful as she wants and needs to be."

Josh squints his eyes to make sure he is hearing me right. When I first met Josh he was innocent and enamored with the process. He was so full of hope that people sometimes referred to him as joyous. Now Josh is dressed in overalls beneath a thick, dark jacket. His hair is covered in white paint, giving him the look of a very old man made out of plaster. He's been doing set design since he left New Hampshire and writing things on the side for the *LA Weekly*. He has the look and feel of a guy who is missing out on something. "You should wash your hair," I say.

"Whatever," Josh says, opening a pillbox and popping something small and blue in his mouth. "It's all deadlines and no money."

"What?"

"The Wayfarer," Josh says, his mouth forming a grimace as he quietly dumps ketchup all over his fries, as if he were trying to silence them. The Wayfarer was the hotel in Bedford, outside Manchester, the only decent hotel in the state. Josh and I had been warned we would never be able to find the Wayfarer, that it took years for political writers to figure out the complicated network of roads that led to the Wayfarer Inn. But it wasn't as complicated as we had been told, especially if you don't actually want to stay there. It was at the end of an unlit parking lot off the tristate to Nashua, next to a Macy's department store. But that was almost a month and thirty-thousand words ago. Josh has an entire room in his apartment filled with pages of writing he's done on Iowa and New Hampshire. They're spread across the floor like a movable carpet. He calls it "The Unpublishable Room." Since then Dean's dropped out and Nader's dropped in. John Edwards is looking at the exit door.

"There are so many things I could have done with my life," Josh says. "Every other writer in town will be writing about the Oscars this weekend. I haven't even turned in my articles for *The Believer*. You should have told me not to bother with New Hampshire." His plate looks like red potato soup.

"You wouldn't have listened to me anyway," I say. "It's up to you to make the best of it."

Josh stares contemptuously at his plate. There is no way he is going to eat the mess he has made. "There was supposed to be an election."

It's a pretty good point. Clearly we had both been thinking the same thing. Our consolation prize for the 2000 debacle was a debate between John Kerry and John Edwards over who could be more protectionist. Edwards is on the way out but his constant harping on trade has begun to turn the party away from taxes and war. The cover story for *Harper's Magazine* this month is called "The Rebirth of Nationalism." The Democrats are defining the election as being about jobs, and they don't mean creating new ones, they mean keeping the old ones from leaving. It's nothing short of a disaster, and what better symbol for the beginning and end of that disaster than a three-star hotel at the back of a parking lot in New Hampshire.

Underlying our conversation is a different problem, a fundamental inability to move forward. We are stuck in the cold swirl of Elm Street, Manchester, in January. The frozen trail over the river from the Econo Lodge to the Holiday Inn. Josh and I are probably the only two people in Los Angeles wearing goose-down jackets. The national press has moved on—they're eating lobster on charter jets with the two front-runners who skip from state to state the way some people check the mail, and even when they move around one state, they take planes. I tried to meet up with Edwards in Albany, Georgia, two days ago. I was in Washington, D.C., and I thought I could take a few quick turns on the North Carolina Express. But it turned out he was going to take a plane from Albany to Columbus, eighty-five miles away.

That was the East Coast. I don't even remember what I was doing there. It seems fitting that the candidates would come to this narcissistic, dystopic wasteland for a debate. Where the runaways arrive every year and claw their way toward a spotlight hoping to stand in a glare of bulbs and stare out at an audience they can't see. That's how you know you've made it in Hollywood, when the applause comes from a place so dark you no longer have to say thank you. Just close your eyes, lean your head back, and take it all in. What does the Hollywood dream have to do with the political aspirations of John Edwards and John Kerry? What could be worse in a man than the desire to be president? John Edwards is spending three days in California, and his campaign says he doesn't need to win any Super Tuesday states to stay viable.[4] He says it's about the delegates.

But the delegates are lining up behind Kerry and that's not what Los Angeles is about anyway. Los Angeles is about need. And Los Angeles is not California. There are a lot of conservatives in this state, and they're a particularly vicious group who elected both Ronald Reagan and Pete Wilson. And when Pete Wilson left to pursue his own White House ambitions he left a trail of scum across the statehouse floor also known as Proposition 21. The idea was to send as many young offenders to adult corrections facilities as possible by mandating they be tried as adults. The proposition was supposed to serve as a landing pad for Wilson's presidential candidacy. When it became obvious that Pete Wilson wasn't going to be elected president, or even White House shoeshine, which would have been an insult to shoeshines everywhere, Proposition 21 was left on the ballot to wither and die. But it didn't wither and die. It sat out in the fields like a weed in the sun. The liberals were too busy fighting the Knight Initiative that outlaws gay marriage and nobody thought a bill as awful as Proposition 21 was actually going to pass without major backing, which it no longer had. It seemed inconceivable at the time that someone would vote to take away a judge's ability to decide whether or not a child should be tried as a youth offender or sent to his or her doom in an adult corrections facility.

But it was an off election, March 2000, and farmers like to be tough on crime. Nobody had bothered to point out the expense, or that judges already had the power to sentence juveniles as adults. Most people just read what they saw on the ballot and checked yes or no. And the ballot read "Juvenile Justice and Gang Prevention Initiative." Six of the most deceitful words ever written. There was no outreach to conservatives. So if Angelyne is Los Angeles, Proposition 21 is Fresno, Bakersfield, and everywhere else. Which leaves no room for San Francisco in the popular equation, which is how it's been for a while now.

Josh refuses to go to the debate with me. "Have a good time," he says. "I'm sure it will be rocking." He takes his food to the trash. "I'll tell you what I'm going to do. In two weeks there'll be a race across the desert in unmanned cars. The Department of Defense will give a million dollars to the winner. Imagine the logistical difficulties. The desert. I'll see you in the sand."[5]

During the CNN debate, John Edwards and John Kerry frequently put their hands on one another's arm. On trade, Kerry insists, "We have exactly the same policies on trade," which may or may not be true. During the debate Kerry successfully steals Edwards's message the same way he stole Dean's message in Iowa. And they keep touching each other's wrists and elbows as he pulls Edwards' message from his sleeves. *John Edwards and I have exactly the same positions on trade.* Dennis Kucinich, as usual, makes the best points. "I think the American people tonight will be well served if we can describe, for example, why we all aren't for a universal, single-payer, not-for-profit health care system." And Sharpton has his jokes: "I will travel all over this country to make Al Sharpton president." But Sharpton hasn't been as funny since it came out that he was getting advice from a senior Republican consultant.[6]

The debate-watching room is designed with a series of monitors, four in each intersection stacked on aluminum trees and surrounded by tables. Along the far wall is a table full of sandwiches and cookies. There's wireless access but you have to pay for it, or you have to ask people from the major networks to share their passwords with you. In the center of the room, close to one of the islands of television screens, sit Adam Nagourney and David Halbfinger from *The New York Times*. Adam is the senior correspondent, one of the most influential political writers in the country. David is the up-and-comer. He's been riding the bus with Kerry since October and now his candidate is making the break and pulling David up with him.

Nagourney rocks as he writes—he seems to be transcribing the debate. He's a small man with a curved back and long arms. When their Internet connection goes down Adam throws his fists into the tabletop. David immediately follows suit. Monkey see, monkey do.

After the debate I meet the columnist Arianna Huffington in the spin room. She's tall and wears expensive clothes. She smells good. I tell her I am lost and I don't know what I'm doing and ask if she can maybe take me under her wing and explain all of this stuff to me. I tell her I wrote novels once, but nothing came of it. I ask her what she thinks of John Kerry and she pauses for a moment and smiles in a way that says she's about to tell a lie. She says she likes him and goes on to explain that what we have is a burning house and we have to focus on putting out the fire.

"Did you notice," she says, trying to be helpful, "Ron Brownstein (the *Los Angeles Times* political correspondent) was asking the candidates about values? But he meant gay marriage. John Kerry mentioned national service and John Edwards talked about a war on poverty. So who gets to decide what constitutes values? Why is gay marriage a debate about values but a war on poverty is not a debate about values?"

I hadn't noticed that. Which is probably part of my problem. But not all of it. Arianna takes me by the arm and introduces me to the big players in the room, but I forget their names immediately so caught up am I in Arianna's smell and warmth. She says to them, "Let me introduce you to Stephen Elliott. He's a novelist." I want to lay my head on her shoulder and tell her how hard it is. I want to tell her I have lost my airline ticket and it's going to cost me a hundred dollars and that I have no place of residence. But it isn't the appropriate place and politics is about getting outside of yourself and your own problems for a little while and becoming fully immersed in the lies and deceit of others. This is the election for the most powerful position in the world.

At some point Jim Rainey comes by to ask Arianna a question. "I see you've met Steve," he says. "Did he use that 'I'm an amateur and I don't know what I'm doing' line on you yet?"

February 29–March 2

San Joaquin; Fifteenth and Guerrero; Edwards Drops Out; Kerry and Edwards?; Removing the Sting; No Room on the Campaign for Love; Trivia Night at Edinburgh Castle

Wilhelmina sends letters from Caracas telling me how much she hates South America. "Who paid for you to go to Venezuela?" I ask her.

"Boys buy me things," she replies.

I take her car while she's gone and drive to San Joaquin Valley to get a look at the land and people who elected Pete Wilson. It's a sick place fueled by an economy that relies on illegal immigrants and a voter base that could best be described as Mean Libertarian. The days blur together between Parlier and Guadalupe and all the cheap hotel rooms with cracked plywood doors. After the CNN debate, the national news stops paying attention to the largest state, the state singled out for the biggest budget cuts by President Bush. California is not in play, which is one of the reasons Texas was allowed to walk in here, hijack our electricity, and bankrupt the coffers. Former congressman Gary Condit lives out here somewhere still scrubbing the debris off his tarnished reputation following the murder of his intern. A classic but irrelevant story at this point. He was having an affair with her and, to protect himself, failed to cooperate with the police, who were searching for her body. Maybe he had something to do with it and maybe not. He was an opportunist, a conservative Democrat, and in the end his own party turned against him. Condit's square face and spiky hair rates only a passing thought in these brown hills. The real action is in Georgia anyway; Kerry's got California locked. But this is my state and I feel I should spend some time here. Plus I'm out of money, waiting for a check to come in so I can start buying plane tickets again.

One of the reasons I got into politics was to escape Wilhelmina but now she's out of the country and I can't stop thinking about her. Heading back into the city on Highway 1 through Big Sur, I reread the note she left for me on yellow Pokémon stationery.

There is no reason in the world for you to ever worry. I will always love you.

Sometimes it takes a lie to know the truth. I pull over near the cliffs north of Half Moon Bay. The Mavericks are turning in the distance. Some of the best surfing in the world, waves thirty feet high out in the ocean beyond the break. The surfers ride Jet Skis to catch them. I look north toward the lights and the city. There's a giant fog bank waiting just past the ranges near Pacifica.

On Super Tuesday I arrive in the evening at Wilhelmina's with a box of chocolates and two nine-volt batteries for her smoke alarm. "You're not eating," she says, sliding her hand inside my shirt and digging a finger into my rib. It's easy to forget to eat when you're on the trail. I set the chocolates on the table and sit on her kitchen floor in front of the sink while she takes out my earrings and cleans them in a coffee cup full of alcohol and wipes my ears with a cotton ball. "You need to clean behind your ears," she says.

"I know."

There's a container of medicated Vaseline on the counter for my split lip. The continual change in climates dries you out and my lip split open in the final days in Wisconsin as the last tip of Dean's candidacy sunk beneath the sea of the election. "I gave you balm for your lips," she says.[7] "Why didn't you use it?"

"I forgot."

Wilhelmina lets out a sigh and replaces my earrings. We don't talk for a while but I know what's coming. Tolstoy once said that the only conclusion an educated person can come to is that life is meaningless. The converse is the question of what do you do when you no longer have anything to strive toward? The first time I met Wilhelmina we sat on a bench near a lake. The second time she kissed me in the train station. And the third time she wrapped me in cellophane and asked if anybody knew where I was. But we've built up a lot of resentments since then. I broke up with her once early in our relationship, afraid she was going to make good on her threats, and she's quick to point out that she could never hurt me as much as I hurt her. "It's busted," she likes to say, "and it can't be fixed."

"I can't see you for a couple of months," she says. "You're becoming too much of a distraction. I need to give my other relationship a chance."

It seems a strange twist of fate that we would break up on the day John Edwards drops out of the race. It's also the day Howard Dean finally wins, taking Vermont with a commanding margin even though he has stopped campaigning. John Kerry now has more than half of the delegates he needs for the nomination making his victory—barring disaster—mathematically certain. And the field is empty except for Kucinich and Sharpton.[8]

"I feel sick," I say, and wonder if it's true. Wilhelmina is still tired from her flight and I'm emotionally raw from dizzying nights alone in the American wilderness. Politics is the emotional edge of any nation. Someone once said every story is a love story or a story about loneliness. Weeks ago, before Wilhelmina left on her trip, she kicked me out of her apartment after the phone rang late at night. I was sleeping. She said someone might come over and I should leave. I guess I knew then that there was someone else in her life who meant more than just the other boys she sees on the side. But on the road I forget. I forget the obvious signs leading up to the obvious conclusions. Everything blurs with the green markers stating city and distance. I think ahead to the Texas and Florida primaries, meaningless and one week away. The floor moves beneath me. I need to rent a room somewhere.

"Don't act angry," Wilhelmina says when I get quiet. "You don't need to be awful." She squeezes my earlobe and I bite my lip. I lay my head against her thigh. It's like my bones are gone. She's wearing sweatpants and a bra; she smells wonderful. Wilhelmina's apartment is always clean. So clean sometimes that it's sterile.

This is not the first time that Wilhelmina has broken up with me. She breaks up with me often. But I know this time she means it. I don't know how I know that. "I have to go," I say. I'm having trouble breathing.

"If that's what you want," she replies, but it isn't what I want. The day I know what I want I'll be finished. She'll write me later and say she went searching for me along Valencia and Mission. She went to all of the bars I go to and drove up and down my streets and stopped in front of my friends' houses but never rang the bell.

She'll blame me for not being there for her, for not communicating well enough. Past midnight, Super Tuesday officially over, I find myself with a group of interns from a San Francisco magazine competing in trivia night at a Scottish pub in the San Francisco ghetto. I have a check in my pocket; my next flight leaves for anywhere.

FLORIDA AND ILLINOIS

March 5–8

John Kerry's Victory Lap; John Ashcroft's Angry Pancreas; Violence in Duval County; Max Cleland's Wounds; Jacksonville; Tampa; Miami; A Bloody Shirt; Broward County; A Long Quote from Larry Davis

I woke up this morning in the Florida home of Larry and Janet Davis. It's a normal enough one-story house, with two bedrooms, tile floors, and a giant refrigerator in the garage. They were already gone. Larry to his criminal law practice and Janet to Dade County where she helps with the psychiatric facilities. You wouldn't know looking at the place that they had played a role in the heaviest political drama of the last twenty years. There was a maid cleaning the house. "Don't drink the water," the maid told me. Or maybe she said, "Do you drink that water?" It seemed like a question. She said Janet had left bottles of water in the fridge for me. I'm not sure why Americans are afraid of tap water but I poured out my glass and took a couple of bottles from the fridge.

It was a cool morning for south Florida, with a light breeze coming from Hollywood beach and a gray haze with sweeps of blue across the bent sky. I came here for Kerry's victory lap. He's getting the last of his free media before a vacation with his wife in Idaho. A lot of the press people have already peeled from the campaign.

Meanwhile, the Bush team is trying to paint Kerry as a flip-flopper, which he is. But a flip-flopper is a big improvement over a president who dreams at night of clear-cut forests, hills like breasts naked of the trees that once kept them safe. George Bush is our first president to actively hate the environment. And flip-flops are better than determined lies. Which brings me to the earliest lie of the Bush presidency. The lie that engulfed this entire humid peninsula and still hangs like a wet reminder of democratic impotence every time an alligator pokes its green snout from the swamp.

I caught up with the Kerry camp at the Martin Luther King Community Center near the Fort Lauderdale airport. I had driven down from Jacksonville where I saw a drunk who couldn't pay his tab beaten in a brutal display of mob violence. There was a moment when I considered paying his bill myself but $170 is a lot of money and it was probably too late to step in anyway. Once those good old boys got a taste of violence they were hooked. I could see it painted on their smiling faces and in the bright sparkles in their eyes. It was two in the morning and the bar was already closed. The bouncer was doing his halfhearted best to protect the drunk who was being punched sporadically in the face while hurling expletives about the cook, the barback, and the bartender's mother. He went too far with the bartender and if that bouncer wasn't protecting him they would have torn him to pieces like a Palestinian mob marching toward the jailhouses in Ramallah, where two Israelis were being held in the fall of 2000. That's another story and a different country, and all that remains of that tragic incident is a photograph of two bloody hands thrust into the night from behind the prison bars.

The situation in Israel is going to matter in this election, though it's hard to say how much. The hard-liners and religious who think the West Bank belongs to the Jews, based on some literal interpretation of the Bible, appreciate Bush's un-thought-out policies. But a well-educated majority of American Jews know exactly what Bush and his southeastern campaign manager, Ralph Reed, former head of the Christian Coalition, have in store for them when push comes to shove. There's an old Jewish saying: "Never leave a thief to watch your house and never trust a pedophile with your daughter's laundry." Or maybe that's not exactly it, but the point remains the same.

Anyway, it was two A.M. in Jacksonville and I asked the bartender if I could get one to go. She was counting her drawer and trying to ignore the screams and slaps emitting from the rear corner. I could see past her that a man in a chef's hat had a firm grip on the drunk's arms. The bouncer was holding two men by their throats.

"Don't open it until you leave, honey," the bartender said, handing me a cold bottle in a brown paper bag. "I wouldn't want to get in trouble." She was wearing a halter top that could have been made from an unmatched sock, cut down the end and then stitched back together.

"Don't worry," I told her. "I'll wait until I get in the car." I have a friend in San Francisco originally from Jacksonville who had tried to tutor me on Florida justice. He said there wasn't any. When I told him I was going to his hometown he refused to speak to me for three days. I pulled away just as the first police officer was entering the lot.

I drove south, thinking about the great theft of the 2000 election. What David Halbfinger referred to as the Democrat's bloody shirt. I slept in a parking lot in Little Haiti. The boys delivering that beating back there could only have been Republicans. The beaten Democrat calling into question their mothers' sexual practices while the hammer continued its downward swing.

Except in 2000 the Democrats didn't even do that. It's hard not to look at what happened in 2000 as part of the game. Like in football, when the ball hits the referee. The ref shouldn't have been there, but those are the rules; the ref is part of the field. It's worse than that of course. And nobody could have predicted just how bad the outcome would be. Johnny Apple in *The New York Times* wrote soon after, that without a mandate it's going to be particularly incumbent upon the Bush presidency to be conciliatory. But the Bush team doesn't play by those rules, and they never did.

To continue with that awful football metaphor for a moment: what really happened in 2000 was closer to the other team catching a touchdown pass out of bounds. The coach has to call for a replay. But the coach didn't call for a replay. The Gore team chose instead to ask for recounts in four counties, the counties that were most favorable to the Democrats. Maybe they thought that the Republicans would also ask for recounts in Republican counties, but it didn't happen that way. That was the first and biggest mistake, the one most agreed upon in hindsight, not asking for a complete recount of the entire state. The Republicans insisted that all of the ballots had already been counted twice, since a win by less than half a percent mandates a recount across the board. But that was actually a lie put forth by Secretary of State Katharine Harris. The votes had not been recounted; rather, the machine tabulations were recounted. Broward County, which completed its recount, proved that a manual recount was possible in all sixty-seven counties, but by then it was too late.

That's just one aspect of a very complicated situation. Katherine Harris intentionally misled the public,[9] but the Democrats didn't call her to the stand—something Judge Terry Lewis in Leon County would not fail to point out later. Bill Daley, Gore's campaign manager and the son of the (in)famous Chicago mayor, retreated to Washington and rejected the idea of questioning Harris out of hand. The butterfly ballots are another issue, but there was nothing to be done about it. Theresa LePore, who approved the ballots, was a Democrat. There was no intentional malice. It was simply unfortunate. Still, when all of the votes were counted by the National Opinion Research Center (sponsored by eight news organizations, including *The Washington Post* and *The New York Times*), it came out that no matter what standard was applied Gore won the state. But a recount of all the votes was not the issue before the Supreme Court so the Supreme Court is not the spot to place the blame. If the recounts continued only in the disputed counties Bush would have won. And of course to think that the Democrats had never stolen an election by much more dubious means would display a willful ignorance of American history.

At some point a person doesn't want to know any more about what happened in 2000. Reading about it has the nauseating effect of a slow murder mystery, intricate and deviously plotted, where you already know the ending. But the more one looks at the issue the more obvious it is that the person most to blame for Gore's tragic loss in Florida is Gore.[10]

This is something John Kerry addressed at the Martin Luther King Center in the Hollywood/Lauderdale Projects. The buildings surrounding the center are dark green, each one stamped "No Loitering No Trespassing." But the people in the neighborhood had no idea what was going on. The Kerry people hadn't bothered to advertise or put up signs. The residents of the community were not invited.

"You don't have to worry about that. I'll keep an eye on it for you," somebody called out as I got out of my rental car and checked each handle to make sure the doors were locked. I was tired and I had a headache and my back hurt. The man was sitting on his porch wearing only purple cutoffs. He looked comfortable and his comfort made him look wise and that made me want to ask him what I should do about Wilhelmina. I had nearly called her the night before from the parking lot of the First Haitian Church. I was drunk and sad but there wasn't much calling her was going to do about it. She likes it when I'm sad, she would have encouraged it. Plus, we're broken up. I wonder if I could hook up with Katherine Harris. But how do you impress a woman like Harris? *Let's steal something really big this time.*

"What are they doing over there?" the man on the porch asked, tilting his chin to the corner where two sheriff cars were parked in a V blocking traffic. "Voter registration?"

"John Kerry," I said. "He's running against Bush."

The man nodded. Evidently the Democrats have been out here registering voters in force. But Florida is also one of the only states to have laws on the books taking away ex-convicts' rights to vote. In truth there's a series of steps convicts can take to have their right to vote reinstated but most people, particularly ex-cons, don't know about that. The direct result is that 10 percent of the black population has been forcibly removed from the electoral process. The Democrats don't lobby too hard against this blatant violation of human and constitutional rights, afraid of appearing soft on crime.

"I hope he wins," the man said.

"I do too," I was forced to admit.

Everything's changed now that the Secret Service is on Kerry's case. But at this point in the campaign it probably doesn't matter anyway. It's a media campaign now—the retail politics of Iowa and New Hampshire and even Wisconsin are a thing of the past. This is a national effort and John Kerry is ready for it. Supporters arrived in buses from the party offices. A single row of black leaders from the community sat along the back of the campaign's reserved benches. Everybody else might as well have been paid actors. This was for the TV and the newspapers. It was surprisingly easy to get past the SS. I showed them a press pass from the Dean campaign dated to December and a passport. They asked for state I.D. and when I didn't have any, they let me through anyway.

"The hotels sure are better," Matea Gold from the *Los Angeles Times* told me. She was referring to the difference between Dean and Kerry. A lot of the Dean reporters had switched sides and a lot of Kerry reporters had left the trail. Many of them had been doing temporary duty, assigned back in November when Kerry was the sure loser. Jodi Wilgoren from *The New York Times* was there, as was Susannah Meadows from *Newsweek*. More important was Gwen Graham Logan, the senator's eldest daughter. When her dad dropped out of the presidential race she went to work for Dean and many people thought she was a shill for her father's vice presidential ambitions. Now she was at the Kerry event.

"Is she working for Kerry?" I asked someone.

"Not yet," was the reply. I saw her lean across the rope toward one of the reporters, gently put her hand on his face, and whisper something in his ear.

Kerry assured the crowd he would be ready for Republican treachery and intends to see to it that every vote is counted. He said he was going to come into Florida with a team of lawyers and contest votes in advance if he had to. "I'm a fighter," he said, which seemed to mean a lot to people here. Nobody wants to be remembered as a coward who had his lunch money stolen. What happened in 2000 was more than just tragic. It was humiliating to every Democrat across the state.

"The night of the election I was with Bob Butterworth, the Attorney General of the State of Florida," Larry Davis told me in his office after the Kerry event. Larry was sitting in a large leather chair and his partners frequently poked their heads in the door to crack jokes. Occasionally the phone would ring and Larry would pick it up and say something like, "Yeah, well, you're going to have to do some time. Be at the court at nine A.M." I quickly decided that if I was ever on trial for murder Larry is the guy I would want to defend me.

"Butterworth was the chair of Gore's statewide effort. He and his wife, Martha, picked Janet and me up right when the results started coming in and everybody was happy and we went to the Democratic Party party and the Dems were winning. They had called Florida. It was a done deal and Butterworth wanted to go down to Dade and see the people in Miami.

"So, um, so we're heading down to Dade county and I'm driving his car for whatever reason, I don't know why, and the phone rings and it's Lieberman. He says, 'I just want to thank the Attorney General.' Two minutes later the phone rings again to tell us Florida is back in play.

"The whole thing was a mess. There were all kinds of problems in Volusia. In Leon County they weren't letting black people vote. Lost boxes in Dade County.

"There's a meeting in [longtime friend and fund-raiser for Gore] Mitch Berger's office and there were like ten of us there and there were some people that had flown in from out-of-state led by John Sasso. He was Michael Dukakis' guy in eighty-eight, when he had been forced out for leaking the plagiarism stuff about Senator Biden, at which point Dukakis' campaign fell apart.

"Anyway, so Sasso was down, along with three or four other guys that had been involved in places like the recount in Indiana. We broke off and they said to me the canvassing board had a lawyer for the entire board. Jane Carroll had a lawyer. And they said Sue Gunsberger should have a lawyer and they asked me to do that.

"So that was my job for however many days it went on. I was in the middle of everything. They're in this big room. Emergency room for the county. Hundreds of people, watchers and counters, just to go through all the cards that were there. And if there was any question about a card it went into this other room and the Republican board was involved. They tried everything to stop us.

"We went on for four days, just to do the votes, seven in the morning until midnight every day. My wife was in Kansas. We did our job. Even with the Republicans doing everything they could to disrupt.

"I really thought it was important. I knew it was important, and I knew there was a lot that could be done in four years. But nobody could have seen this coming. Who could figure 9/11, which changed the equation on everything. I was trying a murder case at the time when a bailiff came in and said a plane just went into the World Trade Center. The judge said keep going. Then the bailiff came back in and said a second plane had hit. That was the end of the day. The guy was found guilty a week later.

"They stole the election but it shouldn't have been that close. How does Gore lose to this guy? I remember the day of the election. We're having this event, it's running late. We have rock bands and all sorts of stuff. So at 1:30 in the morning Gore comes in on a helicopter. Pretty much nobody there was over thirty and Gore shows up and starts talking about the Social Security lockbox. He's talking about Social Security to a bunch of thirty-year-olds.

"If I had known what I know now I would have done more. I would have found those votes somewhere if I had to print them myself. I was hanging out with Mitch Berger not that long ago and I asked him if he ever thought he would get over what happened in 2000. He said, 'I'll get over my mother passing away first.'"

March 9–10

Bringing It Home; Surreal Images of Monster City; Kerry Busts the Nut; Napoleon's Pope; A Ride into Little Kurdistan Late at Night; Punk Rock Lesbians for Anarchy; JB's Pizza; Dan McCarthy Swears to Play It Straight

The primaries end tonight in Chicago. Here the skyscrapers rival mountains, the great American architecture erupting from the plains. Square and solid, the black towers guard this city. The Standard Oil Building, the Sears Tower, the John Hancock. These are not structures to be trifled with. To the west of downtown sits Union Station, one of the great train depots in the nation, a monument to the rail system and slaughterhouses and animal carcasses that made this city great.

Tonight the station is surrounded by yellow jackets and unmarked cars. One thing you never want to do is end up on the wrong side of a Chicago police officer. The biggest difference between the Chicago police and the L.A. police is that in L.A. they were caught. But nobody in Chicago questions a police officer's right to beat a confession out of whomever he chooses. Any half-decent citizen has a friend with a badge and if you can't name that friend within twenty seconds of being picked up beneath the Lake Street el tracks then it doesn't matter what they plant on you because you are clearly guilty of something. I've been on the wrong end of that stick before, more than once. But I'm safe here now—half of my high school class joined the force.

I come in through the press entrance wearing my John Kerry Fun in the Sun pass from Florida, and I'm escorted to the press area behind a giant blue tarp.

"Are you with the traveling press?" they ask me.

"I was in Florida yesterday," I tell them, pointing at my chest. "I've been around."

This is Kerry's primary-night party, though the Illinois primary is not until next week. But tonight the polls close in Florida, Texas, Mississippi, and Louisiana, all going overwhelmingly to Kerry. He has come to Chicago to cement his deal with the old guard.

Inside, Union Station resembles a Roman palace, gigantic pillars rising fifty feet topped with golden leaves buttressing the ceiling. An enormous flag hangs from the rafters. The crowd waits patiently for the procession to arrive at the stage and for speakers to take their turn at the lectern positioned above the crowd like a trophy. The lectern is the first I've seen of its kind in the campaign season. It hovers six feet above with a microphone bending away from its base and leaves little doubt of who is giving the orders and who is doing the listening. It reminds me of Kafka's *The Trial*. The lectern looks like where the priest *didn't* deliver his lecture to Joseph K., preferring instead a cramped altar to speak the truth.

The Secret Service funnels the crowd through the metal detectors into the staging area. People with white tickets stand inside the ropes, near the locus of power. I ask a couple how they got there and they say they are fund-raisers. Then the SS guy collars me and escorts me back to the press area and the buffet. You need an escort to mingle with the crowd. The SS have been weary of the press ever since John Hinckley came out of the pack to put a bullet in Reagan's trickle-down theory.

And the Service Employees International Union (SEIU) is here in force, purple shirts and all. They stuck with Dean to the end. Now the unions have lined up behind Kerry in their final shot at relevance. Clocks are everywhere. Mayor Daley comes first to the microphone and tells the crowd in his nasal twang that John Kerry is the guy who will deliver health care. A pretty unlikely situation but this is Daley's town and he'll say whatever he feels like saying. Nobody contradicts the mayor within city limits. He looks like a pink ham with arms. And when Daley has spoken Governor Blagojevich steps to the podium to pay his dues. They all move aside for Kerry who graciously thanks his wife and their wives. Yes, of course, where would we be without our wives? With Kerry are several veterans from the Swift boat, his band of brothers from Vietnam. He surrounds himself with veterans as an unspoken swipe at the president's cowardice. Kerry says Bush can't run on his record, he doesn't have one. He says Bush is trying to "divide with wedge politics." And if "George Bush wants to make this a race about national security I've got three words for him: Bring. It. On." The crowd chants along with him, signs appear with the slogan. And there he is, the great and final hope, between the pillars and in front of a stairway filled with supporters as if he had sprung from them fully formed draped only in a loincloth quickly replaced with a finely tailored suit. When introducing Kerry the governor talked about change and asked the crowd if they wanted change but he was talking about the presidency. There will be no house cleaning in the Democratic Party if Kerry wins. The old guard is safe and happy with the way things have worked out. When Kerry finishes the crowd erupts, then quickly disperses. Bono comes over the loudspeakers. "It's a beautiful day." Followed by Sam and Dave belting, "Hold on! I'm coming!" By the third song only the devout are still in attendance.

John Kerry is still near the doorway shaking hands with the

money men and ward heelers. The press held at bay. "He's fighting for every vote," his campaign aide jokes. Many of the reporters tell me this is their last day. The real election has already begun.

It's a cold day for March. The wind over the Chicago River is a stark contrast from Florida. I walk through downtown with my hands stuck in my pockets, past the Metropolitan Correctional Facility. The strange orange triangular rock, with slits carved on its face, is anomalous and well hidden within Chicago's mighty façade. Many aldermen have spent the night there when their lucky streaks crashed against Chicago's shoulders. But this is also the city that has made kings. And the people here are proud of the patronage system that keeps this place running so smoothly. The kind of scandals you read on the front page in other cities—*Mayor Gives Enormous Contract to Brother, Sneers at Suggestion of Open Bidding*—don't even count as news here. If you can't get a job working for the water department your father didn't fulfill his responsibilities as precinct captain and that's just how it goes. This is a town that understands and respects power. The subways lurk beneath the city like guard dogs threatening to emerge from the sidewalks if things go wrong.

Cabrini-Green and the Robert Taylor Homes, once the largest housing projects in the world, divided from Bridgeport by the Dan Ryan Expressway. The projects that were built by the senior Mayor Daley to keep the blacks out of the white neighborhoods have been mostly torn down over the past fifteen years. But it turns out the blacks work on patronage just as well as the whites do. Grease the leaders and the troops are kept in line. It's the way it's always been here; it's the way it will always be.[11]

A fine statement for the unions, to end the primaries in Chicago. Nobody tries to put up a show without putting the union on the payroll. And if you come in from out of town you better be ready to pay time and a half, eight hours minimum. And that's just to turn on the lights. But there's something Napoleonic about it as well. With the exception of the firefighters, Kerry won without them. So when the unions came forward it was like Pope Pius VII trying to crown Napoleon. Bonaparte took the crown from the pope and put it on his own head and declared himself emperor. Pius was a practical man and agreed to the order of ceremony as negotiated in exchange for regaining several papal territories. It was a mutually beneficial arrangement and both sides knew the score going in.

The second half of the election has begun now. Even as John Kerry makes his plans to go snowboarding in Idaho Karl Rove is howling from the White House lawn, summoning his minions to begin the task of defining their opponent. The Republican coffers are full but success is not certain. Chinks in the armor are showing, most noticeably in the attacks on Howard Dean. If Howard Dean was really a weaker candidate than John Kerry, and he probably was from the Republican point of view, why didn't they keep that a secret? And what if it is proven that Karl Rove leaked Valerie Plume's name to Robert Novak? Laws have been broken, lies have been told. The skies are dark over the capital and across the Bible Belt. But the Rust Belt is angry, as are the fertile voters of the Mississippi Delta. Who are the swing voters? Where are the swing states? And miles to go before I sleep . . .

VI.   And I Will Show You Rust

Suppose you were an idiot, and suppose you were a member of Congress, but I repeat myself.
— MARK TWAIN

PENNSYLVANIA

April 17–21

Republicans in the Wild; Threats from the Editor; Notes Left in the Stairwell; Quentin Tarantino's Redemption; First-Class Seat at the Apocalypse; Allentown; Harrisburg; Reading; Lancaster; Pittsburgh; Fire over Steel Town

Pennsylvania, the home of acid rain and the American interstate. Tough, independent, and mired in contradiction. Bush lost Pennsylvania by less than 5 percent in 2000. This is why, early in his tenure, he established steel tariffs that he knew to be illegal. Just as the White House knew Bush would never actually have to sign a constitutional amendment banning gay marriage, there was never any doubt that the World Trade Organization would force the U.S. to end the tariffs.[1] But George Bush never cared about that. The steel workers will remember him as the man who tried, unsuccessfully, to save their jobs. And that's all that matters. The coal workers, caked dark with soot, will remember that Bush let them poison the environment for the rest of us. And the backwoods trash that voted for Rick Santorum will also know that George Bush is among them. He is a man full of hate and anger against women who don't know their place, ready to smite heathen living in sin, a vengeful born-again angel eager to mete out God's punishment, watching over them hundreds of miles away on Pennsylvania Avenue.

I know I sound dramatic, but I can assure you it's worse. If you live near Lansing, and clouds appear, and a raindrop lands on your lower lip, stick out your tongue and see if you can taste the metal. Then look west toward Pittsburgh.

I'm downstairs from the campaign office of Senator Arlen Specter, a four-term Republican locked in a vicious primary fight for his party's nomination. I'm eating a cheeseburger at the Firehouse Grill, my second cheeseburger of the day. Specter's being challenged from the Right by Congressman Patrick Toomey.[2] This seemingly meaningless contest for the Republican nomination for the Pennsylvania senate seat will actually have massive repercussions in the presidential election, which is why I'm here.

Harrisburg is the capital of this state that's lost so many jobs due to plant closings and a glut on the world's steel market. Down a tree-lined lane from the Firehouse Grill is the statehouse, and the other way is the Susquehanna River, where birds are chirping on the water as dusk falls and a statue of an eight-foot cow sits on a park bench reading a paper. The sunset is light orange.

I'm drinking a beer and my body is tight from another day spent in a car. You have to be in this state to understand what is unfolding here, the battle for the soul of the Republican Party, and how that will determine the general election in the fall and how Pennsylvania will most likely be the second most important state in that election. It's the ultimate swing state, even more important to John Kerry and George Bush than Florida, rivaled only by Ohio. What happens in the Pennsylvania primary will have drastic repercussions come November and what happens in this primary could shape the Republican party for the next twenty years. I came here to make sense of Pennsylvania after several weeks back home in California. From a distance it seemed that it was a cut-and-dried case of a conservative incumbent (Specter) running against a madman (Toomey). Except the madman was polling at 44 percent, and so I knew there was more to it than I was gleaning from the broadsheets. I knew it had something to do with coal, Jesus, suburban sprawl, and highway congestion. And I knew it was important to the presidential election and the general health of our sickened nation. But when I started to understand Pennsylvania I didn't expect to also understand all of American politics going back to George Washington, but I do.

Back in San Francisco I moved in with three people I met through Craigslist on the northern edge of the Mission District, across from where the projects used to be and where now sit three towering piles of dirt. Just after moving in I threw my neck out while drying my hair and thinking about Wilhelmina. I felt a snap, then a sharp pain that spread like mercury across my shoulders. I was laid up for three days on my new Ikea bed. The satori of American politics feels like that, except without the pain.

I'll try to make this quick. It's the most important point in the whole book and as such it will be easy to attack—hard and fast rules always are. This doesn't bother me, I don't expect consensus. Congressman Toomey's offices are located near the highway at the back of an office park and the buildings are square and functional, like much of Pennsylvania. I put on my pink button-up short-sleeved shirt and walked inside, hoping to be taken seriously.

"Who are you writing for?" Toomey's press secretary asked me. I told him *The Believer* magazine because the name sounds Christian. I hung around the office for close to an hour and picked up a schedule and the literature and watched the congressman on CNN with his staff. One of the girls lamented, "If Bush had endorsed Toomey, he'd be polling 60 percent."

I realized these people were not crazy as I had originally thought. They are pro-life but their real passion is supply-side economics and you don't have to listen for too long to know that they believe in capitalism, privatization, and free markets with a fervor that could only be described as "faith." But they were nice people, well scrubbed and unconcerned with fashion. They offered me water and coffee.

Senator Specter is running as a moderate against Toomey, though most people I know would consider Specter a conservative. We're approaching the point I'm going to make. Specter was instrumental in appointing Clarence Thomas to the Supreme Court, passing Bush's tax cuts and repealing the estate tax.[3] But many Republicans consider him a liberal because he's pro-choice and voted against impeaching Bill Clinton.[4]

In the general election Specter should be a lock, but that's only if he gets past the primaries. The Republican Party has shifted to the Right since 2000 and the Left has moved with them, crumbling on the edges and falling into the sea. Additionally Toomey has a pile of cash, mostly from the Club for Growth, a 527 with strong connections to the Bush administration but also known as a thorn in the president's side.[5] The Club for Growth's stated goal is to make the Republican Party more conservative. President Bush however is stumping for the incumbent, because if Toomey wins the primary, Bush will be less likely to carry Pennsylvania in the fall. And if Bush wins Pennsylvania he should win the election.[6]

Toomey's the kind of Republican who could bring a lot of Democrats to the polls and it would only take a couple of percentage points to lock it down for Kerry in a close election. And if it's not a close election then none of this matters. If it's not a close election something has gone tragically wrong. A week before the primary Specter and Toomey are in a dead heat.

And this is what occurs to me in the Firehouse Grill, with Colin Powell's face on the television screen, silently trying to explain the allegations in Bob Woodward's book *Plan of Attack,* the volume set to mute, the bar crowded and busy with political operatives: the president *is* the center of the political spectrum.

And I don't mean this in some metaphorical way, like President Bush is the center of the political universe. What I mean is that the Left and the Right of politics in America emanate from the president like wings off a bat and run for exactly the same length. Which is why the conservative press laments "Bush Republicans" and the "shift the party has taken from its base." Which is why Patrick Toomey is running from the right in Pennsylvania and despite Specter's best efforts is not considered crazy and in fact he isn't crazy, he's just wrong. But that's why Arlen Specter is considered a liberal Republican and Ralph Nader is considered a whack job by the exact same people who voted for him four years ago. Toomey is as far from George Bush right now as Ralph Nader was from Bill Clinton in 2000, and the ground Nader used to stand on has disappeared, leaving him staring into the void like Wile E. Coyote. Of course, in 2000 the conservative press loathed Bill Clinton[7] and Republicans regularly referred to him as a liberal maniac. The idea of a candidate running to the left of Bill Clinton seemed insane to them. The same way it seems insane to someone with a good understanding of the world now that a person could run to the right of George Bush. Liberals don't even want to begin to start thinking that something to the right of George Bush exists, but it does.

I wake up in the Wellesley Inn in South Reading. I don't know anybody in this state and I'm on my second day of what promises to be a long week of loneliness and like most people I don't like being woken by alarms. The door card promises "superior levels of service delivered in a warm, happy, and cordial manner," but they put me in the handicapped room and at only seven A.M. I'm still on West Coast time. Outside is a wall and beyond that wall a series of strip malls and fields already designated for development. One has to wonder at the final expansion point of Home Depots, Wal-Marts, chain bookstores, Denny's, Old Navys, Bed Bath & Beyonds, and the rest. At what point will the consumer index collapse back in on itself, the chain-store strategy retreat and slowly give life to the merchant class, the mom-and-pop store, and the town square?

Patrick Toomey addresses a breakfast crowd at the Sheraton Reading. It's my first time meeting the congressman.[8] There's orange juice, fruit, and coffee cake. It's not a rally and it wasn't publicized on the calendar. It's a meeting with local business leaders, of whom there are twenty in attendance. The men wear suits and the women wear suits that look like the men's suits—except for Judith J., whose hair is short and dyed blond and who wears a yellow outfit with pinstripes that fits her almost too well. And I'd be lying to say I'm not attracted to Republican women, because I am. I can't help that. She looks like Renée Zellweger with curves and a tan. Her lips are like pillows.

The wallpaper is striped and there's a corkboard ceiling. It's a small room with three tables. I sit in the corner with Lara from the Associated Press and I hear one of the men at the tables declare, "Specter has the best people money can buy. We have the grassroots." And I smile because he is reinforcing my theory that Patrick Toomey in 2004 is really just Ralph Nader in 2000, making allowances for the obvious differences in party affiliation and office, as well as lifetime achievements. But a lot of that has to do with the eight years Toomey spent making himself rich as an investment banker and then as a restaurateur. Toomey was trying to make money while Nader was trying to save the world. But that doesn't mean Toomey isn't just as idealistic.

Toomey is tall and thin and not as smooth as most national politicians. He talks lovingly from the lectern, which has a mike-stand but no mike, about "the supply side phenomenon" and "allowing the markets the magic they can accomplish." He also says he's not in favor of reinstating the draft and believes "we can defeat this insurgency [in Iraq]. It's a limited insurgency."[9]

I'm impressed by his conviction. He doesn't come across as a politician. Instead he comes across as a straight shooter who took a serious blow to the head at a very early age. The shape of his head, which is long and slightly dented above the cheekbones, reinforces this theory. Outside I meet Judith J. and John W. discussing Toomey's talk. I strike up a conversation with the two, curious about how they feel on social issues since Toomey's talk dealt mostly with how best to handle the economy.

"I'm pro-life because of my experiences," Judith says. "Abortions are too readily used as birth control." John nods his head. Judith's smile is a kind squint. I expected hostility from John and Judith because of my earrings and my hair, which is like a sticky, unwashed Afro today. I really need a haircut. The sky is overcast and gray and it's cooler than it was yesterday, almost pleasant. I cock my head to get a better look at Judith and try to understand the abortion-as-birth-control argument. I take off my backpack and lay it on the ground, then I bend down, open it, and take two aspirin. I don't want to scare them off.

"So, church and state?" I say.

"Divorce rates spiked dramatically when they ended prayer in schools in the 1970s," John tells me. "You can choose to believe me or not, but it's a fact."[10]

"That's interesting," I say. And I wonder if the spike occurred when the children who were no longer allowed to pray freaked out fifteen years later, in their mid-twenties. But that doesn't really support John's "spike" theory, so I can only imagine he's referring to the parents being adversely affected as their ten-year-old children replaced school prayer with acid tabs and crystal meth. But I'm not sure. Deep down I think he's making it up, but what's the point in calling someone a liar? And just because I think he's making it up doesn't mean I think he's lying. I think John is as honest as the day is long, but we have different ways of arriving at what we consider the truth. I decide to steer the conversation back to the economy.

"Deficits?" I ask. "Cutting taxes during war?"

"The deficit doesn't worry me," Judith says.

"Economically," John says. "Cutting taxes in time of war is the best thing to do."[11]

"You never pay for war *during* the war," Judith says.[12]

The hotel is built on a hill and the cars are parked in three tiers below us. I thank them both and shake their hands. I feel they've given me a pretty good profile of the Toomey voter and, by extension, the Republican base that George Bush is hoping to turn out en masse in November. But just in case I need a follow-up I take down their information. As I'm walking away I hear Judith saying good-bye to John and then her heels clacking across the parking lot. "Sell, sell, sell!" she screams to him over her shoulder with the enthusiasm of a newlywed declaring her love for her husband while simultaneously trying to catch the next train.

April 22–25

The Hunt Club; Specter Gets Grilled; What Does the Sign Say?; Chiodo's; The Greatest Swing Voter Who Ever Lived; Welcome to Homestead, the Former Steel Capital of the World

The Harrisburg Hunters and Anglers Club should be Arlen Specter's bedrock. He's a staunch gun-rights advocate endorsed by the NRA. Inside there's a moose head on the wall and two stuffed squirrels. The second floor houses an archery range and an indoor pistol range. I ask the lady if I might shoot a gun and she says I should have called a little earlier, they would have made arrangements.

"I've never shot a gun," I say. We're standing inside the shooting gallery in front of half a dozen targets, each with an outline of a man riddled in bullet holes.

"You could shoot one here," she says.

"That would be so cool."

"We shoot PPC," she tells me. "Which is police combat."

I nod, examining the targets. My father kept guns around the house, but I was never tempted to touch one. He sometimes kept a small pistol in his jacket pocket. He didn't drink often, but one time while drunk he invited my sister and me into the backyard and fired a bullet into the grass. "Now you know what it sounds like," he said.

Twenty members show up to hear the senator talk, which seems like a low turnout. It's the same number that showed for Toomey in Reading. It's a big difference from rallies that accompany a presidential campaign and interesting to think that these smaller, determined groups are quite possibly the ones making the biggest decisions. The media have been predicting a low turnout in the primary for weeks and most think that spells big trouble for Specter whose supporters might not be as motivated. Specter is an old man now, in his mid-seventies. I have to wonder why he's even doing this. His cheeks hang down to his jawline and his hair is curly and gray. He's Jewish, which I didn't know before. And I don't think that endears him to the Christian base but it explains his position on abortion.

Specter takes small steps while he talks, creating a little square on the cement floor, and, combined with his curly gray hair, gives the impression of a soft-shoe vaudeville act. "I bring you greetings from the president," he says and forces a smile. He mentions turning old industrial sites into hunting fields. Tells the story of Ruby Ridge, and how a government that was too large got involved with a man who just wanted to be left alone with his weapons, and the tragic consequences that ensued. He mentions that he was on the judiciary committee and was instrumental in finding Randy Weaver innocent of all serious charges.[13] But he spends most of his time telling funny stories about George Bush, which is what politicians do. They tell funny stories. Then, during the question-and-answer, it gets ugly.

"I'm worried about you voting with Ted Kennedy," says Bill, the vice president of the club. "Because I despise that man." The contempt in his voice is palpable. He looks the way a liberal would expect him to look, with a thick handlebar mustache and striped shirt tucked into his jeans. Specter tries to explain his positions, saying the important thing is that he votes with the president. He never mentions the obvious, that it would be impossible not to vote with Ted Kennedy some of the time.

After the speech I stand outside on the wooden porch with Bill while he has a cigarette and tries to unwind. He's a Toomey voter. A man guaranteed to go to the polls. "I vote on social values. I don't even mind paying taxes, as long as we get something for our money. I want smaller government, less intrusion into our lives. I'm against stem cell research and I'm pro-life. I'm against cloning—that's way out in left field."

He strikes me as a military guy and a man for whom integrity plays an important role. Toomey is unwavering in this regard, so I ask him about the president. I ask him about Bush not wanting to go to Vietnam and if that will affect his vote in the fall. "Bush wasn't avoiding going to Vietnam," he tells me. "If he was he would have gotten a deferment. He joined the National Guard to fight."

I try to see what brand of cigarette he's smoking and consider asking him for one though I haven't smoked in twelve years. The Specter caravan piles out behind us. I have to get to Pittsburgh soon. I like talking to Republican voters. It's like trying to participate in an entirely different system of logic. "But his father," I say,

smiling just enough so that he doesn't think I'm making fun of
him but also so he knows I don't quite share his ground, "got him
to the head of the line. There were a lot of people that wanted to
join the National Guard. And the National Guard only meets once
a week. If he wanted to go to Vietnam he could have joined the
military."

"I don't see that as an issue," he says. "I do see that as an issue
with Kerry that the guy after him said he wasn't fit to serve."

Bill is referring to the commander who replaced Kerry on his
boat in Vietnam, a Republican with harsh words for the Democratic nominee. Bill's comments stay with me on the long drive to
Pittsburgh, where I pass a sign that says "Remove Sunglasses" and
another that reminds me to "Be Alert." These are people whose
minds will never be changed. And there's evidence that 45 percent
of likely voters in the general election are like Bill. There's another
45 percent like me and if Bill knew what I really thought he probably would have kidnapped me and presented me to local militia,
where I would likely have been skinned and made into furniture.

That still leaves 10 percent for swing voters and swing voters
don't vote in primaries. But I hear there's a place where I can find
these voters, and that's where I go.

Chiodo's sits across from the Owls Club 1558 and Russian Club
#4 and in front of Joe Delorio's autobody in Homestead, on the
other side of the Homestead Bridge. Homestead is a carbon copy
of many of the small municipalities in and around Pittsburgh. At its
height there were 15,500 steel workers here. But that was during
World War II. Now there aren't any. The sign on the back of the
bar says "Welcome to Chiodo's in Homestead, the Former Steel
Capital of the World." Chiodo's has been around for over a hundred years and under the current ownership for fifty-seven.

Inside Chiodo's the ceiling is strung with souvenirs: old lingerie,
hats, purses, a basketball in a net, helmets, and wooden minicars. I

sit down for a drink with Joseph Chiodo, the proprietor, hoping he'll explain the swing voter to me so I know what to expect in the general election.

"I don't talk politics," he tells me. "But I'll tell you about the steel mills."

"OK."

"There were mills along the river for three miles," Joe tells me. "But that's all gone now. [For] the young people I serve here now, there aren't jobs to be had. What do they do? They take minimum wage in the grocery stores. They have to take two jobs. I've been here fifty-seven years and I can tell you people aren't making enough money to go out. I don't see the economy doing good. This was a happy bar at one time. People still come in and have a few drinks, but it's not the same. [They] used to make a decent living at the mill. The kids that couldn't do well in school didn't have to worry about it, they could get a job. We keep hearing we're going to get jobs back. Where are we going to get jobs back? Pay two dollars an hour in Mexico. I don't know what China pays. Most of the armor you see on battleships, it came from Homestead. Now it's probably made in China. Homestead doesn't make steel anymore."

I finish my drink with Joe while eating a mystery sandwich, which is the house specialty and consists of ground beef, cheese, sauerkraut, and marinara sauce. After a while I want to go but Joe isn't finished talking. Old age is lonely, lonelier even than being thirty-two and driving around Pennsylvania for a week in a rented car. Joe was just two years younger than I am now when he bought this bar after returning from the war.

"The storefronts around here are all empty. The Russian Club across the street has been closed for twelve years. Myself I've been here too long. But I enjoy talking to the ladies. Black, white, I don't care. Used to be a black person would come into a bar and have a drink you'd throw the glass in the trash when they left. I never did that. I'd clean the glass with rock salt, you know, get it good and clean. But I never insulted anyone."

Joe takes me to the front of the bar and shows me an old map of Homestead next to a picture of him and his brother. "We were going to make shoes, but we ended up as barkeeps. I was in the military for five years." Pointing to the map, which shows the area covered with mills, he says, "They were happy when they were working." Pointing to another picture where a woman waits outside the mill on the street while the men collect their pay, he says, "Wives waited by the mill on payday, because their husbands were paid in cash."

I finally leave Chiodo's and walk around Homestead. There are other bars but they're virtually uninhabited. In fact, it's hard not to be struck by how empty the streets are. Most of the buildings are empty too, except for a dollar store and a bank. The storefronts are shuttered and many of the windows are covered in boards. I wonder about this place and if the times were really better when it took 150 men to make a slab of steel. Now they have casters and it only takes fifteen. What is the price of productivity?

Driving back across the bridge to downtown I see below where a shopping mall has been built on the river bank. Amid the neon is a PF Chang's, a Starbucks, and a movie theater. In front of me are the hills and then the Carnegie Mellon Institute, founded by Andrew Carnegie, one of the captains of the American steel industry.

What does it all mean? The international conglomerates have built a settlement inside a town that was famous for its steel, once upon a time. It means Bush and steel tariffs, fighting for an industry that can't be saved and paying lip service to people who think things *used* to be better, and could be again. It means Kerry and NAFTA, trying to explain away his vote as if he were supporting something else. But what it really means is that PF Chang's, a chain restaurant serving Chinese food, has replaced the silos that manned the shore like upturned cannon guns belching smoke and rotating through three shifts of workers just to meet demand. And the old men who mutter into their drinks at Chiodo's about their pensions (which have gone from nine hundred dollars to six hundred) are they the swing voters? What could they possibly want? One could see it all as Joe does, a fight between labor and management that went on for too long and got too personal and now lies at the feet of myopic politicians. But that's the same as saying nothing at all, which goes a long way toward understanding the tenor of the national discussion in its broadest terms, despite the tragedy unfolding in Iraq. Will the next step be more obvious than the last? John Kerry's now preparing the buses in West Virginia to caravan across this state and the other states like it, talking about jobs and the economy. As Toomey and Specter lunge toward their primary date and the Far Right pulls the final peg from Colin Powell's big tent, the Democratic challenger prepares to take another stab at framing the debate.

WEST VIRGINIA AND OHIO

April 26–29

The Jobs-First Express; Wheeling, West Virginia; Down in the Coal Mine; Back on the Bus; Canonsburg; Strip Club by the Highway; Rain in Youngstown; Cleveland Forever

It's morning and everything's calm in Wheeling, West Virginia. Not like last night when the motorcade arrived just after ten P.M. and the Young Republicans, who had been waiting hours, were here to give Senator Kerry a piece of their mind, possibly the only piece. There were fewer than thirty of them on the other side of the yellow tape, kept at bay by the Secret Service. They were young and their necks bulged in our lights. It would be easy and dismissive to refer to them as Neanderthals out looking for a fight, but it would not be incorrect. Close to a hundred supporters were also there with John Kerry signs, held in a separate area. The Secret Service had everything under control. And after John Kerry went into the hotel the two sides could have merged but they didn't. The Democrats were polite and waved signs while the Republicans made lewd gestures. The Republicans were not from Wheeling. They drove in from exurban places along the turnpike before it was shut to make way for the motorcade.

At ten A.M. Wheeling looks like the set of a 1950s film. On closer inspection the businesses are mostly closed and the streets are so empty you can stroll across them in the middle of rush hour without waiting for the light. There's a Chinese restaurant with a façade that mimics a Buddhist temple and a sign saying 1905, the year it opened, hanging above a giant red door. But the building's for sale. It's exactly the kind of depressed small town John Kerry is counting on to win states across the Rust Belt.

A girl at the CVS explains what happened to Wheeling while I'm buying aspirin. I've been getting headaches and I thought it was due to stress, or lack of enough sleep, or the mean letters my father's been sending me. He's upset because, when I was asked by an interviewer about my childhood, I talked about being a ward of the court and the group homes I lived in.[14] My father wanted to set the record straight because I told the interviewer how he had shaved my head and then moved after I had run away leaving me homeless and sleeping on a rooftop. But I was already homeless for six or seven months before he moved and I had no intention of going home and I still haven't. He wants me to know he didn't shave my head, he gave me a haircut. Though he used clippers. His insistence on changing the vocabulary I use to describe possibly the most traumatic moment of my youth gives me insight into the way politicians fight with the media. Is it an "uprising" or an "insurgency"? "Terrorism" or "rebellion"? Everybody always wants to control the vocabulary and family members and politicians are no different that way. My father also says I could have come home at any time, but doesn't explain why he wouldn't give me his address. He prefers to remember the times I came home to shower before he moved, whereas I remember the coldest night in Chicago winter. So when I was caught sleeping in a hallway the summer after I finished eighth grade and the police asked me where my parents lived, I had to say I didn't know, because I didn't. That's when the state took custody, after I had been on the streets for nearly a year. But my father remembers it differently. When two sides refuse to agree things get complicated. *USA Today* ran an article about how the Bush economists think the economy is getting better and the Kerry economists think it's getting worse. We may never know. With such strong disagreements over the most basic facts you'd have to be an egomaniac not to step back once in a while and ask yourself if you're not crazy. But that's not why I'm getting headaches.

It turns out I'm getting headaches from a neck injury and I don't have health insurance so there's not much I can do about it. I figured it out researching my symptoms on the Internet. I buy thirty Tylenol with mint coating and I can feel the cool pills slide down my throat. Meanwhile the girl behind the counter tells the story of what happened to Wheeling. "Twenty-five years ago," she says, "they wanted to open a mall here but the town voted against it. We wanted to maintain the town character. So the mall opened in St. Claireville, Ohio, and put all of the stores here out of business. St. Claireville is less than twenty minutes away on the highway. There's nothing here anymore. The town council can't seem to do anything about it. They've considered casinos and outlet malls but nothing happens and people keep leaving."

So Wheeling's problems are really simple. Except for the larger consideration of urban sprawl that accompanies a new retail philosophy that eschews the mom-and-pop store and fiercely defies collective bargaining. I think of the new shopping center's amphibious assault on the shore of Homestead, Pennsylvania, and compare that with Wheeling's fate. The chain-store developments lay siege to cities like Wheeling with no intention of even moving in. The strategy is not to starve the town into submission. The strategy is to starve the town.

Wheeling is the first stop for John Kerry's Jobs-First Express tour. This will probably be John Kerry's last bus tour until after the Democratic convention. He doesn't travel much by bus anymore, preferring instead to hop across the swing state in chartered planes, but this is a three-day stretch into the heart of the Rust Belt, which, according to Toni Montgomery from the *Florida Observer*, is where the Kerry team has decided they will or will not win the election.[15]

"The Republicans are going to carry Florida," Toni told me a few days ago. I had called him at his home in Florida while driving behind Arlen Specter's SUV outside of Harrisburg. There was a lot of laughing in the background. I asked him what was going on and he told me not to worry about it. He told me there was a girl he wanted to introduce me to. "She rents roller skates on South Beach and she has a degree in psychology." I told him I was still lovesick over Wilhelmina, even though she had been sending me notes warning me not to write about her. The notes freaked me out and I considered going into hiding and then realized I was already in hiding. Hiding in motion. I didn't even know where I was going to stay each night. Who would ever find me? I was going crazy with loneliness at the time and it was getting difficult to focus on the highway.

"How do you know that?" I asked Toni, bringing the conversation back to the Florida electoral college. "You're not even covering the campaign anymore."

"I still get the press releases," he said.

"So do I," I told him. "What are you trying to say?"

"It's simple. If they really thought they could win Florida, Kerry would be here a lot more often and his message wouldn't be geared so heavily to fossil fuel states. Further, he'd pick Bill Nelson or Bob Graham as a running mate, but that's not going to happen."

The problem with Toni is that he's often wrong. On the other hand, he writes for a major newspaper and has access to all sorts of information that I don't have. People tell him things they would never tell me. Toni probably knows Kerry's schedule through September while I only know Kerry's schedule until Wednesday, at which point I'll take a two-and-a-half-hour Greyhound from Cleveland to Pittsburgh, then a twenty-two-dollar airport shuttle from the downtown Westin, pick up my rental car from long-term parking, drive across the turnpike through New Jersey back to Brooklyn, give a reading Thursday night in Manhattan, then catch a flight out of LaGuardia to North Carolina on Friday morning. It seems ridiculous to think about it, and I try not to. And yet I know it was the right thing to do because there's nothing better than three days on the bus with a presidential candidate trying to frame the debate.

It makes me nostalgic and giddy, but Kerry's first day of trying to turn the issue toward jobs and the economy does not go so well. The Republicans have just released a tape from 1971 with John Kerry claiming to have thrown away his medals, only the other day he said he did not throw away his medals, he threw away his *ribbons*.[16] It's another question of rhetoric, similar to the drama between my father and myself. Kerry says he was referring to ribbons, not medals. I say my father moved, he says I could have come home at any time. I say the group homes were rough places. He says the worst thing that ever happened to me was that someone stole my shoes.[17] I say I left home when I was thirteen. He says I left home when I was fourteen.[18]

The thing is, thirteen or fourteen shouldn't really matter, since what we're really talking about is October versus December, and the medals/ribbons flap shouldn't matter either. Because George Bush didn't have any medals to throw in the river and nobody knows for sure whether he did or didn't serve in the National Guard, which was only a once-a-week commitment anyway and not something to be compared with guiding a swift boat down the Mekong. And the questions of Kerry's records should be parlayed with the lack of records on George Bush. But that doesn't seem to be the buzz on the press bus or on *Good Morning America,* where

Kerry gives an interview from a coal mine and defends himself against the Republican allegations when what he really wants to get across is that he's a supporter of the coal industry, of clean coal, and also of steel workers everywhere.

And that's what Kerry tells the crowd of eight hundred at the Wheeling Pavilion and the All-Clad factory in Canonsburg. He says he has "a growth plan that will create ten million new jobs." That he will "end the insane practice of giving companies tax incentives to move jobs overseas. And we will use the savings to cut taxes for ninety-nine percent of businesses that want to expand and create jobs here at home."

He goes on to talk about enforcing trade agreements with China and Japan. It's a direct appeal to the coal and steel workers, the bedrock swing voters of the Rust Belt states, as well as the nation's recently unemployed. He won't talk about environmentalism much over the next three days, except as a way to develop jobs through funding research into things like "clean coal technology," because the states that are really worried about the environment are already locked down. He already has the environmental vote. But even mentioning the environment seems to muddy the message, and most people still don't know what his message is. The people on the press bus don't seem to know what his message is either. The good news for people who care is that John Kerry has a great record on the environment, reproductive rights, and the death penalty. Better still, he's not George Bush, but I've said that already and will probably say it again.

When you're with the Secret Service you never have to worry about traffic jams. They close the highways and I see the traffic stalled for miles between sets of police cars blocking the interchange and waiting for us to pass. I could have been stuck in one of those cars, but I'm not. We caravan through the Appalachian hills.[19] It's a beautiful landscape and it's hard to believe they voted for Bush in 2000. It is harder still to believe that the oldest newspaper in the state, *The Intelligencer,* which was founded as an abolitionist paper, back when West Virginia was still part of Virginia, now runs syndicated columns by Bill O'Reilly, George Will, and Bob Novak, as well as guest editorials from the Heritage Foundation. Did West Virginia know in 2000 what would happen to their jobs and their health care? Did they know their children would be taken for a war of choice thousands of miles away? Of course not. But the larger question is, Do they know it now? All the evidence suggests that they don't; *The Intelligencer* still sells for fifty cents all over town. The worse things go in Iraq the more polls show Americans trust Bush with their security,[20] and instead of focusing on Bush's failure to serve in Vietnam they focus on whether John Kerry threw away his medals or ribbons. And they don't like environmentalists here so although John Kerry is one, he will do his best to convince them otherwise. I just hope they believe him because this is clearly a place that does not know what is in its own interest.

The Jobs-First Express, which consists of two campaign buses, two press buses, a string of cars attached to the Secret Service, and state and local police as well as an SUV carrying the candidate, continues to Youngstown and a fund-raiser in Cleveland. I don't have to buy drinks anymore when I'm with the campaign; all the other reporters know I don't have an expense account.[21]

On Wednesday morning I peel from the campaign, my notebook filled with unfinished thoughts like *You show me coal and I will show you rust*. I'm not sure what half of them mean, and the rest seem senseless or do not lead anywhere. I drive back through Pennsylvania. Arlen Specter has squeaked past Patrick Toomey thanks to a boost from President Bush. After making Bush the cornerstone of his primary nomination, sending out cards with the president's endorsement, and calling Republicans across the state with a prerecorded message from Bush, Specter immediately distances himself from the president, calling the situation in Iraq a "tinderbox" and stating, "I intend to retain my independent voice, a voice I have always had. The 12 million people of Pennsylvania have not elected me to be a rubber stamp, and I will speak out where I think the necessity calls for it." Which is ironic when just a week ago I heard him tell a small crowd that the important thing was that he "voted with Bush 90 percent of the time." But the Democrats in the state weren't listening during the Republican primary, and those are the voters Specter's trying to appeal to now.

It was a close call for Specter: he won 51 percent to 49 percent, illustrating the shift that has occurred among Republicans who seem unanimous behind the idea of tax cuts and for whom deficit is just another word for nothing left to lose. Which is how I feel about parking tickets—you can't bleed a rock. In the age of MasterCard I've always thought that good credit was overrated. Of course it's different when you're a nation and your currency is devalued and the bulk of your cash is spent to service a debt. Especially when the money spent really belongs to people my age and younger. Worse still if you're in a war and that war is getting worse and there is no end in sight and you lie about how much that war is going to cost.

In Cleveland yesterday, before Al Gore showed up at our hotel to give John Kerry six million dollars,[22] but after certain members of the press visited a strip club on the outskirts of Youngstown,[23] I broke away from a campaign stop to speak to a group of nearby protesters. There were only ten of them, a few wore shirts and ties and probably worked for the Bush/Cheney campaign, and there was also a short woman with curly brown hair who was very upset that John Kerry had insulted America's veterans.

"Does it bother you that George Bush chickened out of going to fight?" I asked. I've asked Republicans this question before but I thought I would push the envelope a little bit. The Serbian Hall, where John Kerry was hosting a jobs summit, was in a tough neighborhood, and the streets were blocked by police cars. Six local mayors were with Kerry and the protesters thought it was typical of the media not to pay them any attention despite the fact that they were a pretty small, shabby group.

"He was in the National Guard!" they exclaimed in unison. They said it in an exasperated way, like they couldn't understand why anybody would think Bush was intentionally trying to avoid going to Vietnam. It was no different from the Republicans I had spoken to in Reading or Harrisburg, or the driver who had picked me up from the airport in Portland on the way to my Nike shopping spree, which was the first time I realized that the Republicans were getting their information from other sources and not just Fox News. I'm more and more certain there is a pipe that runs directly into these people's homes playing Christian rock and telling them what to think. But I can't prove it.

They were livid about Kerry's attack on President Bush's National Guard service. I pointed out that Bush had attacked Kerry's service with the medal versus ribbon controversy. They responded that the information wasn't from the Bush/Cheney campaign, but *Good Morning America*. I didn't have anything with me except my notebook and I was wearing my wool sweater. "What if I told you the Republican National Committee supplied that tape to *Good Morning America*?" I asked. "Would that change your mind?"

"We have the right to ask," the short lady told me. I closed my notebook and smiled. The general rule of journalism is never to ask a politician because they'll never give you a straight answer. But this lady already knew that tape came from the RNC and had decided to lie to me anyway, at which point I walked away. But maybe I shouldn't have. Maybe I should have grabbed her sign and torn it in half. It probably would have earned me a beating and it wouldn't have been worth it. The Kerry bus would have left without me but not before erasing my hard drive which I had left open in the press filing room. The Republicans would have stolen my money and left me to fend for myself in the Cleveland ghetto.

To go to New York you leave the turnpike for Highway 78 in the middle of the state, cutting around the capital. The 78 will take you within four miles of Allentown, in the Lehigh Valley. The Lehigh Valley voted overwhelmingly for Patrick Toomey in the primary. These are the hills and the coal mines that will elect the next president. Bush will come through the Rust Belt next week, on a three-day swing through the same places Kerry has just been. While John Kerry's sweep was titled the Jobs-First Express, Bush's roadtrip is called the Winning the War on Terror tour.[24]

The problem, of course, is that we're not winning the war on terror. Painting something on the side of a bus does not make it true. A strong argument could be made that we're not even fighting a war on terror. General William Odom, a member of the conservative Hudson Institute, told *The Wall Street Journal* yesterday, "We have failed [in Iraq]. The issue is how high a price we're going to pay." The common wisdom is that Iraq is going to get worse before it gets better and it may not get better. But nobody thinks people will vote on that issue. Which is why Kerry came through here trying to convince people they're poor and Bush is trying to convince them they're rich.

"Give the check back if you're against the tax cut," one of the Bush supporters told me yesterday. "The tax cuts are working," she said. "All you have to do is go to Wal-Mart and you can see it. People are buying things."

It will be a while before I understand the Rust Belt in full and I don't think I'll ever understand the Republicans, but that won't stop me from trying. Oddly enough Maureen Dowd laid it all out in her column this morning: "Mr. Kerry errs on the side of giving the answer he thinks people want to hear, even as Mr. Bush errs on the side of giving the answer he expects people to accept as true." Which pretty much puts it all out in the open, unless one is paying attention to the details. But the details don't matter. What's relevant is that when asked a week ago if he owned a gas-guzzling SUV, Kerry said no. Which turned out to be a lie along the lines of "I did not have sex with that woman." The SUV is owned by John Kerry's wife. A small lie, no doubt, but telling in a much larger way. Essentially, John Kerry bends the truth to accommodate whichever constituency is in the room. And yet I would do anything to help this man become president, which is personally sad as it symbolizes the end of my idealistic youth. It's a slippery slope once you buy in to what Marc Smith calls the Big John Scam.[25]

In these hills and the malls surrounding them, this strange swath of land that swings noticeably every four years, there is only one truth that can be verified and is absolute: No Republican has ever won the White House without winning Ohio. A lesser truth is that if Gore had carried West Virginia he'd be president right now, but Clinton ignored the industry and his vice president paid the price. What else do these hills contain besides steel and coal and doctored memories of better times? The residents stand waiting for some good news at the ATM while rockets pound Fallujah. The cameras catch it all in green with night-vision lenses. The troops are finally coming home, flags draped across their coffins, the pictures the administration tried to keep out of the news.[26] Today the president and vice president sit together behind closed doors providing explanations to the 9/11 Commission. But that's not what it's about on the turnpike or the churches of Allentown and the townships surrounding Toledo, where preachers follow gospel with tutorials on the joy of supply side economics; and a breeze passes along the congregation's feet and the congregation sways, eyes closed, dressed in their Sunday best like Baptists at a revival. One member cries, "I have seen the lord." Another thinks, "I too can be rich and then these tax cuts will be mine."

The danger of these hills is that even with the modern highway system you can still get lost in them. These are the places where Democrats turn from their message and while grasping for swing voters they alienate their base. The majority of Democrats who care about the environment and the quagmire in Iraq will not be turned on if the bulk of rhetoric coming from the campaign deals with protecting jobs in industries that should probably be phased out altogether.

I pull into a service plaza and fill up the tank. It's cool and it's going to rain soon. Gas is $1.80 a gallon. I use the bathroom but I forget to put my shoes on and approach the urinal in wool socks, which turns out to be a mistake. I buy one more cup of coffee to last me the final hundred miles to Gotham, and I stand by the car for a moment, squinting at a cobalt sky.

Three Points of View on George W. Bush

The economy is moving in the right direction, and don't let anyone tell you otherwise.

—DICK CHENEY ADDRESSING WAL-MART EMPLOYEES IN BENTONVILLE, ARKANSAS

Digression

YOU—*How to Meet the President; The Taxes You'll Pay Later*

It's not easy to meet the president, but it can be done. The important thing is to sleep in your friend's house in Dupont Circle. She's a lawyer who also paints and she has a small dog. The night before you meet the president you'll watch *The Sopranos* with her, the episode where Tony Soprano's daughter gets engaged and his cousin is promoted to managing the casino. Also the episode where Vito gets caught giving a blow job to a security guard outside the construction site. *The Sopranos* has nothing to do with meeting the president except that it's during *The Sopranos* that you'll find out your flight has been cancelled and you need to change airlines. Here is the connection between organized crime and the President of the United States you have been searching for all your life.

Go to sleep early. The small clock your friend leaves on the coffee table will not go off at five A.M. like it's supposed to but your internal alarm will jolt you awake at 5:22 A.M. and you will look wild-eyed until the shapes around you make sense in the dark. The difference between someone who meets the president is the difference between someone who rolls over, pulls on his pants, shoulders his backpack, and walks out the door—and someone who gives up and goes back to sleep. If you go back to sleep you'll remember this failure for the rest of your life and will never again question why things didn't work out for you quite the way they should have.

If it's raining heavily there'll be a cab downstairs waiting for the neighbor and that neighbor will be going to the same airport you're going to so you're in luck. Cross the Mall and pass the tiny lights of the Treasury Building, drive over the Potomac, swinging sharply to the right away from Pentagon City. Ignore the short, blocky buildings with barricaded windows that house the nation's machinery. Don't question what you're doing; it's not that kind of a thing. Meeting the president is about finding purpose and being open to the unexpected, like the first time you caught yourself dancing to Justin Timberlake. The streets are so dark and wet they glow.

Part of meeting the president is forgetting the book you were reading on the origins of Fascism.[1] It will still be there when your friend wakes up two hours later, rubbing her eyes, confronted with the mess you left behind. She lacks the thirst for power that fuels the nation's capital. She just wants a nice house and then maybe later a child. She's going back to California, and she'll comfort herself with that thought, the percolator whistling, while her dog wraps himself around her ankle and your first plane begins its descent into Detroit.

But you can't fly into Detroit unless you find out about the bus trip several days earlier when it's mentioned in *The Note,* the daily brief rounding out all of the political stories published by the major papers every day. If you don't read *The Note,* your chances of meeting the president are zero. Because it won't be mentioned anywhere else. Some of the events, which will be scheduled across Michigan and Ohio, where votes matter, will be called Ask President Bush. The tour will be called the Yes, America Can tour. And the point is to inspire colorful stories in the local media. There won't be anyone there to Ask President Bush unless their local Republican office invites them ahead of time. It won't be listed on the president's calendar, ever. For security purposes, the president's schedule is not published. For political purposes, only Republicans are invited to media events.

To find out where and when the first event will be you need the phone number for the Bush/Cheney 04 press office. If you're traveling with John Kerry at the time you can get that number from Michael Roselli, the senior producer for CNN. He always has a book open, something literary, and is a calming presence in what can be a very stressful environment. Michael has all the phone numbers you could ever need.[2]

When you call you'll get a recording that says the bus tour information is not available yet. But it's just a test, think about it. You have to prove you are serious to these people. If you go to the BC04 Web site, you'll see an entire section dedicated to all the good the president is doing for the environment. Remember the smog stacked over the skies of Houston and the off-duty policemen there working security for the oil companies dressed in full uniform while taking orders from marketing executives. You have to know not to trust anybody. Look at his skin, thick from Texas sun, and his lips that have all but disappeared in his last three years in office.

People who trust never meet the president.

If you call over and over again and you're never away from your phone and you say things like, "Salon.com is a major news source!" and act surprised when they say they've never heard of it. Then at three P.M. on Saturday, two hours before the deadline, they will fax you one page with a paragraph worth of information to your hotel near the interstate in Chapel Hill, North Carolina. The fax will say "Sensitive Information" across the top and it won't be addressed to anyone.

You'll need an editor in New York willing to fax your social security number on company letterhead on short notice. Don't promise him anything and he will promise you nothing in return. It's a tacit agreement—nobody assumes the risk. All he asks is that you don't act like that guy who ran around the Kerry camp dressed in a Viking outfit and wrote that spiteful article for *Rolling Stone*.

If you have an editor who works on Saturday, and you call often enough, they'll put you on a press list for the first event. If you want they will reserve a spot for you at the airport and you can see the president depart Air Force One. But they won't let you in the motorcade so it's one or the other, the airport or the event. It's a bus tour so you ask if you can get on the bus and Sarah Thilman tells you there isn't enough room, which you know is a lie. She says not to worry—they will give you great support. They will write your story for you.

This is how news is made. They write it, shoot it, and deliver it to the media. Some journalists, like Adam Nagourney, refuse their handouts. But more often than not what you read in the paper is written by the campaign.[3] They will take pictures for you. They will have helicopters shooting video, providing coverage of the buses between events. They will e-mail you everything that happens and you can publish their photos and their words of the events for free. You don't even have to give them credit, which is what happened last week when *Good Morning America* and *The New York Times* ran with a video of John Kerry in 1971 saying he had thrown away his medals. Neither mentioned the Republican National Committee as the source of the videotape. People will say it's evil to print news spoonfed from partisan sources without acknowledgment. But you know the difference between evil and lazy better than anyone. You're an expert in the evil versus lazy argument.

"That's not really interesting to me," you'll tell Sarah. That's what you have to say if you want to meet the president. After a couple of minutes Sarah will ask if she can call you back shortly. But Sarah will never call you back and she will never answer the phone when you call again.

It doesn't matter, you're on a list, and you can parlay that list to be on more lists. When you get to the airport watch the cab door—if you bang your elbow it will bruise and for a moment that pain will distract you from everything that has ever happened in the world. And don't forget to thank your friend's neighbor for letting you share the ride. Keep moving because when you stop moving you'll have to answer the question that every runaway has to answer at some point, *Hey kid, what are you running from? You can't run from fear.* Go to the front of the line because your plane is about to leave. If the man in the pinstripe suit with only a thin beard along his jaw outlining his face will not let you in front of him, the man behind him with the thick T-shirt and unwashed hair will tell you to go ahead. Take fifteen milligrams of speed inside the terminal because it's important to be awake for your country, especially in times like these. Remember, your original flight was canceled because of weather conditions. Buy a copy of *The Economist* before boarding the plane and flying into the storm.

May 1–6

ME—The Burning McDonald's; Questions for the President; The Rise of Capitalist Nationalism; South Bend; Niles; Kalamazoo; Detroit

There's a McDonald's burning in Niles, Michigan. I see the plume of gray smoke just as I cross the border from Indiana and the time zone changes. Traffic is diverted from 13th Street onto 15th and then back to 13th and then Eagle Drive. A plumber was soldering a pipe near the roof and the insulation caught on fire. At first I thought it was a terrorist attack—the president's motorcade was scheduled to cross in front of that McDonald's at noon after the president gave a speech endorsing an Indiana congressman on the steps of Air Force One at the South Bend airport. But the time change threw everything off. The airport is only thirteen miles away but Niles Senior High School is an hour later. The burning McDonald's will haunt me for two days as I try to decipher the message beneath the message underlying the president's visit to this state that has lost a disproportionate number of jobs during the Bush presidency.

I arrive at the high school an hour early and they give me a local press pass. A Young Republican from Notre Dame University escorts me to the gym, where high school students—boys in tuxedos and girls in red glitter dresses—are performing a dance around the stage. The boys face forward and the girls back, then they switch, singing the whole time and waving their hands. Bush will stand on that stage shortly to address the crowd. I'm excited and wired and before the president arrives I call Chrissy in Chicago. Chrissy's not really my sister, but sometimes I call her my sister anyway. My real sister's name is Victoria.

"Guess who's going to meet the president?" I say.

"Who?"

"Me," I tell her. Then I hang up and turn off my phone.[4]

The crowd at the school gym are all local Republicans and they got their tickets through a connection with the mayor or some other official. It's a stacked crowd and the fashion statement of the day is American flag clothing. Girls wear American flag skirts cut above the knees and men wear ties painted with the Stars and Stripes. The gym is strung with awards the local teams have won over the years. The event is called Ask President Bush and these are the people who are going to ask him his questions and when he arrives they go nuts.

The president lets the crowd clap for a while, then waves his hands, signaling them to sit down and they do. Laura Bush introduces the president. She's wearing a fuchsia jacket and dark pants. Her husband is wearing a charcoal suit. She's slim and has a kind smile. She tells the story of George's run for Congress and how she spent a lot of time in the car with George and by the end of it "he convinced me to vote for him." It's a hit, the crowd loves it. Laura Bush is a sweetheart. She will sit by the stage and motion to her husband when it is time to go.

"Think it's all right if I take off my jacket?" the president asks. "We're not in Washington anymore." I'm fifteen feet away from him. There is a black velvet rope and then seven rows of seats and then a square stage three feet high where the president stands. Next to me is a riser built from plywood, filled with dirt, and covered with a sheet of plastic. I tell myself that my goal for the day is to find a Republican to like.[5]

"I told the people back here they have the best view," Bush says, referring to the rows of people behind him looking at his ass. It's a funny joke, and there's more to come. When Bush laughs his head shakes. It's a quiet laugh that comes from a place deep inside. There's something strong in the way he speaks, something muscular about the way he holds his body with his head forward over his collarbone and his nose and lips sharp like an eagle's.

"I'd like to have a dialogue with you," Bush says. "I came here to ask for your help."

"Oh brother," the lady next to me whispers. She's from the local newspaper. Next to her is Adele Straub from 92.1 FM radio. Adele won't stop clapping at everything the president says. She's ecstatic. It's the first time I've ever seen a member of the press actively and openly endorsing a candidate from inside the press area. Adele is small and wrinkled and reminds me ever so slightly of the old ladies who arrive to see the pope give mass at St. Peter's. They will claw you to death and step over your dead body in their heels in an effort to get closer to the pontiff.

It's a short speech and Bush spends much of it speaking about the war in Iraq. "The best way to protect the homeland is to stay on the offensive and bring the killers to justice," he says. "I looked at intelligence on Iraq and saw a threat. . . . Saddam . . . ties to terrorist organizations . . . See, not only did we make America more secure by getting rid of Saddam, we are changing the world by insisting freedom and democracy prevail. . . . Freedom is the almighty God's gift to each man and woman in this world."

Every time he makes a point the crowd erupts in applause. But I don't feel more secure. I wonder if I can return God's gift and exchange it for a new Sony PlayStation. Each time the crowd claps I imagine another McDonald's bursting into flames.

There's major differences between Bush's approach and John Kerry's. Bush is short and to the point and he says things that may or may not be true[6] but he is incredibly succinct and easy to understand. There's no room for second-guessing. You either accept the facts of what he is saying or you resolve yourself to calling the president a liar. It's totally different from Kerry who leaves ample room for splitting hairs as he straddles the issues while forging an unlikely coalition of miners and environmentalists.

Bush continues about how the attacks of September hurt our economy. A baby starts crying and the mother rushes the baby out of the room. She must have known the baby would cry. Bush says the best way to generate economic growth is to let people keep more of their own money. "The tax cuts we passed came at the absolute right time." He speaks of inheriting an economy in decline and turning it around. The further he goes the stranger I feel.

"We can't have a vibrant economy unless you become less dependent on foreign sources of energy." He says we will move toward things like reusable energy but it will take fifteen (fifty?) years to get there. I'm pretty sure he said fifty years but I decide to give him the benefit of the doubt. "We got to use the resources we have to get there. . . . We need to be exploring for energy."

Everything the president says is easy to digest and makes sense on some basic level. Outlining a problem and providing a solution never takes more than three sentences, which I find reassuring. America is more secure as a result of invading Iraq. We're going to create clean energy, but first we're going to dig up some oil and mine the hell out of Pennsylvania. People get tax refunds, then they go out and spend their money, and every time someone spends money it creates a job. Except of course that the country has lost jobs. The genius is undeniable and beautiful—you accept it or you don't, there's nothing to argue about.

I'm stunned by the president's charisma and humor. He cracks me up several times and at one point I find myself on the verge of clapping. But his real appeal is very animalistic. The strength he radiates is the strength of a man who does not waver. I decide that if there was no government, if the waters had risen to swallow most of the continent and anarchy reigned across much of the world, and people were living in caves, I would want George Bush to defend my cave. He would be my first choice to stand in front of the entrance wearing an animal carcass, ready to club to death any mammal that crossed within fifty feet, while I stayed inside with the women, trying to stay warm cooking scraps over our tiny fire. But we're not there yet.

After the president's speech five speakers are called upon to say how tax relief has made their lives better. The president prods them along, like a game-show host, periodically stopping them to explain what they are saying to the rest of us. "Let me stop you there. You hear what he said, 'partnered with businesses' . . . Now two or three jobs, that might not sound like a lot. . . . It's a market-based approach. . . . And you used that money to hire people didn't you?"

"Yes I did, Mr. President."

"Let me tell you something about Dan. He got laid off right after September 11th. Why don't you pick it up from there?"[7]

After the five speakers Bush takes questions from the crowd and the questions are so soft that I have to wonder if the people asking

them weren't planted ahead of time. The first questioner is His-
panic and wants to know how he can help convince his fellow His-
panic voters to vote for Bush in the fall. The president responds
with a sentence in Spanish and finishes with, "This team understands if you own something in America you have a vital stake in
the future of our country." Another questioner is African American
and asks essentially the same question. "I repeat exactly what I said
before to my Latino friend here." Both questioners are exception-
ally large with big shoulders and giant bellies and over six feet tall,
though that's probably not relevant. They give accent to a room
that otherwise could be compared with a cold gallon of milk.

Two children are called upon, a little girl with curly hair and a
young boy with his blond hair cut close to the scalp. The boy
wants to know why the president came to Niles, to which Bush responds, "Because I want to get out of Washington. Because there's
good people here." The girl wants to know Bush's highest priority
in his second term and he tells her his highest priority is to keep
America safe.

Nobody asks how he intends to cut taxes, pay two-hundred billion dollars for war in Iraq, and trim the deficit simultaneously. Or
why, if his environmental record is so good, groups like the Sierra
Club are not supporting him. It's not that kind of crowd. The only
difficult question comes from a woman who complains about the
funding being cut for the volunteer program she works at.

"National funding?" the president asks.

"Yes."

"That's what you get for trying to cut the deficit," he says, and
he laughs from inside, his body moving slightly up and down like
an accordion, his head moving forward and back on his neck. But
nobody laughs, so he makes another joke. When that doesn't work
he promises to have his people to look into it and then calls on
someone else. The next person asks how the president's faith in
God affects his daily routine.

When Bush leaves he leaves quickly. His press pool is whisked away to the buses at the back of the motorcade. The cameras are taken down and I'm left standing behind the rope next to a square filled with cement. I've got a lot of questions but no answers. I've been up since five this morning and I'm four hours away from the suburbs of Detroit where Bush will have his last rally of the day near the GM technology center. The event itself starts in five hours so there's little time. They wouldn't let me on the press bus, they wouldn't even consider it. The door closes behind the president and the national media as they speed off to their next stop in Kalamazoo. I'm left behind.

I corner the little boy with the crew cut on his way to the door. "When did you know you were going to ask the president a question?" I ask. He's with his mother and his mother is smiling. I have a presidential press pass hanging around my neck. It says "White House Press Pool" and it is six-sided. Behind that are two laminates for John Kerry's bus tour through this same swath of state. I want to get this small boy to confess. He's ten years old, but he lives inside the pipe. There's a blueprint inside his head that contains a detailed map of the end of the world. If I had two days alone with him without his mother watching I could coerce him into giving me all the secrets of an administration that operates behind closed doors, only releasing documents in precision attacks against its enemies. I need to know what he knows.

"I decided earlier today." He grins like a liar but he's too young to understand that so I don't read too much into it.

"Were you surprised when they called on you?" I ask, tightening the noose.

"I guess so."

"Did you know in advance you would be called on?" I say, going in for the kill.

He pauses. And it's really a dramatic pause. And maybe I'm the only one who notices he turns his head in a style that could be called defiant. By this time the local camera crew have arrived and are filming the boy. "No," he says and I know I've lost another small battle in this war of attrition.

The president stops in Kalamazoo before heading to Detroit. I skirt along the bottom of the state on Michigan 60, a small two-lane road that crosses a hundred miles worth of farms and lakes. There's no cell phone reception and great distances separate the houses. The dirt is turned in row after row, the fields bump against and are surrounded by trees. It's a flat, quiet horizon punctuated only by the occasional gas station. These are core Bush voters, from the emptiest place in America.

I cut up on Highway 69 to 94. The highways are still open but the police cars sit on top of every overpass ready to shut the roads. Here's a trick. I'm the only person on the interstate who knows the president is coming this way except for the administration and the law enforcement. Every officer in the state has been called on to help protect the president. I'm two hours away from a rally that starts in two hours. I give the car some gas. It's a Dodge Neon, the cheapest thing in the Hertz lot. It's not a car with a lot of acceleration and there's no scan feature on the radio. I push the car to eighty and it shivers. As it goes past ninety it begins to quake and the side panels release a plaintive metallic whine. The police watch me pass but they don't go after me. They can't, they're waiting for the president. They stare from the overpasses and the meridians and the turnabouts in the center of the highway. I burn past them all, just ahead of the motorcade. Twenty miles outside of Sterling Heights, Cheap Trick comes on the radio. *Didn't I didn't I didn't I see you crying.* Cheap Trick knows: When the president's coming, it's all right to speed.

The final event of the day is at the Jerome Duncan Ford Theatre on Freedom Hill. It's a small amphitheater, similar in shape to the one where I saw Ozzfest in Scranton, Pennsylvania, in 2002, but smaller.[8] Still, there are at least five thousand people in attendance, and probably as many as ten thousand. It's motorcycle awareness month and among the shirt-and-tie Republicans there are bikers and women with many earrings in full leather outfits.

I'm the last to arrive and park my car a mile away on the muddy edge of the stadium grounds. My name is not on the list at the media table but I show them my pass from earlier in the day so they give me another pass and let me in. Passes beget passes. There's a band playing and when the motorcade pulls into the lot they show the picture on the giant overhead screen. One of the first things the president tells the crowd is that he's proud to be here and that he got here, "On the George. W. Bush. bus!"[9] The crowd goes nuts, and he lets them.

The speech he gives is similar to the speech he gave earlier, except more aggressive toward Kerry. This is either because of newspaper filing times or the larger crowd or because they didn't want to see headlines that read "George Bush Starts Off Bus Tour by Crushing Beer Can on Kerry's Head." But here, speaking to an immense and adoring crowd, he goes on the offensive.

"I'm running against an *experienced* United States Senator," he says, leaning over the podium, speaking into a mike, the corners of his mouth pointed down with pleasurable disgust.

"We love you!" some girls scream from the upper area of the stadium on the lawn.

"He's been in Congress long enough to take both sides on just about every issue," he continues. "He's been on both sides of big issues. And if he could find a third side . . ." Head front and back, body up and down. He goes on to talk about the SUV controversy. How Kerry spoke of his SUV while in Michigan, then denied having an SUV on Earth Day, and then cleared it up by saying the SUV belongs to his family. "Now there's a fella who's getting a lot of mileage out of his Suburban." In my notes I write, very funny SUV story, with an arrow pointing to the quote.

Then things get scary. He talks about the "terror regime in Iraq."[10] He finishes the thought with, "Either take the word of a madman [Saddam] or defend America. Given that choice I will defend America every time."

"I'm not sure those were the choices," I say to the cameraman next to me but he refuses to look away from the lens. People are always ignoring me. The giant crowd is chanting, "USA! USA!"

I turn to Amber Hunt Martin from the *Detroit Free Press* and say, "Every person in this stadium thinks there's been a decrease in terrorism since we invaded Iraq." She nods her head and kind of laugh/smiles. There's no mistaking the fear. This is a crowd that could turn on us and she doesn't want to be seen as a partner to dissent. The local media area is in the very center of the amphitheater, the best seats in the house. The National Press area is far off to the side ready to beat a hasty exit. We're surrounded by a violent jubilee and if she agrees with me and the crowd turns on us, there will not be enough security to stop them from tearing off our arms.

Then Bush says, "America will never turn over national security decisions to leaders of other countries. . . . It is not enough to serve our enemies with legal papers. . . . We will not stand for judges . . . who try to remake the values of democracy by court order."

The crowd loves him. He's a rock star. He has everything going for him except his record. And for a moment I think Kerry doesn't have a chance. These people love this man deeply. And the only thing that snaps me out of it is when someone in the local media says to me, "He's going to have a hard time carrying Michigan."

When Bush leaves the speakers blare soul music. I don't see any black people in the crowd. There is a family with a sign that reads, "Assyrians for George Bush." Of course, white people like soul music just as much as black people do. Still, there's this girl in pinstriped pants. She's with another girl and two boys and they're both incredibly satisfied with this experience of seeing the president and she's dancing toward the exit and it strikes me as wrong. But maybe it's the pants. How much more interesting would it be if, instead of "Signed Sealed Delivered," they were playing "I Don't Know Why I Love You" by the Rolling Stones?

I move with the herd toward the exit. I'm staying the night in the Fairfield Inn in the middle of a cluster of mid-level hotels on Van Dycke, just over the border in Warren. The room rate is forty-nine dollars a night for two twin beds and a small TV. I realize that I'm very tired. More tired than a person should ever be. I feel tense and weird. There's a pool in the hotel but it's way too cold outside to go for a swim and will be for a while still. Sticks and leaves float along the surface. My white sweatshirt is covered in ketchup. McDonald's restaurants are spontaneously combusting across the state as the Bush campaign prepares to bed down at the Sommerset Inn in Troy. Was it really a plumber who started that fire with a soldering iron at nearly the exact same time the president arrived for the first stop of his first bus tour of the electoral season? Or was it part of something bigger, that giant cloud of thick gray smoke? A consequence following an act.

The important thing is not the McDonald's. If every McDonald's across the state burned to the ground it wouldn't matter as long as no one was hurt. Many in the health industry would see it as an improvement. But what is important?

The day's contradictions burn through me. The nationalism in a town where just about every car contains a catalytic converter or fuel injection system built overseas. All of the chants of "USA! USA!" Walking away from the stadium I was immersed in pieces of conversation: "Whenever somebody mentions Hillary's name, I just want to smack them. . . . How stupid do they think we are? . . . They make me so mad. . . ." There was a different quality to the talk, a quality missing from liberals when they talk about Bush with an equal, and yet somehow less violent, hatred. "This is how I talk to liberals," a large man in front of me wearing a cowboy hat demonstrated by pounding his fist into his palm. It was cool and the sun was down; I wondered what he needed the hat for.

And there it was on the stage. All of that talk about how we would never let another country make our decisions for us. The chants. Our God from whom it is divined we spread democracy.

War will make us safer; in fact we are already safer because we are at war. It would be so easy to panic.

But then that reporter calmly stated that Bush would have a hard time in Michigan. She seemed so sure. She had not just driven 230 miles across the state at an average speed of eighty-five miles an hour all the while watched by police cars radioing ahead from every bridge. And she hadn't had to wake up at five o'clock in the morning to catch a flight from Washington National into South Bend Regional airport where there are four video games from the late eighties inside terminal A.

I'm not saying she doesn't work hard. Just that at the rally she was probably looking at things with a clearer head than I was, and probably with more experience.

And that's the hope I wake with as I stare from my window to the courtyard and the giant streetlight there like antennas and the sign on its base—"No Parking Fire Lane." Continental breakfast is served from six to nine. There are free Frosted Mini-Wheats in the lobby. I love Frosted Mini-Wheats, one of life's great pleasures. I haven't seen the last of the president, not by a long shot. Today Bush flies into Ohio and the buses will meet him there. But I have to take a different route, west to Chicago, where I'll pick up Chrissy and continue to Iowa in the third person. There I'll meet Bush amid the corn-soaked fields. I've got to drive, drive, drive, back across this state and stay within the speed limits and hope that none of the troopers recognize my car from the day before. I have to make sure the McDonald's are still standing before I venture forward to the next logical step.

May 7–9

US—The Next Logical Step; The Ballad of Christine Bell; Shifting Points of View; Chicago; Dubuque; LaCrosse

Chrissy Bell and her brother Steve Elliott drive west from Chicago to Dubuque starting on Highway 90 and staying west across the

two-lane toward Iowa as the interstate twists north. Chrissy wants
to buy a house on the Illinois border out here one day, somewhere
to go on weekends with friends and for family gatherings, but
that's not why they're here. They pass through Galena's quiet hills
and the valley. They pass towns with redbrick buildings and artisan
communities where chain stores aren't allowed and they argue
about the future of towns like these.

Chrissy and Steve get a room at the Juliene in Dubuque, a hotel
formerly owned by Al Capone and used as a hideout during the
1920s. That night they watch as an old couple dances across the
floor, a white-haired lady playing piano accompanied by a man
rattling a pair of spoons. The dancers two-step slowly around the
linoleum. Steve sits at his table, his beer in front of him on a napkin, wondering if he will be that happy and in love late in life. His
sister sits at the bar talking to a lighting technician who was a DJ
in East Dubuque twenty years ago, "when things were really hap-
pening."

The dance floor is eight feet square. On his third beer, still nodding his head and watching the senior citizens, Steve thinks, Those
old folks can really swing. He taps Chrissy's shoulder on the way
out and she says, "OK, hon, I'll see you later." The technician says,
"You should have seen it. In December you couldn't tell the snow
from the cocaine."

Before six in the morning Steve wakes up feverish and goes for a
walk through downtown. Last night Chrissy had wondered when
he'd get married and have children. "I can't have children," he told
her. "I need too much attention. I'd be jealous of the child."

Chrissy shook her head. "I think it's great that you have such
insight into your flaws. But have you considered trying to
change them?"

"I have," he responded sadly. "Takes time."

Now his ears are ringing and he has a headache. He takes two mint-coated Tylenol and follows the cool pills with a biscuit and a bottle of water from the McDonald's. The sun is just out and the protesters are already gathering in the park, along with some workers from the John Kerry for President office. One of the workers used to work for John Edwards and he recognizes Steve and asks if he is still writing for *GQ*.

"Not really," Steve says. "I am in a way." He's stuck in an old lie, the lie he first told the campaign workers in order to get access. At least that's what he tells himself, *I did it to get access*. He's writing for *GQ* the way he has always written for *GQ*, which is to say that he isn't writing for *GQ* at all.

The protesters are up early because if they aren't across the bridge by eight they will be denied entrance to the river district, which is where the big hotel and convention center is, right next door to the casino on the other side of the road leading out of town.

When Chrissy wakes at eight A.M. Steve is back in bed with a wet towel across his eyes and his computer open next to him playing ocean sounds.

"What's wrong with you?" she asks.

"I'm hungover."

"That's impossible. You only had three beers."

"Impossible things happen all the time," he says. "You'll have to go without me."[11]

Chrissy leaves Steve in the hotel room with the wet towel over his face and marches to the giant glass convention center sparkling on the edge of the shore. She's met by a Secret Service officer with short hair made into hard, tiny spikes by a tablespoon of super-hold gel. His head resembles a baby porcupine. He points her toward a table where a volunteer leads her behind the building and hands her off to another volunteer who checks her name against a list and then hands her a White House press pass and escorts her to a waiting area where men in rumpled shirts are standing around having a cigarette. She's amazed that the press pass Steve said would be waiting for her is actually there. He told her the other day, "Come meet the president. I'll get you a press pass, it's easy. They'll give one to anybody." She's led inside and given a place in the center of the room on a three-tiered riser where she sets up her camera and attaches her new 200-millimeter zoom lens. Steve leaves for the river half an hour later, green-faced and covered in a thin layer of sweat. He drops his coffee on the sidewalk outside while adjusting his backpack, which he likes to wear strapped across his stomach and his chest. The cup lands upside down, the lid shooting off into the grass, the brown liquid puddling in the cracks in the walk.

"Oh no," he says, staring back across the bridge. There is nowhere to get another cup between where he is and the convention center. If he wants coffee he'll have to go back, but then it would be too late. They'll close the bridge; he'll miss the event. To his right the casino sits on the water open twenty-four hours a day. He tells himself a couple hands of poker will wake him up, but then confesses his own lie and trudges toward the back entrance where he asks the press liaison if there is any coffee to be had to which she responds, "No." He sits on one of the chairs reserved for national press and promptly falls asleep.

It happens like this: there are three thousand people in the room. There was an article in *The Daily Telegraph* about a seventy-seven-year-old veteran who wanted to attend the event and waited an hour for a ticket. Before giving him a ticket they asked if he was voting for George Bush. He said he didn't know who he was voting for yet. That's why he wanted to meet the president, so he could make up his mind. "I'm sorry," they said. "We're only giving tickets to people who sign a pledge to vote for the president." When he refused they called security. In the newspaper he was quoted as saying, "I don't like to lie."

So everybody in the room is Republican but they don't all look the way Steve and Chrissy expect them to look, though most of them do. Pixeled among the suits and ties and blue skirts and white tights are girls in red T-shirts with multicolored hair and boys with surfer haircuts not dissimilar to the New York–based novelist David

Amsden's. There's a punk rock element to supporting George Bush. Perhaps even a backlash against parents that were too understanding, a youthful search for structure in a world that seems unmanageable. The beginnings of this idea swim upstream across the muddy swamp of Steve's feverish mind.

At one point Steve opens one eye to see Chrissy staring down at him, smiling, her hands on her hips. Her long black hair tied in a ponytail, her round face a cross between a mother and a young girl. "You look like shit," she says.

Behind Chrissy everything appears infused with a dark green, like those awful night-vision photos out of Iraq. "Aren't you supposed to be taking pictures?" he responds.

"No, seriously," Chrissy says, pulling a napkin from her pocket and wiping Steve's forehead with it. "In all the time I've known you you've never looked worse than you do right now."

As the music starts the bay doors compress twenty feet into the ceiling. The light pierces the hall and the George W. Bush bus pokes its nose into the light. The crowd roars. Chrissy thinks it's the most phallic thing she's ever seen, the bus swollen with blue and red stripes, rented from Canada, driving through a lit opening, greeted with the screaming orgasm of Iowa's conservative base. The bus windows are tinted, the front grill seems to be grinning. The crowd breaks into a chant, "Four more years! Four more years!"

Occasionally Steve wakes to the president speaking, "Serious challenges . . . serious answers." But as soon as it's over he walks back to the hotel for one more hour of sleep so that he's ready for the big event in five hours at a baseball field in Wisconsin. On the way back to the hotel, he passes a group of protesters with a sign, "Tony Danza Supports ACT. Hey George, Who's the Boss Now!" He doesn't know what they mean but he knows they don't like George Bush and that means Tony Danza doesn't like Bush, either. Chrissy and Steve saw Tony Danza last night on Main Street, outside the Underground Sports Bar after they viewed the final episode of *Friends* together before returning to the hotel to watch the old people dance. The final episode of *Friends* was a disappointment.

"How are you going to work that into your book?" Chrissy asked.

"The final episode of *Friends* failed to live up to its potential, just like our generation," he responded.[12]

"Oh, that's good."

Steve wondered if Tony Danza was here to support Bush and Chrissy said, "No way. He's too dark to support Bush." Passing the signs he realizes she was right.

It's 120 miles north on a slow road into La Crosse, Wisconsin, with helicopters hovering overhead all the while. Just across the border, around the bend near a Fleet and Farm, Chrissy pulls the car over to take a picture of a marine chopper that has come to rest in a field. It sits there like a giant bug, its dark chin angled into the grass. Two marines in white helmets stand in the dirt waiting for the propellers to spin and then, in an instant, they disappear inside the machine, which lifts several feet from the earth and is gone.

"I could see how you could get addicted to this," Chrissy says. She's enjoying herself; she loves doing new things and meeting new people. Earlier, while Steve slept she went to the local grill for a sandwich and a bloody mary and the people there gave her the entire history of the town. She met a woman who wrote an advice column in the local paper and confessed to never once receiving a request for help. She wrote the questions and answers herself.

Chrissy and Steve have known each other seventeen years. They were in their early twenties when they started referring to each other as sister and brother, mostly so people wouldn't read a sexual element into their relationships. They've slept with each other's friends and the only time Chrissy ever gets mad at him is when she breaks up with someone and he takes her boyfriend's side. She often dates strong men, bikers and truckers, men with large fists. She's three years older than Steve so her boyfriends are often older as well. Sometimes Steve looks up to them, especially Opie, who lived above a bar on the ragged outskirts of Milwaukee and taught Steve how to play dice in Steve's final year of high school. Just outside La Crosse Chrissy reaches over and rubs his arm.

Sitting on the crowded second riser that has been built on the pitcher's mound and reserved for local press, Steve says, pointing at Chrissy, "If you lost some weight there'd be more room for the rest of us." Some of the journalists laugh uncomfortably. They know that joking about a woman's weight is a dangerous thing to do.

"Aren't you taking your author photo on Sunday?" Chrissy says. "Because I'm worried about that zit between your eyes." Steve rubs his finger across the zit between his eyes. "Don't touch it," Chrissy says. "You'll make it worse."

There are seven thousand people in the stadium. A giant red W sits on a large iron pole. The gestures are iconic, the bus, the W. It's all branding. They play the music from *The Natural*. The same sign hangs behind every podium where George Bush speaks: "Safer, Stronger, Better."

Laura Bush introduces the president and tells the joke she always tells, about driving through Texas with him when he was running for Congress and how by the end of it he had won her vote. And the president laughs like he's hearing it for the first time, like she caught him off guard with that one. She says, "My husband treats the men and women he meets with dignity and respect." Behind her on the scoreboard is an advertisement that reads, "Rely on Your Home Team, Grand Slam Service." Behind the billboard are rows of yellow and white striped tents.

"I like her," Chrissy says of the president's wife. "She seems like someone I could hang out with."

"Yeah," Steve responds. "She's nice."

George Bush follows his wife. Tells the crowd about all the jobs he's created. "We've added 1.1 million jobs since August . . . I'm running to make sure America is the greatest economy on the face of the earth." Steve is tired of disagreeing with him. He wants what the president says to be true. But he's not a Ph.D. in economics. He does know that under Bush the country has lost more jobs than it's gained. "Al Qaeda is wounded but not broken," the president continues. "Regimes in North Korea and Iran are challenging the peace. . . . Today no one doubts the word of the United States of America."

I do, Steve thinks to himself. The baseball stadium is at capacity but it doesn't begin to compare with Wrigley Field. If the stadium were in Chicago, Little League would play here. The president loves baseball.

"Because our coalition acted, Saddam's torture chambers are closed."

"Did he just say what I think he said?" Steve asks, but nobody answers. Nobody ever answers Steve, or at least he feels that way. He looks around quickly, more alert than he's been since they crossed out of Illinois. The crowd is cheering, their applause like thunder. An entire set of bleachers is filled with military personnel jumping up and down, threatening the structure's foundation. The event started forty-five minutes early because of a storm warning. The sky is gray.

For several days pictures have been all over the news detailing brutal torture of Iraqis by American soldiers in Saddam's old torture chambers. *The Wall Street Journal,* *The Washington Post,* and *The New Yorker* have all run extensive articles affirming that the pictures are only the tip of the iceberg. There are more pictures. The torture was widespread and endemic and occurring for a year and not just in Iraq.[13] Some editorialists are still referring to "isolated incidents" involving a handful of soldiers, but those editorials are not written by people who read long-form news because anybody who read the longer pieces in just about any paper would know that it wasn't true. There were no isolated incidents, there was widespread abuse spawned by a broken administration that had publicly stated that the rules of the Geneva Convention did not apply.[14] A lot of people, like Steve, think that if we already hadn't lost in Iraq, then we have lost now. The pornographic nature of the photographs will keep them alive on the Internet forever. According to Karl Rove it will take a generation to get over those pictures. The war in Iraq is over and we have failed. So Steve's surprised that the president is referring to Saddam's closed torture chambers. Chrissy stands on the riser above him, rapidly shooting the president's determined face.

Steve's been traveling with Bush all week and it fits right in with everything the president says. The worse the economy is, the more the president insists the economy is doing great. The more people are killed, the more the president insists we are winning the war on terror. When pictures of prisoners stacked naked in giant piles or being pulled along on a leash by a female prison guard are played on every news channel in America, the president takes credit in front of seven thousand loyal Republicans for closing Saddam's torture chambers.

Thirteen hours earlier, at six in the morning, Steve stood against the Holiday Inn on Main Street gripping the building as the sidewalk rose to meet him and he waited to vomit into the grass. He remembers it clearly now. Steve quickly runs through the counterarguments: maybe Saddam's torture was worse, at least in our society these things can come to light and something can be done about them. But none of the arguments hold water when pursued even the slightest distance. Maybe if they had changed the name of the prison things would have been different. It seems, in the moment, to be the president's biggest lie yet. Bigger than saying John Kerry is in favor of a bill placing a fifty-cent tax on a gallon of gas, even though Kerry voted against that bill. All lies seem small in comparison to the picture of the man in the hood, a shawl or something draped over his naked body, standing on a box with his arms spread and electrodes attached to his fingers. Nobody wants to believe they come from a culture capable of that. But if one believes that all men are created equal then one must also accept that there are no limits to set on man's inhumanity to other men.

"Because we acted, an example of democracy is rising in the Middle East."

It's too much, but somehow the clouds hold. Even though it doesn't rain a strong wind blows down from the hills surrounding the town, kicking up dirt and biting at the crowd, many of whom are only wearing T-shirts. Chrissy brought a jacket with her because Steve told her sometimes these events get cold. Political rallies do funny things to the weather. Steve wears a T-shirt, a sweater, and a purple jumper.[15]

The sky darkens until deep gray, all hints of blue hidden behind the mass of clouds. Just past six o'clock, the president closes as the wind reaches beneath his collar, "We know that, for our great country, the best days lay ahead."

Outside the field, Chrissy photographs the protesters and Steve contemplates the police boats motoring up and down the Mississippi, then falls in with the crowd toward the entrance. He listens for the conversations of the Republicans as they pass the protesters lined on the other side of the Secret Service tables. Many of the protesters are dressed like clowns in baggy American flag pants and look like Ken Kesey's Merry Pranksters from forty years ago. The loose flags they wear are the opposite of the well-tailored flag clothing worn by the Republicans. They bang drums and wave signs that read, "Bush Lied, People Died."

"So what if he lied?" one woman says. "Everybody lies."

"Do we have to walk right in the middle of these morons," someone else says.

"Get a job."

"Take a bath you dirty hippies! Yeah, I said take a fucking bath."

An old lady with curly white hair and a red leather jacket pushed past in a wheelchair says to the protesters in her quiet, sick voice, "Go home you weirdos."

The protesters scream back, "Open your eyes!"

One of the soldiers waves his arms in front of the protesters. "What is wrong with you?" he yells. He's so upset he can't believe it. He jumps up and down landing with his knees bent and his arms spread and smacks his forehead with his palm. How could these people possibly not think America is safer, richer, and better? They'd probably prefer it if Saddam was our president. But thanks to George W. Bush, Saddam Hussein sits in a prison cell. Idiots! Before things get worse a policeman slips a firm hand below the soldier's elbow and escorts him away.

As Chrissy and Steve drive back on the tollroad toward Chicago the clouds break open and sheets of rain pour from the sky. Steve holds the car steady at seventy miles per hour. In the near distance forked lightning cracks the horizon.

"I wonder if a car has ever been hit by lightning," Chrissy wonders. She's a pipefitter with the Chicago local and she's already reminding herself to call in for work in the morning. Once she clocks enough hours she'll be eligible for health insurance for the rest of her life.

"Of course," Steve says. "Everything's happened."

She says she's not worried because the car is grounded and Steve asks if she's sure and she admits she isn't. He jokes that she's a fountain of bad advice, reminding her of how she told him that, if he was going to gamble while drunk, the game to play was roulette, and then another time when she cautioned him to drink whiskey instead of beer because beer wasn't healthy. And how when they first met he had a thousand dollars saved from cutting french fries at Freedy's Fine Dining on a Bun,[16] and she convinced him to blow it all on a road trip. She told him that people who save money are cheap and he didn't want Chrissy to think he was cheap. He's never saved money since.

"You know what's scary?" she says as they pass Madison and the lightning draws closer. Somewhere out in the black lie the Wisconsin Dells and a giant water park and Devil's Lake, where the water is so clear you can see to the bottom even where it's twenty feet deep. Earlier they'd seen a pickup with a sticker that said "Union Republican." Chrissy was distraught. As a union member going on ten years her dislike of Republicans runs deep and has a rich history to support it. "All that stuff about the economy. About how the tax cuts are fueling job creation. He's so obviously making that up and all those people believed it. Also, all that nationalism stuff, about how tough we are and how we're not going to let other nations tell us what to do. Those people in there were like white hairless gorillas. You know what else, it was all scary, everything that man says is scary. You told me he was charismatic but he didn't seem charismatic to me."

"He was probably under stress because of the prison abuse scandal and all the people calling on Rumsfeld to resign. You should have seen him in Michigan."

"You don't need to make excuses for the President of the United States. He's old enough to take responsibility for himself," Chrissy says, as they pull into the lot at the Motel 6. "Listen. I know you're going to write mean things about me and I don't care."

"Shut up. I'm not going to write mean things about you. I'll tell everybody you're pretty and you have good skin, both of which are true. You also have a great sense of humor."

"Write that I'm looking for a doctor to marry but I don't want children," she reminds him, laughing, jerking the handle and running from the car.

"OK," he says, following her with the two bags he's been living out of for longer than he cares to remember. "I'll write that."

VIII. Summer's Promise

You must be careful what you pretend to be. Because in the end, you are what you pretend to be.
—KURT VONNEGUT

June 3–9

Chicago; Burlington; The Trouble with Small Planes; Howard Dean Takes His Revenge

There are only two months left before John Kerry comes from behind the curtain at the back of the Fleet Center and accepts the Democratic nomination for president of the United States. There won't be much horse-trading going on; Kerry's got the nomination locked down tight with everything under the protection of the old guard. Following the massacre on Super Tuesday, Kerry rolled across the field guaranteeing seats at the convention to all the moneymen and low-level operatives with allegiance in their precincts. Nobody gets more than their due and all the right palms are greased, which is exactly how everything was supposed to work out until Howard Dean came howling out of the Vermont wilderness getting the kids all jazzed up with his antiwar rhetoric and health care for all combined with his radical position on balancing the budget. The movement caught Kerry like a flat tire in the middle of a sandstorm and for a good while in the fall of 2003 it looked like the presumptive nominee was going to be shipped back to Boston to watch the Democratic Convention on satellite TV from a secret room deep in the bowels of Teresa Heinz's mansion.

But it didn't work out that way, proving yet again what James Carville and all the other wizards are quick to point out: nobody wins on the strength of new voters. The Dean campaign was a disappointment but if politics is about anything it's about not learning your lesson. And in fact, the greatest strength of the decision to agree upon a Democratic nominee early is that it has given the young voters a chance to drop out for a while and recharge. Youth is fickle, and it's unlikely that anyone could hold on to the youth vote that long. The young are easily disillusioned, which is what happened when McGovern was swept to the nomination in 1972 and then fed to Nixon like slop to a pig when the hippies and freaks found out Saint George was just as human as the rest of us. But now, with the primaries done, the kids are tuning in again just in time as the rock and roll bands are starting to get into the act, spearheaded by organizations like Music for America and Punk Voter as well as hip-hop summits that are popping up across the nation. Still, the mess in Iraq looms large and Ralph Nader is the only antiwar candidate left standing. Which is pushing Howard Dean back into the fold to cover Kerry's flank from the left and remind everyone, particularly the idealists, what happened last time.

With all that in mind and the country silenced by the death of Ronald Reagan, a man credited with ending Communism and killing seventy thousand innocents in El Salvador, his casket draped in an American flag as a hundred thousand mourners file past one at a time, I board a turboprop back to Vermont to sit down with the former governor and work things out. Small planes are the only kinds that fly into Vermont, eighteen rows of three seats. The best thing about them is they don't have televisions. But they shake a lot, and they're often cold.[1] I called the Dean office, now named Democracy for America, about a week ago and asked if I could interview the governor.

The press secretary, Walker Waugh, had read my stuff in *The Believer* and was excited for me to come out. He scheduled me for fifteen minutes at 10:30 on Wednesday morning. I borrowed Chrissy's camera and bought a digital tape recorder at RadioShack for thirty-nine dollars, the Olympus VN-1800. In HQ mode the 1800 is supposed to get forty-five minutes of uninterrupted high-quality digital recording. I considered a microphone and a PC link to convert the recording into MP3 format, as well as headphones, but my bags were already too heavy and my back was starting to hurt again. It was summer and the Midwest had turned hot and wet, the way it always does this time of year.

On short notice the direct flight to Burlington was more than four hundred dollars plus twenty-five dollars for the cab. The closest hotel room available over the Internet was the Best Western Windjammer next to Interstate 89. The Windjammer has an all-you-can-eat salad boat and a sports bar, which is where I was when Walker called me on Tuesday evening to tell me that the governor didn't want to do an interview with me after all.

"Why not?"

"We're not granting interviews to novelists."

I calculated my expenses and figured that the campaign owed me in the area of five hundred dollars. Apparently what happened was Walker passed along the request to Laura Gross, former NPR public relations flack and new communications director for Democracy for America. Laura wanted to know if I had interviewed any of the other candidates, and I had when one takes into account the day I spent with Dennis Kucinich. But that wasn't enough for Laura who pegged me for a hack and issued the decree about interviews and novelists. So I contacted an editor at the *San Francisco Chronicle* and they agreed to run the interview on their Web site, but by then it was too late, or at least that's what I was told.

Of course, that may or may not be the real story. So far, Laura hasn't responded to my inquiry but I think she will. The only problem is, a communications director is not much different from a publicist or a spokesman, so there's no reason to believe that she's going to tell me the truth. In fact, I would bet against it. She'll tell me the governor is too busy, which is almost certainly a lie.[2]

More likely is that Howard Dean, like all of the other national politicians with only a handful of exceptions, is still trying to control the media. Dean, perhaps more than any candidate since Richard Nixon, actively disliked the press corps. And he disliked them so personally that it became a liability. At one point Howard barked at the reporters, "Get a life." Dean thought he could bypass the press and take his message straight to the voters but it turned out he was wrong. One of the results of Dean's attitude toward the press was the press's attitude toward him. But Dean supporters still blame the media for poor coverage of their candidate and CNN went so far as to issue an apology. In a recent interview with *The Progressive,* Dean said the press was a "failed institution," pointing out that the majority of media was controlled by just eleven corporations, and one of the questions I was hoping to ask him is what exactly we should do about that.

But I wasn't going to get to ask the governor anything and I wanted to know why Howard Dean had decided to screw me in particular, especially since I had supported him, even taking his side against the media and stating publicly that Fox News should not be allowed on any campaign bus. I told Walker that everything I spent was coming out of my book advance, which was pretty much gone already though Picador is promising another small check. Nonetheless, I was the one taking the hit. I had already written two mega articles on Howard Dean as well as a full-page op-ed in the *New York Daily News*. Why kick me in the ass?

"I know," Walker said. "I totally agree with you, but it's beyond my control."

I could hear he was telling the truth, that it was either Laura Gross or the governor himself who was out to get me. But I still didn't know which one or why.

"I'm coming over anyway," I told him the next morning.

"Oh, please don't do that," Walker said. He sounded like someone worried about losing his job. We both realized at this point that Walker was really the one who shouldn't have approved my request for a press pass. I didn't want Walker to get in trouble, but I was in Burlington, Vermont. What else could I do?

"It's really not a good idea for you to come here," Walker argued desperately for another fifteen minutes. Which made me think that all of the explanations I had for Howard Dean and his partner in crime, Laura Gross, trying to screw me over were possibly wrong. In fact, maybe they were still angry with me over the bet I had made with Jeanie Murray, Howard Dean's Iowa State Coordinator.[3]

I learned a lot since that fateful day and have since correctly picked the dates that Wesley Clark and Howard Dean were going to drop out of the race, sweeping up bus money from Toni Montgomery and Philip Gourevitch. I still lose a lot of my bets but by much closer margins. When I thought I lost five dollars back in January I had no idea how much I was in for until today.

Eventually Walker realized that I was coming over no matter what so he tried to hedge by asking me to wait until four and offering a few minutes with Laura as an olive branch. Initially I accepted his offer. I wanted to ask Laura to her face why she had barred me from seeing the governor so I could call her a liar. But then I realized what Walker was doing, trying to keep me away until the governor was gone. I decided to head over there anyway.

The Dean campaign has lied to me too many times; if I waited until four they'd move the entire building.

Democracy for America is headquartered in the UBS building, the same one Dean for America was located in. To get there, you head south five minutes from Burlington to Shelburne Road, Highway 7, turn left at the Denny's, stay left over a bridge to Vermont Gas. Then you turn left again at the Chittenden County Correctional Facility, passing Kidstown and arriving at the four-story building across from a row of housing developments behind the overpass.

DFA still occupies the entire third floor and the reception area is covered in pictures from Howard Dean's heyday during the Sleepless Summer tour, when ten thousand turned out to see the governor in Seattle. The photos, which feature supporters lined up against police barricades and the governor addressing packed auditoriums, provide a vibrant contrast to the office, which is quiet and drastically underpopulated, like a company that has gone out of business leaving a handful of accountants to sort through the books. In those situations all the regular employees get screwed except for the mail person who is usually deemed too necessary to let go and offered a small stipend to stick around. The 250 former staffers have disappeared into the political wilderness. The floors are still mauve with the same low-hanging corkboard ceiling, which seems more oppressive without the din and excitement. Near the reception there's a hand-stitched quilt.

Walker Waugh meets me in the entryway. He's about six feet tall and very good-looking. Skinny, with the top two buttons on his shirt undone and with curls that don't quite meet his shoulders, he looks like a young Robert Plant. He apologizes again and I tell him it's not his fault, though in a way it is. Then we talk about Democracy for America.

"The purpose of Democracy for America is to push a political movement," Walker says. I ask him if he means something similar to what Newt Gingrich and Ralph Reed did in the early nineties, which was a comparison Dean had made. "Yeah, except without the ideology and the lies and with better intentions." Every two weeks DFA endorses twelve progressive candidates running mostly for offices like alderman or city supervisor or judge nationwide. "We call them the Dirty Dozen. When we endorse them we help the candidates in a number of ways. First, by linking to them on our Web site. That's the biggest way." They also give the Dirty Dozen candidates a forum through the Democracy for America Web site, which still gets some traffic, though not the millions who used to pass through Dean for America. Dean also goes to fundraisers to support the candidates.

The other side of Democracy for America is Howard Dean's role as a surrogate for John Kerry. "John Kerry takes precedence," Walker tells me. "When Kerry asks Dean to go on the radio to talk about health care, for example, we push back all of his other events. But we plan to keep going past the election."

The problems with DFA are obvious. Why would anyone care? Ralph Reed's Christian Coalition had a vast network of churches to tap into a population unaware of the constitutional mandate separating church and state. Newt Gingrich was a congressman. I like Democracy for America's mission, though clearly journalists are not banging down the doors to get inside, which makes the whole thing even more insulting. I hang out with Walker for half an hour on a short tour through the semideserted offices. Laura Gross's door is closed and so is Howard Dean's. Dean has moved into Joe Trippi's old space.

"What happened to Trippi?" I ask Walker.

"Nobody's heard from him in a while. He started a group called Change for America, but I don't know if they're doing anything."

It's been just under a year since the first time I came here in July 2003. Zephyr Teachout was busily blogging away and happy to explain to me how she had left everything, packed up her car, and moved to Vermont. She works for ACT now. Dean's office door was open that day and a photographer from *Time* magazine was inside taking pictures while Howard talked on the phone. Trippi's door was open as well, with Trippi rattling off statistics to two or three field operators. During that first tour I walked close to Dean's office and he looked up slightly and someone standing behind him just out of view shut the door on me. Dean's always shut the door on me, but this is the first time the door has been shut in advance.

June 10–21

Return to Lake Eden; Through the White Mountains; Lewis Rickel Discusses Ronald Reagan and Central America; Portland; The Truth About Hardwood Floors; The Benefits of Charity; A Small House and a Pretty Wife; The Senator from Maine; Double A Baseball, The Sea Dogs Get Beat; Lemony Snicket; Tobias Wolff; San Francisco, Los Angeles; What's the Point of Being Josh Bearman?; Dick Cheney Lies; Bush Backs Dick Up; Five Miles on Sunset Boulevard; An Unclear Sky; Baton Rouge; John Edwards Addresses the Louisiana Democrats; Revelations in New Orleans; Café du Monde; Cheney Lies Again; Wayne Parent Explains Louisiana Politics; Bourbon Street; Breakdown in the Big Easy; Chad Prather, M.D.; Monica Chavez Gets Married; Low Ceilings in the French Quarter; Michelle Orange Tells Me What My Problem Is[4]; Dick Cheney Drags Down the Ticket; Running Out of Steam; A Thousand Dollars Wasted; Cheney Lies, He Lies, He Lies

June 22–24

Milwaukee; The Green Split; What's Wrong with Ralph Nader?; Romance in Brew Town; Bikers for Cobb; Medea Benjamin; Camejo Rising

San Francisco is overcast in June. The ocean is still colder than the sky and the air cools just above the sea, kept low by an inversion blanket two hundred feet over the earth. A strong wind blows from the west, passing the tankers and fishing boats and pushing the fog far past the coastline all the way to the bay, so even the Mission District is full of cloud. In the hills the fog seems to hang from the gutters as if caught. Closer to the beach, the air is as wet as a roll of toilet paper dipped in a glass of water. Golden Gate Park is lacquered in dew and the bridge is lost inside the damp haze. They call it June Gloom but it's actually very comfortable compared to the swampy heat of New Orleans and the Florida panhandle. I'm not all that fond of heat.

I had been home less than forty-eight hours, sitting in a coffee shop with two thousand dollars in my pocket.[5] It was a dark café that had changed its name three times in as many years but never once changed the menu. The food was awful. I was going to have a cup of coffee and then continue on to the bank when I got a phone call from Ralph Nader's press secretary, Kevin Zeese. Kevin was on his way to the Green convention. Impulsively I said I would meet him there. The only demon I had yet to confront before John Kerry accepted the Democratic nomination for president of the United States was Ralph Nader.

"I worked for Nader last time," I said to Kevin. "I drove a van."

"Really," he replied. "How do you feel about him now?" I wanted to tell him that a few days ago I was in Baton Rouge eating étouffée with John Edwards and spent two nights wandering Bourbon Street before realizing I was looking for something that doesn't exist. But Kevin didn't have time for that. This would be a big weekend for Ralph Nader. Kevin told me that most of the resistance they got came from liberals.[6] He said the conservatives didn't give them such a hard time. I didn't ask him why he thought that might be; it was so obvious. Maybe I should have told him: if your enemies like you, you're doing something wrong.

I went home and tossed the two thick rolls of bills onto the bookshelf and threw some clothes in a bag. I called the airline from the taxi and made a reservation on a plane that was leaving in an hour and a half. The operator wanted to know before booking my ticket if I thought I would make it and I told him I thought I would. The cab driver told me to do it all while I was young.

In the Denver airport, halfway to Wisconsin, I got a note from a friend inviting me to a reading and I thought, no, I am a ghost. This is what my life has become. From the outside the Denver airport resembles a giant white circus tent, the steel built to look as if it were billowing. I lived here before, an hour away in a ski resort. I was twenty-six years old and had just skied for the first time down a small hill in northern Wisconsin. It was a Christmas present to my fiancée, and she spent most of the time sick not wanting to go outside but I liked the feeling of moving fast, even on man-made snow. It seemed like a reason to live for a little while. I broke up with her and left for Colorado two weeks later and spent a season learning how to snowboard while bartending in a timber lodge two mountains back from the employee dorms. And on weekends I came over Loveland Pass into Denver to see what there was.

The Milwaukee hotels are booked full. It turns out there's a music festival at the same time as the Green Party nominating convention. The music festival is the biggest in the world and it lasts for eleven days. Poor planning on my part. I didn't know that when I left the café in San Francisco hours earlier. Ralph Nader picked his vice presidential nominee two days ago: Peter Camejo, the former Green candidate for governor of California. Over the next two days the Greens will choose whether or not to endorse Nader and then Nader will go to Portland and Seattle and try to get on the ballots there. I'll go with him and make up my mind about him this time around.

It shouldn't matter but it does. The Greens have ballot access in twenty-two states. Democrats are fighting desperately to keep Nader off as many ballots as possible. I bought groceries yesterday because I thought I would be home for at least three days. Earlier today I made two avocado sandwiches and left one on a plate in the refrigerator. I thought I was pretty smart for making two sandwiches because usually I only make one and forget about the second half of the avocado. But as I fly toward Milwaukee the second sandwich remains in my fridge, where it will turn brown.

I forgot other things in my rush, but that was the worst of it. Especially now that I am on a plane and hungry and there are these two awful children on the seat next to me crying. I feel sorry for their mother. The one baby, the loud one, sits in her lap grasping for her breasts, fully naked except for his diapers and a pair of light brown socks, tears streaming down his face. The other baby, in a powder blue bodysuit, cries in little fits to compete with his older sibling, a small bubble of spit bursting from his tiny mouth. He squirms away on his back, kicking to the edge, and nearly falls headfirst from the chair. His mother keeps him safe with her other hand, her long fingers stretched across his thin belly as she struggles to dress the older boy. Her hand becomes a cage for the child.

I blame George Bush for my hunger and the screaming children, and also Terry McAuliffe. If Terry McAuliffe hadn't pushed all the primaries forward in order to anoint an early nominee for the Democratic machinery to rally around things might have been different. Instead, people are obsessed with the vice presidential nomination, but it's the equivalent of the NBA draft—it doesn't really matter until it happens and you'll know the answers soon enough. When I saw John Edwards a few days ago in Louisiana he essentially repeated his speech from the primaries except this time he replaced his own name with John Kerry's. All the local operators were there, the governor, both senators, the head of the state party. There were about fifty tables with five to ten people per table but some of the tables were empty. Three reporters from the local papers and one from the AP were on hand to ask the senator if he was going to be the vice president.

"Would you like to be the vice president?"

"I'm going to leave those deliberations to John Kerry."

"Has John Kerry talked to you about being vice president?"

"As I said, I'm going to let John Kerry answer those questions."

"But if you weren't letting John Kerry answer those questions, how would you answer them?"

"As I said . . ."

None of it mattered and no one cared in any meaningful way. The reporters were uninterested in their own stories. I had been wasting my time. And more important, my money. I had to stop and remember why I got on the campaign trail to begin with. It wasn't to hear would-be vice presidential candidates not answer questions. But I couldn't blame him for not answering the questions—they weren't worth answering. So I asked about Dick Cheney's recent statements linking Al Qaeda and Saddam.

"I'm a member of the intelligence committee," Edwards told me. "And I can tell you he's wrong."

"Why don't you just call him a liar?" I asked.

"Why don't you do that?" Edwards said, with that boyish smile and good skin he has. He seemed to think that because I was wearing a press pass I wouldn't say such a thing. As a journalist I wouldn't want word to get out that I held a personal grudge against a member of the current administration, which would play right into Republican conspiracy theories about the biased left-wing media.

"OK," I said. "Dick Cheney's a liar."

On Edwards' way to the ballroom, before wrapping his arm around the state party chairman and his wife, I asked him whatever happened to Jennifer Palmieri, his former spokeswoman, who had assured me John Edwards was the *only* candidate who could beat Bush.

"She's working for John Kerry in Ohio now," he told me.

"I liked her," I said.

"I liked her, too," he replied, pausing for just a second, something that might be a memory moving across his constant smile.

Which brings me back to the beginning, on my way to Milwaukee and then Portland and Seattle, to reunite with the Greens and Ralph Nader. The plane lands in the middle of a thunderstorm, and in fact our plane is the last to land before they put a halt to landings and wait out the lightning. It's the same weather I remember last month driving to Chicago from La Crosse after George Bush looked right at me in the middle of the crowd and said, "Because our coalition acted, Saddam's torture chambers are closed." And the sky cracked and split over the dells. There's been eight inches of rain in Wisconsin since then. People have lost their homes to floods.

Walking along the wet streets surrounding my hotel I ask myself if all of this was worth it. I don't know yet what the price of this year on the road has been for me. I know that it ended my relationship with Wilhelmina but that was probably a good thing. It wasn't very good for my teaching career. I know that I missed the opportunity to publicize my novel because I never knew what town I would be in, so I wasn't able to do very many readings. I know that I've lost weight and my skin is bad and I missed a good friend's wedding. And I know that my father and I are on worse terms than we've been since I left home at thirteen. I'm not sure my father and I will ever reconcile. I doubt it. You travel without your support network. It's like living without skin.

I'm hungry, but the restaurant attached to the hotel closed at eleven. The only way to get any food is to wait in line at the drive-in. I stand between a Volvo and a Z28 huffing gas, waiting on a Whopper, a bag of fries, and a fake chocolate shake. It's midnight and the rain has stopped and the only light comes from the Burger King and the gas station. There aren't any sidewalks in this part of town.

When the cashier sees me at the window without a car he doesn't seem to know what to do. He holds my order, deciding whether or not it's OK to serve someone without a car. He looks around, but there's no manager in sight. The Volvo is getting impatient and lets out a small beep. It takes the cashier more than three minutes to count out thirty-four cents in change.

The Green Party nominating convention is at the Hyatt Milwaukee City Center, not far from the Hilton and the indoor water park there, and perhaps it wouldn't matter if it didn't tie in so closely to who will win the presidential election this year. But it does, or at least that's what people think right now. What's happening among the Greens is endlessly interesting and complicated, situated on the blurry border between realism and idealism, illuminated beneath the pride and ambition of three men: David Cobb, Peter Camejo, and Ralph Nader.

David Cobb was the national legal counsel for the Greens and the de facto head of the party, as well as the founder of the Texas Green Party. Now he lives in California and he's running for the Green's nomination for president. Cobb is promoting a safe-state strategy. That is he wants to convince people in states that are solid red or blue that they're wasting their vote by not voting Green. But in contested states, swing states like Ohio, he wants to encourage people to vote their conscience, which most people interpret, correctly I think, as encouraging Greens to vote for John Kerry.

Recently Ralph Nader, who had not been campaigning for the Green endorsement, said he would accept the Green endorsement after all. Many of the delegates here want to endorse him, especially now that he's named Peter Camejo, a prominent Green Party member, as running mate. Though Nader declined to attend the convention and never joined the Greens himself, Peter Camejo will try to get the Greens to endorse Ralph anyway. It's a cynical move on Nader's part because, along with seeking the Green endorsement, he's been accepting nominations from the Reform Party and the Populist Party, anything to get on a ballot.

At the Hyatt, Cobb and Nader/Camejo signs compete for space

among the glass railings circling the elevators. Both Cobb's and Nader's signs are green but Cobb's are darker green. On the second floor there are rows of tables selling T-shirts and bumper stickers promoting their candidates. I meet a worker from the Nader/Camejo ticket and he tells me he won't back Kerry until Kerry comes out in favor of true proportional representation.

"What's good for the negro is good for the Nazi," I remind him, and what I mean is that proportional representation helps both sides, Far Right and Far Left.

"What!?"

"Somebody else said that," I tell him.

He thinks that Nader is going to get in the presidential debates this time.

"That's not going to happen," I say. "You can't possibly think that."

"It could happen if Bush wants it to."

This is his first election. He says he spent the last eight years doing his Ph.D. I feel superior to him and that makes me realize how rare that feeling has been on the campaign. I always assume the reporters from the big papers and other people on the campaign trail know something I don't. But he clearly knows less than I do. And that's part of the thing. Part of being political, really political, is being wrong a lot of the time. You have to put yourself out there, take a stand on unlikely issues, and fervently believe things that are almost certainly untrue. On a couch in the lobby of the hotel a woman from Michigan tells me that the conflict between Nader/Camejo and David Cobb is probably good for the Greens and good for John Kerry, too. I nod my head yes. Yes. I am here again, among the believers. Men with long hair and women without makeup, students in T-shirts that say "Don't blame me, I voted for Ralph Nader." There's something great about it. These people are fun. Of course, fun can be dangerous; recently a man in New England fell out of a Superman roller coaster at Six Flags Great America and died.[7]

When I see David Cobb he smiles and gives me a big hug. "Stephen Elliott," he says. "The guy that stayed on my couch." He doesn't mention finding the diary entry that I left behind, detailing my fantasies of having sex with his wife.[8] "Why the blue tag?"

The blue tag he's referring to is a media credential stating *The Village Voice,* which is not entirely accurate. Ed Park, the editor of the literary supplement, asked me to write about Ralph Nader several months ago. When I asked him if he was still interested in a piece about Ralph he told me no. So really, the credential is just another lie. But I'm writing a book—surely that's worth something.

"Man, how can I take you seriously as a journalist when we shared a joint together?" Dave says, pinching his fingers together as if holding a roach. He puts his fingers to his lips and then opens his hand as the invisible joint disappears. Dave's sentiment is real but we didn't smoke pot together. I haven't smoked pot in years. Still, I feel a strong bond with Dave. For the rest of the convention Dave introduces me to people as a former Green who is now a big-time journalist.

I run into Peter Camejo in the skywalk connecting the hotel with the convention center. Peter was running for the Green nomination before he agreed to be Nader's running mate, which really begs the question of why he agreed to work with Nader when, if he had gotten the Green presidential nomination, he would have been running *against* Nader. I ask him if he really thinks he can get in the presidential debates.

"I think there's a small fighting chance," he says. He walks quickly and talks seriously. He strikes me as someone who is trying to radiate love but deep inside holds a core of anger. "The polls show 65 percent want us in the debates. Our position is if over 50 percent of the population want someone in the debates you respect the rights of the people."[9]

Peter Camejo and David Cobb have their own debate in a room not big enough to hold a thousand Greens, on the second floor of the Midwest Airlines Center.[10] Camejo tells the crowd, "I want to debate Dick Cheney!" and people go nuts. I figured out earlier that he doesn't really think that's possible but he's tapping the vein of hope that runs through the Green Party. Only a fool would believe that Dick Cheney is ever going to debate Peter Camejo.

Camejo attacks David Cobb and the safe-state strategy. He compares the Democrats and the Republicans, points out that John Kerry voted for authorizing troops in Iraq, and tells the audience we have to say at some point, "I will never vote for them again." Camejo looks like a grandfather, fragile and friendly, soft and wrinkled. When he smiles his eyes squint upward in contentment. But he doesn't speak in the soft and friendly way hinted at by his facial features. He believes the differences between the Democrats and the Republicans are cosmetic. He says, "The corporate world has two parties, and one of them is for fooling us . . . Let's scorch the Democrats!"[11]

Cobb is reasonable and allows that Kerry is bad but George Bush is dangerous and we have to take Bush seriously. To my surprise, Cobb is a natural orator. He speaks into the cheering much the way John Edwards and Dennis Kucinich do. I ponder voting for Cobb, since I live in California. But then I have to ask myself if I really want to grow the Green Party. I'm not sure I do. When the debate ends the Greens start yelling at each other, angry over the perceived background maneuvering of the Cobb campaign to keep Ralph Nader off the ballot. The nomination rules have been rewritten so that a candidate can win the nomination with less than a majority of the vote. The Greens are in crisis and are not likely to survive. And I wonder if David Cobb hasn't sacrificed himself, and the Green Party by proxy, on behalf of the greater good. It makes me want to vote for him even more, though I know I won't.

Nobody has heard of David Cobb outside the Green Party faithful. And by the time this is over that will still likely be the case. Ralph Nader is the Green Party's only chance at relevance in the near future, and that's no chance at all. Nader has never cared about building the Green Party, which for David Cobb and his supporters is a fatal flaw. I sit with David for half an hour at a booth in the back of the hotel diner. I find his safe-state strategy appealing because it shows an intellectual engagement with a concept that probably runs counter to his own instinct. David justifies all of it by saying that the Green Party is "bigger than any one candidate." But David doesn't know that he's speaking with an apostate. I have lost my faith. I've been raising money for John Kerry in California and sending it out of state. Before we finish eating David tells me that he split up with his wife, so if I'm still interested it doesn't matter to him anymore.

The cracks are everywhere. The stress of 2000 is returning to break down the house. Party members openly denounce one another. The question of whether or not to campaign in all of the states is a pivotal one. No matter what happens the Greens are likely to lose half their members.[12] Outside the hotel there is music and people dance in the streets. People are hooking up and drinking and making out.

At the Nader/Camejo rally a woman in the back of the room asks Peter Camejo, "If Nader wants our endorsement so bad, why did he wait so long to ask for it?" The simple answer to her question is that Nader thought he could get on the ballots without the Green Party but has found that harder than he thought. If Nader had openly courted the Greens, he would have had their endorsement. "You see," Camejo says, opening his hands toward the woman but looking away from her, "we're worrying over petty, meaningless issues." From there he talks about war and people dying all over the world.

On Friday night, the day before the Greens will make their decision, a decision that is almost certain to have undesirable consequences either way, Ralph Nader calls from Washington, D.C. "I want you to consider," he tells several hundred assembled Greens. "We will be stronger together. This coalition also could be very beneficial to the Greens in terms of their own resources, in terms of visibility, in terms of enduring on the ballot." He says he doesn't want to interfere with the Greens' business, as long as they're able to choose a candidate in a democratic manner with the majority of the vote.

Peter Camejo lays it out in starker terms. "Two wings of the same party, the party of money," he says, referring to the Republicans and the Democrats. "Don't be afraid to be Green. Don't be afraid to stand up to them. The Democratic Party is what makes the Republican Party possible. I have seen what America is." And here he could be referring to his brother, who was tortured by the CIA in Mexico before being sent to a Mexican prison for two and a half years. Or he might be talking about the time he had to hide in the airport control room in Colombia because the CIA instructed the Colombians to throw him in jail.[13] "I know what this is about," he continues, speaking directly to the guilt and disillusionment that set in among party members following George Bush's inauguration and subsequent scrapping of the Kyoto Protocols. The realization among many Nader supporters that in 2000 the cost of their intransigence was too high. To them, Peter Camejo says, "John Kerry is not going to make this world better."

June 26–29

Ralph Nader

If somebody asked me if I regretted working for Ralph Nader in 2000, I'd say maybe I do. I'd say it depends. I'd say yes most of the time, but not always. I was tuning in after a lifetime of tuning out—how could I regret that? I didn't do it for myself. I did it because I thought it meant something, and most of the criticism I've gotten since has come from people who didn't do anything. But I was wrong on so many levels. I thought Bush and Gore were the same, and they're not. But the majority of people who now say, "I told you so," were in fact not doing anything. Most of them never told me anything at all. When I campaigned for Nader I didn't go through any swing states. I spent most of my time in shopping malls in places like Platt, Alabama, taking threats from security guards working for minimum wage without health care. I was working for minimum wage without health care myself, driving a van with a Nader sticker stuck strategically over the *Diesel Only* instructions on the gas tank. We were in the Deep South, but there was another van and that van spent three full weeks exclusively in Florida, and I've often thought, What if that had been my van?

In the end, the Green Party rejects Ralph Nader. Four hundred and eight delegates vote for David Cobb on the second ballot to give him the nomination that includes automatic ballot access in twenty-two states and the District of Columbia. Hundreds of Nader supporters walk out forming a splinter organization, Greens for Nader. In Cobb's acceptance speech, he takes great pains to praise Ralph Nader, the good he's done, the visibility he's added over the years. He points out that Ralph Nader is the reason he went to law school. But the next day the only quote to run from David Cobb in the Associated Press is, "The Green Party has gotten out from under the shadow of a man who has probably cast a larger shadow than any other living American."

With David Cobb presiding over the Greens, Nader arrives in Portland and I'm there to meet him. I caught an early flight out of Milwaukee, stopping over in Phoenix and arriving in Oregon just in time. The flight was more expensive than it should have been, but this is no time for saving money. Picador has come through with a chunk of change to help me finish my book; they're hoping to send it to press before the election. They figure it's their only chance at making their money back.

Nader's in Portland because of a state law that allows a candidate to qualify automatically for the ballot, *if* he can gather a thousand supporters in one room and get them all to sign a petition. The hall they've rented for the occasion is at Benson High School, on the northeast side of the city, and holds 1,200.

The protesters are out in full force in front of the school. Billionaires for Bush are there to thank Nader for helping their candidate. They wear fake furs and blow exaggerated kisses. They've set up a bed near the end of the sidewalk where two of them roll around in fake money. It's good weather for a political event; the weather's so nice you can barely feel it. I'm wearing a new T-shirt and I talk to several of the "billionaires," pointing out that in 2000 it was Billionaires for Bush *and* Gore and the group had protested both candidates equally, essentially supporting Nader. On their Web site in 2000 they had run a list of donors who had given money to both Democrats and Republicans, hoping to buy influence no matter who won. None of the "billionaires" in Portland knew their own history, the role their own group had played. This is about memory. None of them had been "billionaires" in 2000.

Near the entrance to the school there's a man in a George Bush mask handing out thank-you letters and he reminds me of the theater we did in 2000 where we would don Bush and Gore masks and put on puppet shows in the street. The League of Conservation Voters is also in attendance, also handing out flyers. I try to speak to one of their members, but when the head of the group sees him talking to me, he tells the guy, "It's time for you to go." The LCV has strict rules about members speaking to the media. Like everybody else, the LCV wants to control its message, perhaps everybody except Ralph, who in 2000 openly encouraged us to engage with the press. "When you're in a town, stop by the local newspaper," Nader told me the first time I met him. "See if you can get them to write a story."

"The progressive community feels very strongly that Ralph is working with the enemy," Matt Blevins, the state director for the LCV, tells me. He explains that they're not trying to limit press access just that they're worried that the average member wouldn't know the answers to the questions. He says he's happy to answer any question I have. I ask him whom he voted for last time and he tells me he voted for Gore in 2000 and Nader in 1996.

"That's quite a track record you have," I say, because I don't believe him.

The Democrats openly harass the crowd and most of the crowd takes it. One Nader supporter gets angry and violent and tears up one of the Democrat's signs. "Fuck you," she says, near tears, her hands bunched in fists at her waist. "My father was a veteran and he died thirty years ago and you people have no shame!" The sign blows into the gutter and everyone waits to see what's going to happen. The woman has a square, unhappy face and straight hair hanging over her shoulders, with bangs cut above her eyebrows. It takes me a second to understand that she's talking about Vietnam. Of course. Vietnam, a mistake made by Democrats and made worse by Republicans. Over fifty thousand Americans, millions of Vietnamese, Agent Orange, napalm, the draft. And now we're in Iraq. Thirty years after her father was killed the Democrats and Republicans are still in power. She stands toe to toe with the protester, her forehead in front of his nose. He wears a cheap tuxedo, a thrift store impersonation. How much violence has this woman stored and what else has she done with it? But she doesn't hit the protester, a Democrat, who has no idea what she's talking about. She walks away from him. The protester says meekly, "My father was a veteran, too."

Stalking along the edge with a press pass I become invisible and anonymous. And it's not much different from being in a zoo— passing the cages and fences, glancing briefly at the animals. Occasionally one raises your curiosity and occasionally you raise the curiosity of one of the caged beasts in return. Except a zoo smells different, and not too many people go to the zoo alone.

I've been insisting all year, every time I'm asked, that I'm not going to make a conclusion on Ralph Nader until I see him. The arguments against him—that he's an egomaniac, a tool of the Republicans, a man driven solely by a desire to destroy the Democratic Party that has slighted him—are all too simplistic, anger expressed as rational, and easily dismissed on their own terms. The editorials question Ralph's motives but rarely come to a relevant conclusion.

The crowd stretches all the way around the school into a park. Republican radio hosts have been urging their listeners to attend this event, to help put Ralph on the ballot. Citizens for a Sound Economy, the same group that ran ads attacking Dean as a latte-drinking liberal, has been operating phone banks, calling conservatives to persuade them to get to the school and endorse Ralph's petition because it will help Bush beat John Kerry. They are not the majority, but they're possibly 5 percent. The Republicans add a strange tint to the crowd, like flakes of shit-brown on a tie-dyed T-shirt. And the Democrats have encouraged attendance as well. Moses Ross, the spokesman for the Multnomah County Democratic Party, sent an e-mail to members asking them to attend and take up seats in the hall, instructing them to "politely refuse" to sign the petition.

It begs the question of who's using whom. On the face of it, attempting to keep a legitimate candidate off a ballot is immoral and undemocratic. Democrats don't care about that this time. They fought fair last time and got their asses kicked. But the long-term consequences of a Democratic Party that is not just corrupt but is supported by members who accept corruption as the price to be paid is yet to be seen.

The Republican presence in the crowd is obvious and disarming. I see one lady with coiffed blond hair and lips painted a conservative cherry red, if such a thing is possible. "Did you vote for Nader in 2000?" I ask her, and she says no. "Who did you vote for then?"

"George Bush," she replies.

I ask another group, "What does Ralph Nader look like?"

"I don't know," a man says. He's in his sixties with a floral-patterned shirt, a ring of white hair around his tan pate. He's with his wife and a friend and his friend's wife. His friend also wears a greenish shirt and has a similar haircut.

The auditorium quickly becomes a sauna, with most seats filled.

Counters for the Oregon State Office stand at all the entrances wearing jackets or vests with official patches on their chests. The Republicans sit toward the back, on the sides. Near the front, where it's hotter, the demographics change. There are few Republicans in the front rows. The convention is called to order. A man in a dark suit calls for Ralph Nader's nomination by voice vote. The crowd screams "Aye!" He reads the rules and continues down the slate for Peter Camejo. He states that each vote is separate and, if contested, does not affect other votes. The whole process takes about twenty minutes and when the petitions are signed the Republicans and Democrats quickly leave, smiling, proud of themselves, clever.

"This is what democracy looks like," the speaker says.

Ralph Nader approaches from the left and the people still in attendance break into applause. With the Republicans and Democrats gone, as well as the supporters who didn't have the time or inclination to stay, the crowd thins to seven hundred. This is my first time seeing Ralph this year, and I'm curious as to what my own feelings will be. I still feel his magnetism, which is like the magnet of a father to a son, though I've never felt this way toward my own father. My own father is inconsistent and forgives easily. His temper is a storm of unpredictable violence, but when the screaming's over he'll come to your room with a bowl of ice cream and ask why you're crying. Nader is the consistent father, unrelenting, sure of himself and what he stands for. Nader is a man who takes himself very, very seriously. And it reminds me of why I don't want to vote for David Cobb or Dennis Kucinich. I like them as people but don't want to vote for someone as insecure as I am. I want a president who has something of greatness. And if I can't have that I'm willing to compromise.

"This candidacy is not going to flatter voters," Nader says, palms pressed to the podium, staring into the audience, one of his eyes open slightly more than the other so that his face appears slanted. "We want voters to rise to the occasion." He speaks about sports fans for a while, the millions of them and how they understand the most complex facets of their games. "Is it too much to ask tens of millions of voters, with so much at stake election after election, to be as diligent as sports fans?"

As Nader continues on the responsibilities of citizenship I feel the creeping tide of idealism spilling across my own pessimistic synapses. What if he had done things differently? What if he had run for Congress, built a political base, and tried to change things that way instead of always working from the outside-in, trying to change the system without joining it while the system came together and closed ranks against him until he decided it was necessary to run for the top position, determined either to save or destroy the entire framework of American government. And I guess the answer to that question is Bernie Sanders, the independent congressman from Vermont.[14] Which is to say, he would be liked and admired by both progressive independents and progressive Democrats but at the end of the day he wouldn't have much of a say in things.

The Nader supporters want people to remember Nader's gigantic accomplishments: automobile safety, the clean air act, consumer protections, food labeling, the safe drinking water act, the Occupational Safety and Health Administration, the Environmental Protection Agency. But by focusing on Nader's accomplishments they betray a fundamental misunderstanding of the human condition not dissimilar to the argument so many Jews still make when defending Israel's occupation of Palestine. "If they hadn't invaded us in 1967 we wouldn't be in the West Bank and Gaza." As if Palestinians, the vast majority under age forty, were going to remember or feel responsible for anything that happened in 1967. I never understood the argument; it's an argument that has nothing to do with a solution. History is only useful when it just happened or supports something you already want to believe. And what the vast majority of progressives remember, driven primarily by their profound hatred of George W. Bush, is that Nader's candidacy cost Al

Gore the election. And that's the only memory of Ralph Nader they have. There is nothing else to take into consideration. "Don't turn off politics, because if you do, politics will turn on you in a very disagreeable manner," Nader says, and listening to Nader speak, I'm remembering what drew me, and so many others, to support him in 2000.

"Is it time to give voters in Oregon a chance to vote for renewable energy?" he asks. "To vote on the failed war on drugs where nonviolent drug addicts are imprisoned instead of rehabilitated? Time to give voters the chance to vote against the Patriot Act and its renewal next year?" Occasionally protesters interrupt Nader. They jump screaming as if their seats were on fire, unraveling signs and shouting obscenities as they are escorted out. They always leave easily. As soon as someone puts a hand on their shoulder they turn and walk out the door. At one point Nader says they'll be sure to return the favor at the Democratic National Convention. But I doubt that. If Nader showed up at the Democratic Convention, there would be nothing left beyond a few pieces of spine and a ragged trail of blood draining into the city's many underground tunnels and throughways.

"To vote on capital punishment or the prison industrial complex . . . the bloated, redundant military contracting process that is eating one half of our federal expenditures . . . reform of our tax system where there's more tax on labor than there is on pollution . . . to be presented with a strategy and a plan to abolish poverty in America . . . When you evaluate the Democratic Party, don't just evaluate them for what they won't do, evaluate them for what they won't stop . . . They're laughing at us. [They're saying] we're going to take your hard-earned money and there's nothing you can do about it. And if you don't like the way your forests are treated, your rivers, your air, too bad."

After Nader's done I ask his coordinator if they're all going out for a party or something and he says they are. But I'm not invited.

I have a friend in Portland, on the southeast side five miles away from the high school and he's left the door open for me. I hang around the school for a little while but nobody offers me a ride so I stand outside a rock-climbing gym until a taxi comes along.

In the morning the news reports are unsure if the event last night qualified Ralph Nader for the ballot. They collected 1,100 signatures on 950 sheets of paper. Most people don't think that's enough of a margin of error to withstand the Democrats' challenge. A certain number of the signatures are almost certainly forgeries produced by the Democrats in attendance to cast doubt on the validity of the petitions.

I think of Matt Blevins, the LCV leader who last night dismissed his volunteer in order to control his message and then told me that he voted for Ralph Nader in 1996 and Al Gore in 2000. I can't prove he was lying but he paused before answering and it seemed like the message he was trying to communicate was that there was a right time to vote for Nader but that time was long past. The correct answers are so easy to give later down the line. In 1996 the Democratic Party said that Ralph Nader's candidacy was going to throw the election to Bob Dole. The Democrats who said that were wrong.

Nader gives his next talk in Seattle, at the University of Washington's Kane Hall, which is part of an area of campus that's all concrete and straight angles. There aren't as many in attendance to see Nader as there were in Portland and the protesters aren't here either. The room holds three hundred and is only two-thirds full. It's a quiet Sunday in June, and outside an easy breeze floats over the hills from Puget Sound. Seattle is a city that should mean something, the birthplace of grunge rock, the WTO protests in 1999. In the 1990s Seattle was arguably the most culturally influential city in the nation. Runaways from all over the country arrived at the park in Capital Hill, where they hung out all day under the trees and got their food and shelter at a church nearby. The kids still run away to Capital Hill, but Seattle is not a mecca for protest or rock and roll anymore.

The flyers advertised a five-dollar cover charge but the cover is not enforced. The rules in Washington are different. Washington is one of the easiest states in which to acquire ballot access. The laws permit rolling conventions, which essentially means you can keep collecting signatures every day until you have one thousand, as long as you declare each day a convention with a small notice in the newspaper. It's almost impossible *not* to get on the ballot in Washington.

Still, it's hard to believe that only two hundred people are interested in hearing Ralph speak. At the super rallies during the last election, thousands packed into stadiums to see him. He is less popular this time around.

Nader talks first about the Congressional Black Caucuses, how they had demanded he drop out of the race. "It didn't matter that [in 2000] we campaigned in poor areas that wouldn't even be on the screen for Gore or Bush . . . They're worried about the one million Democrats that voted for me in 2000. What about the eight million Democrats that voted for George Bush? I went into Ward Eight [in Washington D.C.], where sixty-seven thousand people live and they don't have a single supermarket even though we've had a black mayor in Washington, D.C., for thirty/thirty-five years. . . . And the Congressional Black Caucus is saying, 'Don't mess up our little party.'" Nader's disgust is palpable. He's disgusted with the Black Caucus, disgusted with the Democrat's efforts to keep him off the ballot. A lifetime of service and here is his reward. With regard to Howard Dean, who blasted Nader for accepting support from Republican groups, Nader says, "I think Howard Dean should go on the Jay Leno show because he's becoming comedic."[15]

"He fucked me over, too," I say to no one in particular.

It all seems personal now, which surprises me on some level. It didn't seem as personal yesterday, which is probably why it's a good idea to hear every politician twice. Nader doesn't appear capable of accepting that someone would disagree with him, and it explains why so many of his closest partners over the years are no longer with him. He points out that, of all the entertainers who supported him in 2000 (Michael Moore, Phil Donahue, Eddie Vedder, etc.), only one, Patti Smith, supports him this time around.[16] He presents it as a strength, something to be admired, the integrity of continuing even when all of your friends think you're wrong. But I don't think that's strength.

Over the evening I begin to see that a relationship with Ralph Nader is unsustainable. At some point you will let him down and when you do he will turn on you without hesitation. Of course he would welcome you back if you admitted your misdeeds, kissed the ring, and begged for absolution. But what's the point in asking forgiveness if you know you'll do it again?

"I'm sure you've met your share of what we call viral liberals," he continues, looking up from the lectern. Nader's face is filled with small lines and the right front of his nostril appears swollen, as if he has a blister on his nose. But I think his nose has always been that way. "So seized with fear they'll go to the end of time. Once you have an 'anybody but Bush' mind-set, it doesn't matter who you are, you will stop thinking. . . . That's why we call it a virus."

The crowd claps in approval through the speech. There are only the devout in the hall tonight.[17] Ralph continues on to John Kerry, wants to know why Kerry's not winning in a landslide, criticizes the Democrats for cowardice, and points out where it's gotten them so far. "If you cannot stand up for the workers whose lives are being lost due to occupational diseases, if you cannot stand up for forty-five million Americans who don't have health insurance, who are you standing up for?" He lists the letters that he's sent to

Democratic leaders, which have gone unanswered. He talks about veterans groups writing to George Bush and Bush not responding to them. He spends a lot time talking about the disrespect and disdain that politicians have for the people and for Ralph Nader in particular.

"They shouldn't blame Ralph," a journalist from Germany tells me. She wears a tight green T-shirt that hugs her muscular arms. "Last time the Democrats lost by five hundred and twenty-seven votes. If the Democrats can't get five hundred and twenty-seven votes, it's their own fault."

"He asks a lot from people," I respond. "I think maybe he asks too much."

When Nader's done we head into the University District for a hamburger and a beer. I tell her I don't have a place to sleep tonight and she tells me she has a child and a small, messy apartment that's not open to me. We sit at the bar, which closes early in the summer, and we talk about travel and writing books and the difficulty of relationships. She was with a man for seven years, a writer, and he was always writing. "He was good in public, but he never shared his feelings with me. He didn't want to be bothered because he spent all of his time writing. At first I admired it, but then I realized it was just an excuse." We shake our heads in agreement: writers are messed-up people.

She leaves me at a motel beneath the Space Needle, just north of downtown. The hallways with their anonymous carpets stink of soap and beer, and the bed sheets are striped green and orange. I stare from the window across the street to where the nicer hotels are. The street itself is six lanes and many blocks with no turns or stoplights. Down the middle is a five-foot concrete barrier. A pedestrian would never make it across.

In the morning I hump my bags downstairs and start toward the airport. I'm getting tired of carrying two bags with me everywhere, but I'm not sure how else to go about things. The bags start light but then get heavier as I gather books, reading them and then stashing them in my pack to give away when I get home and in the meantime always buying more. The café near the bus stop doesn't have a bathroom. I wonder how Ralph Nader would feel about a place that sells coffee but doesn't have a rest room.

I'm glad I came to Seattle to see Ralph Nader a second time. You can't know a politician after just one speech. I feel better about my lost idealism now, knowing that I could never have lived up to his standards. I'm not sure anybody could, which may be why he never married or had children, though it wouldn't explain at all why I never married or had children. Nader's right when he says if you support a politician without demanding a mandate then the politician will give you exactly what you asked for, which is nothing. You can't stab a nun and still consider yourself a good Christian. Still, the relief comes from realizing an ideal as unattainable, and maybe the best analogy is to losing your virginity. On the one hand, you'll never be a virgin again. On the other hand, you can have sex now.

Officially, Ralph Nader is not yet on any ballot and the Greens are nose-diving into irrelevance. David Cobb is a nice guy but not a person you would actually want to run the country. It's possible the Greens will be less than an asterisk next to Ralph Nader when the victors publish the history fifty years from now. And I wonder if we'll look back on this time with an honest memory, if such a thing is even possible. Will someone write a book about America's historic rejection of third-party candidates at the beginning of the millennium? And if so, will anybody read it?

IX · The Rising Curtain

> That is why you can write a novel about a man, but about a
> crowd—never. If the crowd disperses, goes home, does not
> reassemble, we say that the revolution is over.
> —RYSZARD KAPUSCINSKI

July 11–25

*Just Getting Started; Slow Train into Beantown; Ethan Hawke; Thomas
Patterson; What Bearman Knows; A Map of the World, Actual Size*

I had arrived early in Boston thinking that if I could understand
Boston, then I could understand the Democratic National Convention. And if I could understand the DNC then I could understand the election and what the world is going to look like in the
early months of 2005. That was my basic plan leaving the capital
and heading north through Gotham to Back Bay Station. But it's

not as simple as that. In the week before the convention the city seemed to exist in a nervous calm, like a child waiting to be hit. I had been given some phone numbers for friends of friends but it turned out most of them had left town for the month, hoping to avoid all the politicians.

I called various people associated with and producing the convention but nobody would agree to talk to me. I stopped by the DNC headquarters and they wouldn't let me inside. They're on the fourth floor of a giant office building near the original statehouse and not far from where Paul Revere made his ride. The city is filled with monuments to the American Revolution, and it's hard to deny our revolution worked out pretty well. We could have ended up with Stalin or the Ayatollah Khomeini. It took us over two hundred years to officially certify a policy of preemptive attacks. Most countries get there quicker.

I called the DNC offices from the lobby reception and they told me I couldn't come upstairs. There was a guard posted at every elevator in a buttoned white shirt and black jacket. I had walked three miles through the Boston Commons and then Chinatown. And when I found out they wouldn't let me upstairs to see the headquarters, I lay down on a stone bench near an indoor fountain and put my hand over my face and didn't move for a while.

The DNC has decided to script the convention from start to finish, determined not to make unintentional news of any kind. All news will be hand delivered to the press in carefully written releases, speeches, and staged events. All of the decisions have already been made and so, according to one definition, there won't be any news in Boston this week at all. But there are other ways of defining the news.

I meet Josh Bearman the Thursday before the Democratic Convention not far from where I've been staying.

"Yo," Josh says, and we clasp hands and do one of those man hugs where you shake hands then wrap your arm around the other person's shoulder, leaning into each other so your collarbones touch for a moment. He's got two small bags with him and is wearing gray corduroys, a beaded necklace, and a striped red and blue shirt with a flower pinned to it. He's grown a beard so he looks like a young rabbi. But fashion is not important here. He's staying at a frat house at MIT and we walk there from the station.

But I didn't even want to talk about Josh yet, except to say I'm glad he's here. I've been lonely, which is part of being on the road all the time and something one learns to live with, like sleeping on a floor. When the convention is over I'll go back to San Francisco and stay there. I'm going to have to learn how to interact with people again. While I've been gone, all my friends have gotten married and bought houses.

Anyway, I was lonely, but now Josh is here. And the rest of the people I've met over this past year are also funneling into this patriotic city as if they were intentionally trying to help me tie up all of my loose threads and place this story in context, if such a thing is possible.

"Nothing is knowable," Josh tells me. We're on the Charles River, on the other side of the highway, walking toward the Harvard Bridge. The esplanade is filled with shadows and dark statues. He's been looking into what can be known for the *LA Weekly*, but he can't get anyone to publish his story. Nobody can figure out what he's saying. He's been talking to pollsters from the 2000 campaign and trying to get into the organizations that collect data for the presidential candidates.

"It's beyond secret," he says, referring to the various research organizations. "They might have fifty rooms, or different areas, each one doing some research, aggregating data. Their methods are proprietary. So if people knew how they conducted their polls and collected information they wouldn't have anything. The campaigns hire these guys to help them figure out what people want and where they can expect to win votes, where they have a chance, where they don't. It's all about allocation of resources. But here's the crazy thing—they're always wrong."

We take the steps up to the Harvard Bridge. There's a thin haze, and the light from the hotels cuts patterns in the sky. There's always a nice breeze over the Harvard Bridge; I've been coming here to clear my head. We linger for a time, our arms on the beams, elbows inches apart, staring out across the river. Josh has invented a term for our relationship:

> **bro-mance** /bro-mans'/ *n* Ardent, platonic emotional attachment or involvement between two men. Activities that might be construed as *bromance* include sharing ATM passwords, setting aside large chunks of time for each other without specific plans, comforting each other when one party feels insecure, reading in each other's company.

When I first met Josh he was a video game expert and he had just finished a long article on giant hamsters. But then he became obsessed by politics and his obsession led to a breakdown near the entry ramp to the Hollywood Freeway. Ultimately he didn't find what he was looking for in politics, which if I were to guess is something just short of the meaning of life. So instead he's spent the last three months trying to simply figure out what is true, only to come up empty.

"In 2000, all the polls were wrong," Josh says, running his fingers through his beard, the water drifting beneath our feet. There's a lot of water in this town. "Preference polls, state polls. Later they looked back and said, 'Well, this is why Gore lost here. Here's what went wrong.' But that's bullshit. The only knowledge that means anything is predictive. If you can't accurately predict the future what's the point of studying the past? The past will happen on its own, you don't need to analyze it. You might just as well dissect a baseball game."

On the other side of the river, Josh's frat is a gray cement building at the edge of the MIT campus. There's a pool table and a Ping-Pong table in the front room. I say that if it comes to it I will beat him at Ping-Pong. The guys staying in the fraternity are truly huge, boy giants, mostly shirtless, muscles rippling across their chest and arms. I tell Josh that gigantic athletes at a premier engineering school prove that each group has a similar makeup, once the first variable is found. In other words, there are just as high a percentage of athletes among engineers as there are among poets.

Josh shrugs his shoulders and tells me I'm just articulating a basic sociological idea known as the self-similarity principle, a mathematical concept from fractals and complexity theory. I tell him it's like craps. Once you roll a six your chance of the second die being a six reverts back to one in six. If you go to Vegas and you don't know that, you're in big trouble. But Josh isn't a gambler and has stopped listening. His ear is pressed against the wall, waiting for music, trying to determine if he'll be able to sleep here.

"So what I'm saying," Josh says later in a hotel bar, "is if the polls are always wrong, why do we bother with them?" We're in the lobby of the Sheraton, ground zero for many DNC delegations including Ohio. "Here's something else. With only one exception—Warren Buffett's Berkshire Hathaway, which is really only important because it is such an exception—no mutual fund has ever beaten the stock index."

"That doesn't make any sense," I say.

"When something's true it doesn't matter if it makes sense. It's like this. If you invested in the technology stock index, that is, spread your money evenly across every technology stock, you would do better over ten years than you would in *any* technology mutual fund. Even though those fund managers work day in day out, making phone calls, shifting cash, digging up inside information." While Josh is explaining this to me he moves his hands around to illustrate a guy talking on two phones at the same time.

"I lost a lot of money once on the stock market," I say. "I'd been given six months' severance. I figured easy come easy go. At the time I thought it would all come back to me. But it didn't."

Because Josh has been talking all night about things not being knowable I decide to tell Josh my theory, that everyone says it's a close election, but there's no reason to think that. I say all this hype of the close electorate, which the Democrats have used as an excuse to keep Nader off the ballot, is pure voodoo. Look at Reagan and Carter in 1980, neck and neck until the very end. I ask Josh, if Kerry wins big in this election, who's going to apologize to Ralph Nader? It's the political equivalent of weapons of mass destruction. You can't undo going to war once you find out that the reason you went to war is false. In that same way, after the election you can't undo blocking Nader from getting on the ballot. I tell Josh that it fits in perfectly with what he's now saying about the unknowability of all things.

"No," Josh says. "Forget about Nader. It's going to be close. Kerry's going to win 270 to 268."

With all that in mind I went to the media party at the Boston Convention Center on Saturday night. It was the only party to which I was guaranteed entry. There have been lots of rumors floating around about all the events in Boston this week. Ted Kennedy is having some kind of exclusive clambake, and Tuesday night San Francisco mayor Gavin Newsom is the guest of honor at the *GQ* party. *Newsweek* was said to be having a party at the same time as the media party, but that turned out to be a lie. There are thousands of journalists with full credentials in this town, and not enough party invites to go around.

The problem is, they all think that because they're journalists they should get everything for free. They should always be given access, a VIP pass, and a drink, whether they're going to write about your event or not. Which is why Josh and I weren't even able to get tickets to the Rock the Vote event even though we've been trying for over a month and Josh went to the other Rock the Vote party in Los Angeles. It doesn't matter. Half the country's media has now fully descended on Boston and they all want to shake their asses with the kids.

I want to jam out, too. But I can already see that my plans are backfiring for this week. It would be nice to think of life as just one big party but then there's what life really is. We have to decide how much we want to sacrifice for the environment, how much we want to tax the rich, how we want to deal with other nations, how many wars we want to fight, how seriously we want to be taken in the world. Iran is financing political organizations in Iraq, and North Korea is stockpiling nuclear weapons. The 9/11 Commission is writing about an assumption train, and the Iranians are saying don't come driving your assumption train over here.

The media party was open to *all* credentialed media. All you had to do was RSVP. Anybody who typed an e-mail on the Internet could have gotten in. But only a press person would know that. Anyway, the shindig was in the new Boston Convention Center in the South End. The entrance was a red carpet and all along the carpet were volunteers clapping and yelling, "Welcome to Boston!" I had to ask if I was in the right place, just to be sure.

"Yes," I was told. "And we're happy to have you."

So that was the first thing. The DNC was using their volunteer base to hang outside the convention center and make the press feel important. And why not? The Kerry camp has always been adept at that little game, preying on writers' insecurities and accommodating them with conscientious handlers, good food, and nice hotels, rather than access and straight answers. The Kerry campaign has taken over, railroading Dennis Kucinich at the Platform Committee and installing operatives and liaisons at the highest levels of the Democratic Party.[1]

Inside the media party there were fountains and open bars with only top-shelf booze. Josh ordered a Jack and Coke and ended up

with a Maker's and Pepsi. There were roast beef carveries and fon-
dues, and various gourmet restaurants wheeled samples of their
best entrées across the center. There were also marching bands, a
dance floor, and an indoor Ferris wheel. At the end of the night
Little Richard came out to play a set.

Little Richard told the crowd of reporters to put away their tape
recorders and cameras. "You've been stealing from me my entire
life," he said. "Taking my music, not giving me a dime. I'm nearly
seventy-two years old. Look at me, I invented rock and roll. I love
this country but I was young then. I'm older now."

Outside, rows of white cabs waited to whisk the reporters to
wherever their next stops would be. Buses were ready to shuttle
large groups to Braintree and Logan Airport. I was full on free beer
and roast beef and the city was right in front of me, spread out like
a portrait of itself, just the other side of the Broadway Bridge.

Still, I was having a hard time. The more I looked, the further
everything seemed. Toni Montgomery had told me that everything important happens away from the convention floor in places
like this, but I was starting to disagree with that theory. I had
thought I would come to Boston and write about the parties and
the backroom deals, who is speaking and who isn't speaking at the
convention. I was curious about the tiny protest yard just outside
the Fleet Center where they intend to keep the protesters in a
caged lot covered in black net, divided by the steel girders propping
the highway, soldiers stationed overhead along the edge of the
ramp above the closed-down North Station, surrounded in barbed
wire, rifles at the ready. Days earlier, the soldiers were already
watching, dressed in camouflage, adjusting their scopes. The protest
yard only accommodated a thousand and the city had promised to
rotate protesters in shifts. And people were wondering how far our
democracy has gone.

The newspapers are already filled with news from the various
parties associated with the DNC. The gossip columnists are out in
full force. The broadcast networks have slashed their coverage of

the convention to three hours, less even than the five hours they offered in 2000. Their excuse is that the convention will be covered live by several cable channels, but that fails to differentiate between the intentional and accidental viewer, especially in a year of dramatically increased interest in the political process.

That's what I was thinking about, leaving the party and stepping onto the Broadway Bridge. The bridge is under construction and wooden planks lead across twisted steel rods and pipe. It would have been easy to make the wrong step and turn over the edge. It had gotten late, past midnight, the convention center still a sea of bulbs and expensive dresses, and Little Richard still screaming "Tutti Frutti." And I kept thinking: *focus on the issues*. The convention is the only time in this election cycle when John Kerry is going to address the country with a lengthy speech. And the only way to differentiate myself from most of the journalists would be to write about the actual convention itself.

"Didn't think it would be so hard to get across this bridge," a man said, coming up behind me. He was dangerously drunk, tripping over the ankle-high borders and various pieces of building equipment scattered on the planks. He was tall and at least ten years older than me. He seemed very unhappy.

"This is crazy," I said. There were people walking across the other side, where there was a functional sidewalk. There was no reason at all for us to be walking where we were.

"A mess," he said. "Boston is nothing but one big construction scandal."

On the other side we fell in step together. He explained that he was a writer but didn't write about politics. Not anymore. He wrote about finance now for various large publications. He asked me if I needed a ride and I said I did.

His car looked like a teenager's bedroom, books and papers and food wrappers scattered across the seats. Underneath the clutter the seats had lost their upholstery and were reupholstered with T-shirts and other fabric. Or so it seemed.

We drove into the center of the city and quickly got lost. "I hate this city," he grumbled. He was trying to get back to Cambridge. He had a child and the child was already asleep but he felt he should get home. I didn't ask if he had a wife or if there was somebody else there. I figured it was none of my business. He said he'd drop me off on Massachusetts Avenue and I said that would be fine.

"I wrote a book once," he said. "Long out of print. Published in 1980. Goddammit." He laid on his horn and blew through red lights. I was sure we were going to get arrested. He was driving the wrong way down a one-way street, ducking into parking spots to avoid crashing. "That's my big regret, never writing another book."

He wanted to know what I made of all this and I told him I'd been on the trail for a year now and he nodded. "I think it's important," I told him. "I think that the country should know where John Kerry stands on things. People should watch the convention because otherwise all they're going to hear about is parties and road closures and horse race stuff, and that's bullshit." I was surprised at myself for what I was saying and thought maybe I should go to a strip club or something before going home, just to get back to reality a little bit. I should never have visited with that Harvard professor.[2] It was his fault for placing these evil thoughts in my head.

"You think that?" he asked, stopping the car in the middle of Beacon Street and leaning his head against the glass.

"Sure," I said. "People have a responsibility to pay attention. All they're going to get is John Kerry's side of the story. But that's important, too."

"You're not going to sell many copies that way," he said. I nodded. His book was out of print, he was drunk, and his child was asleep. I liked him and wished we had more time to talk about his book and what he's been doing for the past twenty years. But he had to go; there simply wasn't enough time to take in everything. That's why every picture is just a snapshot. We say we look at things in miniature to better understand and help us with our conclusions, but in fact there isn't any other choice.

I thanked him for the ride and got out, walked up Mass Ave. past the Berklee College of Music and the headquarters of the Christian Scientists. The Christian Science Center is bordered with neatly clipped linden trees and features a twenty-eight-story administrative building set upon a fourteen-acre stone mall with a reflecting pool and fountains where the neighborhood children play in the summer. You're not supposed to swim in the pool and the water recycles over a long rock table but appears extremely still. It's such a small town. Boston's packed with slanted roads and even when you get lost you still end up where you're supposed to go, just by default.

July 26–28

A Letter from Iraq[3]; The Convention Begins; The Triumph of Hope over Fear—Barack Obama; Jesse Jackson; John Edwards; A Gambling Boat from a Prison Town on the Outskirts of Chicago; Unfurling the Sails

In the morning the whole world is a deflated air mattress squeezed between a piece of wall and a large desk, with a view of the bottom of an open door leading out to the porch. I look up to either side of the door. I feel like I've been smacked around with a pipe. It's almost impossible to sleep now that the Democratic Convention has started: every night there are parties and every day there is politics. When the bars close at two, other places open to finish what was started.

Thirty-five thousand people have funneled into Boston to take part in the Democrats' great infomercial. The city is filled with politicians, activists, and political junkies. There are also thousands of journalists and they're all complaining about the convention being too scripted. "They're like the Republicans," several journalists tell me, which is true except for policy and how they would run the federal government. Otherwise the speakers at the convention are on message, with every speaker offering personal assurances of

John Kerry's integrity and a reminder of Kerry's service during Vietnam. It makes me think of the Stalin trials, the various Bolsheviks brought out to confess to Trotskyite plots to sabotage the Socialist Republic. And then Bukharin, in dozens of unanswered letters to Joseph Stalin, "Koba, do I too have to die?"

But maybe that's the difference between terror and hope. Terror is when you confess from fear, and hope is when you give yourself because the other options are so unthinkable. Hope is jumping from the attic window of a burning house because your chances of survival are better, even if you land in a garbage pail full of cowshit and three-week-old bananas. Terror is walking back into that house at the point of a bayonet because burning to death is quicker and less painful than whatever they've been doing to you in those soundproof rooms beneath various government offices in small cities along the Mississippi.

Hope is a nice theme for the Democratic Convention. It's in the talking points, and every speaker hits on it with only one exception, Al Sharpton, who points out, "If George Bush had selected the Supreme Court in 1954, Clarence Thomas would never have made it to law school."

But Sharpton, Kucinich, and even Bill Clinton are all overshadowed by Barack Obama, who lays out the best of the Democratic Party in a speech that will be remembered long after the moneymen and Evangelicals have driven this country into the ground. "On behalf of the great state of Illinois, . . . land of Lincoln," he starts, before continuing into his father's upbringing in Kenya and migration to America on a college scholarship. He talks about America's promise, its diversity, and how hard work is rewarded.

"Even as we speak, there are those who are preparing to divide us. . . . Well, I say to them tonight, there's not a liberal America and a conservative America—there's the United States of America. There's not a black America and a white America and Latino America and Asian America; there's the United States of America. The pundits like to slice and dice our country in red states and blue states; red states for Republicans and blue states for Democrats. But I've got news for them, too. We worship an awesome God in the blue states and we don't like federal agents poking around our libraries in the red states. We coach Little League in blue states and have gay friends in red states. There are patriots who opposed the war in Iraq and patriots who supported it. . . . The audacity of hope! . . . In the end, that is God's greatest gift to us, the bedrock of this nation; the belief in things not seen; the belief that there are better days ahead. . . . Jobs to the jobless, homes to the homeless . . . and out of this long political darkness a brighter day will come."

It's an amazing speech by the young black Senate candidate from Chicago. It's so good that even the journalists applaud and every delegate jumps from his/her chair. I feel stoned when I hear it, and I think sure, why not? Let's figure it out. And the thing is, every single person in the Fleet Center is addicted to this stuff, so it's like being high with twenty thousand people at the same time. In fact, it's so great that nobody notices the foundations of the building cracking along the barbican.

While Barack Obama waves to the crowd, one arm wrapped around the waist of his pretty wife who is trying to kiss him and whom he kisses on the mouth but maybe not quite the way she wants to be kissed, a stone at the edge of the building rolls off toward the Charles River. Obama's wife is holding him close. She knows their every move is being broadcast to every city in the world and millions of viewers across America. But she can't seem to help herself and for just a moment presses her body against her husband. He feels her desire and keeps a reasonable space between them, rolling his shoulders back, smiling and waving. There'll be time for what she wants later, in the hotel room in the dark with the cameras off, the intersection of hope and desire, which is one way of looking at politics, in the best of times.

And in the worst of times, the meeting of anger and need. The volunteers without passes, fanning out across the city, wearing white polo shirts and offering assistance to all the visitors in the town. The anonymous workers who can't get into the event and are only trying to help—they are either hopeful or angry, two sides of the same coin. And their vessel, which is steered by the ones willing to go without sleep or food for days just for the brief pleasure of addressing a crowd that isn't even listening, for three minutes, long before the prime-time event. Obama and his wife on stage, symbolic of the leadership and their foot soldiers, intent on keeping the focus on hope and desire.

I want to pause the world for a moment here. Obama has his hand around his wife's waist. He is waving to the crowd. Everyone is up out of their chairs and a giant image of the couple plays behind them on a wide screen. I am on the floor. I had traded up for a floor pass and am crushed near the photographers' gallery. The photographers are fighting each other as usual, elbows flying everywhere near the velvet ropes. I keep three Ohio delegates between the candidate and myself. I feel like I am lifting off my toes.

Which is to say that I didn't notice it either, the shift the building made. It must have been sudden, perhaps at the very end of the speech. Nobody in the center was going to notice anything in that moment, not even with the entire structure shifting a full two feet. The crack started near the protest pen, the area below the highway, roped off and covered in the big black net.

The crack started there and by the time Obama and his wife had left the building, ostensibly for some fund-raiser at one of the major hotels, but perhaps for somewhere else, by that time the crack had spread completely around the building and in the morning, by the time people noticed, it appeared like a black line wrapping the base. A clean line as if someone had done it intentionally, but I wasn't so sure.

Wednesday morning I arrive back at the Fleet Center and that's when I notice the crack. I'm still thinking of the intersection of hope and desire and wondering if I haven't read too much into the affection between Obama and his wife. After all, what is youth without passion?

The lack of sleep is starting to get to me, and I feel pretty sure I'm not thinking right anymore. Or maybe I'm seeing things clearly for the first time. I meet Josh just inside the Fleet Center. He's waiting at the Dunkin' Donuts wearing a tailored English suit, his beard is coated in pomade.

"What happened to you?" he asks. I stare into his shiny facial hair. The pomade has made his beard straight so the tips hang almost to his Adam's apple.

"I couldn't sleep," I say, and then lower my voice. "I kept hearing Barack Obama saying, 'Not a liberal America or a conservative America—United States of America.' I don't even believe that, but I can't get it out of my head." I give Josh a dollar. "I'm under a lot of stress."

"You've got to get some sleep, bro," Josh says, handing me a doughnut and a cup of coffee. "What was the last thing you did that wasn't political?"

I think about it for a minute. "I saw *Catwoman* on Friday." Josh looks at me like I've got a lobster sticking out of my nose. Friday was my last chance to see the movie. I knew I'd be too distracted once this whole thing got under way. It had to be opening night or not at all. The theater was nearly empty so I took my shoes off and propped my feet on the chair and watched Halle Berry's transformation. The movie was over two hours long and I didn't even notice. Though it did strike me as strange when her leather suit was cut up all of a sudden, even though she hadn't even been in a fight yet. I didn't much care.

"Whatever," I tell Josh. "Don't judge me."

"Yo, yo, yo, who let the grouch out? Bromance, remember?" We lean in together, separated by two coffees and two doughnuts, and touch our cheeks.

"You notice that crack around the building?" I ask Josh, nodding toward the doorway.

"That's always been there. I noticed that on Sunday."

"I don't think so," I say. "I don't think that crack was there."

"Sleep," Josh says, leaving me for the heavy donor booth on the sixth floor. "Go home and come back later. You're not going to catch any of this stuff if you don't get a little shut-eye."

But I decide to stick around. By the time John Edwards comes out the center is packed to bursting. I'm on the floor again, crushed in a sea of shouting Democrats waving signs and I look up into the rafters and see the balloons—red, white, and blue, strung with nylon through the beams. I try to count them but they're so high up and they're so many. Ten thousand? A hundred thousand? Balloons of all sizes. Waiting, waiting.

"How great was Teresa Heinz Kerry last night?" John Edwards asks, shining down on the adoring crowd. The last time I saw Edwards I had a plate of crawfish in my lap and was one of six journalists in Baton Rouge. It will be a long time before I get that chance again. Edwards pumps his fist as the crowd cheers. "I stand here tonight ready to work with you. . . . And we have so much work to do. . . . We shouldn't have two public school systems in this country: one for the most affluent communities and one for everybody else. It doesn't have to be that way. We can build one public school system that works for all our children. . . . How are we going to pay for this? We'll roll back the tax cuts for the wealthiest Americans, close corporate loopholes, and cut government contracts and wasteful spending. . . . I mean, the very idea that in a country of our wealth and our prosperity, we have children going to bed hungry . . . it's wrong." Edwards squints and grips the podium lightly. His smile, the same one he's relied on for so long, maybe a little more serious now, and his squint with just a touch of harshness, ever so slightly, more serious than before. "So when you return home . . . when your brother calls and says that he's working all the time at the office and still can't get ahead . . . when your

parents call and tell you their medical bills are through the roof—
you tell [them] hope is on the way." As Edwards finishes his speech
blue and white signs appear in the audience, each of them reinforcing the message, *Hope Is on the Way*. Some of the signs go up before
Edwards finishes, and the handlers hiss into the crowd, "Lower the
signs! Hey! Lower the signs!"

When Edwards finishes the crowd goes crazy once again. Edwards' children join him on the stage and he dances with his little
girl. She wears a white dress with frills and he pulls her up by her
arms and puts her back down, laughing, on the stage. The band
starts playing and the delegates jump and wave their arms and then
I feel it. There is no doubt what it was. The building has shifted
again and is steadily sliding toward the water.

July 29

*It's a Boat; The Honorable Max Cleland; Jim Rassmann Cleans Up His
Act; Wesley Clark; The Band of Brothers; John Kerry Reporting for Duty*

Sometimes, on the sea, it feels like I never left, like I've always been
here. On the day John Kerry is scheduled to accept the Democratic
nomination for president I meet Josh and Zephyr Teachout in the
hospitality lounge in the media tent. The media tent is lashed to
the Fleet Center by yards of sturdy rope, but to get there you have
to cross a shaky log bridge and hold on carefully to the line. It's
impossible to go between the center and the tent without getting
your feet wet, as the bridge dips inches below the water when you
walk across it. But the view from the bridge is fantastic. Seagulls
overhead, the water is flat all the way to the horizon.

"I have something to ask you," Zephyr says as I join them. From
the window I can still barely see the port of Boston as we float past
the Cape, and also a man trailing behind the ship holding a wire,
balancing on a surfboard. It looks like Jim Rainey from the *Los
Angeles Times*. I wave and he waves back.

The table is covered with empty beer cans and newspaper and everyone is acting as if nothing is unusual, so I try to play it cool myself. That's the first rule of not getting caught, just act like the people around you. Anyway, I don't want to be the first person to point out that the Fleet Center is a boat. If nobody wants to take a cold hard look at the reality of the Democratic Party I don't see any reason to burst his or her bubble.

"Why didn't they trust you at the Howard Dean campaign?" Zephyr asks. Zephyr was one of the very first people I met on the Dean campaign over a year ago. I've always liked her.

"I don't know," I tell her and then go on to explain the bet I made with Jeanie in Iowa, but Zephyr interrupts me.

"No, I know about that. It was way before Iowa. It was in December. They were cautioning everybody not to speak with you. They said you couldn't be trusted. I got in a lot of trouble for sleeping on your hotel floor."

What Zephyr is saying goes back to the beginnings of my time on the trail. They were giving interviews to Fox News and treating me like the bad guy. "I always felt like an outsider," I tell her. "Nobody would talk to me."

"I know. I'm asking why."

"I guess I don't know. I had figured it was just because I wasn't writing for a major newspaper. But I guess it was something more than that."

"It was something way more than that," Zephyr says.

Inside the center the halls are crowded with nervous excitement. All of the delegates arrived before five so they could shut the doors and push away from the dock. Everyone made it on time except for the candidate and his band of brothers, the men he fought with in Vietnam. But when I ask someone where they are I'm told that John Kerry served his country admirably and that his father was a pilot in World War II. This is how the convention has been from the start—everybody stays on message. Nobody deviates from the script.[4] That's how they get in your head.

Across the red carpet blue markers poke from the floor announcing the states of the delegations. Behind the delegates is a four-story podium for giant television cameras. Around the sixth floor, on top of the skyboxes, an electric banner circles with slogans like *A Stronger America*. The banner switches between red and blue, and digital eagles fly forward with their wings closed against their breast. Directly above the stage is an American flag painted on glass and barreled in dark wood, and it resembles nothing so much as it resembles a door, like the door above my air mattress turned horizontal. Speakers hang from the light fixtures curling away like snakes.

I trade in my media credential for a floor pass but when I try to enter the floor I'm told the floor has been closed. I climb back up the stairs where I'm told that if I leave I will not be allowed to return. All access has been stopped. You are either on the boat or you are off the boat but at this point we are all on the boat, whether we like it or not. There will be no opportunity for second-guessing. I can watch from the side or I can drift into the hall and do my best to follow on the television sets inside the press filing room. So instead I take a seat on the steps next to and below the reporter from *Mother Jones*. I look up and see that Josh is seated to the right of me.

"What are you doing here?" I ask. "I thought you were supposed to be hanging out backstage. What happened to your all-access pass?"

Josh shakes his head. He's wearing a button-down shirt, blue jeans, and a Gilligan cap with assorted fishing tackle pinned around the headband. He looks more normal than I've ever seen him. "I wanted to be with you for this," Josh says. "Bromance." He hands me a Flintstone chewable vitamin and a bottle of water.

With three hours to go all motion has ceased except the steady rocking beneath the building as the Democrats chart their course. Willie Nelson steps onto the stage and everyone claps and Willie breaks into a beautiful rendition of "Living in the Promised Land." I nod my head to the music, thinking about what Zephyr told me back in the media tent. They were all so dry sitting there and my feet were soaked. The Dean campaign was onto me all along and they wanted nothing to do with me. I can't pretend it doesn't sting. I've never taken rejection well.

While Willie is singing I wonder if this is what it felt like on the *Titanic*. Nowhere left to go, nothing left to do, committed to your fate, jamming out to slow rock and roll and waiting to sink below the waves. But it's not a good analogy. If you were on the *Titanic* and you didn't get a life raft you were totally fucked. The rafts were mostly reserved for the rich, which is what always happens when the poor don't stand up for themselves. But even the rich didn't necessarily make it out. This is different, primarily because nothing is known. We may hit an iceberg, but it's too soon to say.

After Willie, Carole King comes out to play. By nine o'clock the walls and the ceiling are mostly gone and it's nothing but sky and wind. The pool reporters are all here today, the ones who have been following Kerry across the country. They are now typing away, blocked from the stage by TV screens, blind to the bigger picture, with the large blue ocean spread out before us. Nedra Pickler from the AP is over there and I want to go and hug her. She was always so nice to me.

"How about that breeze?" I ask Josh.

"Yeah," Josh says. "A breeze."

"Delicious," I say. "That's what it is."

"Don't worry," Josh says. Josh always liked Edwards first and Kerry second. He saw all of it coming in January. He never fell for any of what Dean was offering, or Kucinich, or even Nader. He was plugged in from the get-go.

"I'm not worried," I say. "I feel fine. I just wish I had some taffy."

The final speeches are made by Kerry's children who assure everyone that their dad is a good dad, a man full of love and integrity, running for president because it's the right thing to do. I lean back against the separators. They're so fake, I think, but who isn't? As they get older they'll learn to deliver their lines with more feeling and then one day they won't even know the difference. Which is when I notice the helicopters.

"Holy shit," I say. Three dark green choppers, fifty feet above the stage, but nobody looks up. Everyone is focused on Vanessa Kerry. Then the ropes are lowered, bundling in black spools near the stage entrance, and the band of brothers rappel from the crafts to the platform: Jim Rassmann, David Alston, Skip Barker, Steve Hatch, Mike Medeiros, Pat Runyon, Wade Sanders, Del Sandusky, Fred Short, Gene Thorson, Jim Wasser, Drew Whitlow, Bill Zaladonis. It's all the guys from the Swift boat, all of them as calm and happy as if they never went anywhere without a chopper and a length of cord. Then Max Cleland wheels onto the stage.

Cleland was a senator in Georgia, but he lost his seat in a tight race in 2002. Saxby Chambliss, his opponent, in a model of Republican treachery, ran advertisements equating Max Cleland with Osama bin Laden and Saddam Hussein, seeking to portray Cleland as soft on security. All of which is ironic since Cleland lost both legs and an arm in Vietnam. Saxby got out of serving in Vietnam on account of a trick knee.

"Ladies and gentlemen," Cleland says. "I'd like to share with you my story of how I came to know and love John Kerry. . . . While John Kerry was earning a Silver Star . . . I was being treated at Walter Reed Army Medical Center in Washington, D.C. I was twenty-five years old. My body was broken and my faith was shattered. One day, on leave from the hospital, a friend was pushing me around the city in my new wheelchair. In front of the White House it hit a curb. I fell forward out of the wheelchair. There were cigarette butts and trash all around me. I remember trying to lift myself up off the street. I was angry at the war. Saddened that veterans weren't getting good care. And frustrated that people in power weren't listening. Those were difficult days for me.

"But I ultimately realized that although I had lost a lot, I still had a lot left. . . . I decided to run for the State Senate of Georgia. I won, but when I got there, in 1971, I was a lone voice. Then I heard this young veteran on TV speaking about the war. It was John Kerry. He put everything I was feeling into words. . . . John Kerry has never let me down. . . . He is an authentic American hero. He is the next captain of our ship of state. And he will be the next president of the United States."

"You hear that?" I whisper urgently to Josh. "*'Ship of state!'* They know it's a boat. Thank fucking God! I was beginning to think I was the only one."

Kerry comes out from behind Cleland to mad roars of applause. A wave rocks against the stern, splashing over delegates from Puerto Rico and Democrats Abroad. The stage is full with the same speakers I saw in Des Moines, Iowa. Never in my wildest dreams would I have thought to transpose that night, on the state county fairgrounds, eating a corn dog while Teresa Heinz compared Iowa to Mozambique, to the Democratic National Convention in July.

"A great American novelist wrote that you can't go home again," Kerry starts, lifting his hands from the podium.

"That's true," I say to Josh. "I can't go home."

"OK," Josh says.

"My parents inspired me to serve, and when I was a junior in high school, John Kennedy called my generation to service. It was the beginning of a great journey—a time to march for civil rights, for voting rights, for the environment, for women, and for peace. We believed we could change the world. And you know what? We did.

"But we're not finished. The journey isn't complete. The march isn't over. The promise isn't perfected. Tonight, we're setting out again. And together, we're going to write the next great chapter of America's story.[5]

"We have it in our power to change the world again, but only if we're true to our ideals—and that starts by telling the truth to the

American people. That is my first pledge to you tonight. As president, I will restore trust and credibility to the White House. . . . I will be a commander in chief who will never mislead us into war. I will have a vice president who will not conduct secret meetings with polluters to rewrite our environmental laws."

"Dick Cheney sucks," I say to Josh.

"With great faith in the American people, I accept your nomination for President of the United States." The crowd erupts in applause, but Kerry is nowhere near done. He's got an hour to fill and he's only on page two of his speech.

"Standing with us in that fight are those who shared with me the long season of the primary campaign: Carol Moseley Braun, General Wesley Clark, Howard Dean, Dick Gephardt, Bob Graham, Dennis Kucinich, Joe Lieberman and Al Sharpton. . . .

"Now I know there are those who criticize me for seeing complexities—and I do—because some issues just aren't all that simple. Saying there are weapons of mass destruction in Iraq doesn't make it so. Saying we can fight a war on the cheap doesn't make it so. And proclaiming mission accomplished certainly doesn't make it so."

Josh's phone rings and he wraps a coiled earpiece into his left ear and clips a wire to his shirt. "So far so good," he says, tucking his chin into his collar. "Close the deal."

"As president," Kerry continues, moving his arms freely, opening his hands toward the audience. "I will wage this war with the lessons I learned in war. Before you go to battle, you have to be able to look a parent in the eye and truthfully say: 'I tried everything possible to avoid sending your son or daughter into harm's way.' . . . And on my first day in office, I will send a message to every man and woman in our armed forces: You will never be asked to fight a war without a plan to win the peace. . . . To all who serve in our armed forces today, I say, help is on the way. . . .

"For four years, we've heard a lot of talk about values. But values spoken without actions taken are just slogans. Values are not just words, they're what we live by. They're about the causes we champion and the people we fight for. And it is time for those who talk about family values to start valuing families. . . . When I was a prosecutor I met young kids who were in trouble, abandoned by adults."

"That's what adults do," I say to Josh. "They leave you to your own devices. When you're a kid in the system it's like being in a wilderness and the adults are like giant bears. You have to try not to disturb them. There's this danger all around you, and there's no protection. There's nothing you can do once they turn on you."

"Easy," Josh says, his hand on my chest. "Ride this one out."

"We value health care that's affordable and accessible for all Americans. Since 2000, four million people have lost their health insurance. Millions more are struggling to afford it. . . . America will stop being the only advanced nation in the world which fails to understand that health care is not a privilege for the wealthy, the connected, and the elected—it is a right for all Americans. . . .

"And now it's time to ask, What if? What if we find a breakthrough to cure Parkinson's, diabetes, Alzheimer's and AIDS? What if we have a president who believes in science so we can unleash the wonders of discovery like stem cell research to treat illness and save millions of lives? . . .

"I learned a lot about these values on that gunboat patrolling the Mekong Delta with young Americans who came from places as different as Iowa and Oregon, Arkansas, Florida and California. . . . We were literally all in the same boat.

"It is time to look to the next horizon. . . . The sun is rising. Our best days are still to come."

"I've got to go," I say, and I bolt out, up and across the press tables, toward the convention floor. Music is playing. I grip the Plexiglas and balance along the thin porch behind the *New York Times* reporters. Every candidate for the Democratic nomination has joined John Kerry on the stage. His family is there; the Edwards family is there. They're holding hands, waving. The seated delegations have disappeared and the walls are gone. The point of sea and sky looms ever closer.

It's not supposed to work this way. The edge of the world is not supposed to exist, but there it is. The heavens are filled with red, white, and blue balloons showering the deck. The balloons are everywhere and if you look up one of them will land on you and block out your view of what may or may not be clouds. I focus on moving forward. I want to get close to the stage, or as close as I can. I want to be there when whatever happens, happens.

I climb across the photography podium and the rows of chairs folded backward. I wade through the balloons, which are now waist-deep. I can't even see the ground. And just as I'm about to touch the stage the Fleet Center meets its event horizon. I fall forward, trapped for a moment below the celebration. I hear the soft whir of propellers through the din of cheers. I struggle to my feet but am immediately thrown back as I reach for the stage. The Kerrys and Edwardses are nowhere to be seen. The other candidates are still there, ten feet way, shaking hands, covered in confetti, looking startled, grasping for the microphones as the Democratic Party tips gently, then lunges violently into what happens next.

Notes

I. LOOKING FORWARD TO IT

1. Name and details have been changed to protect Wilhelmina's identity. Names of other nonpublic figures have also been changed where appropriate to protect their identity.
2. I did write a four-hundred-word piece for the January 2003 issue of GQ for its special section, My Worst Job Ever. I wrote about working the midnight shift in a pornographic bookstore during my junior year of college. The article was reprinted in South Korea.
3. Charles Taylor was still in power in Liberia at the time so this was actually a pretty funny joke. Now, with Liberia out of the news and Charles Taylor in exile, the same joke doesn't go quite as far.
4. John Heckenlaible of Ambath Corporation had not heard of the Hawkeye Hotel when I called, but pointed out that by publishing this sign we were slandering his corporation. "What if we honored our warranty?" He asked. "What if the sign was wrong?" I tried to explain to him that all I was saying was that there was a sign that said this but he kept interrupting to protest that I was dragging Ambath's name through the mud. I told him I had no position on Ambath either way. For all I know they're the Ben & Jerry's of bathtub liners (and by this I mean they are a socially conscious business). Nonetheless, the sign exists. Or does it?

   In a follow-up call with the Hawkeye Hotel the owner stated that he was dissatisfied with the liners and dissatisfied with the company, but he didn't want to be sued so he had taken the signs down. He used a product called Dispray, which he blames for ruining the tub, along with faulty measurements on the part of Ambath. He said the salesperson told his wife it was OK to use Dispray but that he didn't have it in writing. The salesperson, he said, no longer works for Ambath.

   The next day Heckenlaible called me again. He'd been looking into the Hawkeye's allegations. "We installed four products in September of 2000," he told me. "We found out they were using improper cleaning materials and in spite of that we replaced each of the products we installed in 2001. We found out they continued to use the wrong materials, which ruined the second set of free liners."

I thanked John and said that his account squared pretty much with the account of the Hawkeye Hotel. Since both sides agreed that the Hawkeye had used the wrong product not once, but twice, I was coming over to Ambath's side. John asked if I was still going to mention the sign I saw in the bathroom of the Hawkeye and I said I was but I would footnote his concerns, at which point he grew upset.

"How about if I was writing an article about you that said, "Stephen Elliott beats up grandmothers?" He asked. "And if I footnoted that it wasn't true, would that make it OK? Do you see my point?"

I told him I did see his point.

5. Kate O'Connor is the only person who currently travels with Howard Dean on the campaign trail. She was Dean's Chief of Staff while he was governor of Vermont and people in the Dean for President office refer to her as the Travel Chief of Staff though she insists she doesn't have a title. She's worked with Howard Dean for thirteen years.

6. People hate me for this but I don't care. The winner is the one sitting in the White House and is not defined by who got more votes. As for the Florida election it was within the margin of error and too close to call, though if all the votes are counted Al Gore does win. Anyway, anyone who thinks only Republicans steal elections needs to read Mike Royko's classic, *Boss*.

7. Alex actually didn't want to talk to me. She seemed very turned off by my presence despite my enthusiasm to find a copy of her documentary *Journeys with George,* which I hear is excellent. Six months later we will attend a caucus in Iowa together and she will ask Joshua Bearman not to quote her name in an article he writes for *The Believer* magazine.

8. It has been widely circulated that Howard Dean blew it on *Meet the Press* when he was unable to answer a question about the number of people in the military. Rush Limbaugh called it a "crash-and-burn appearance." But it's been widely circulated that Rush Limbaugh is not very bright. Defenders of Dean state that his answer, "Probably between one and two million" is technically correct. There are 1.4 million Americans in the military.

9. This might no longer be true but it was true at the time and that's what matters. The summer of 1995 was the greatest summer of my life.

10. By this comment I don't mean that Jennifer Palmieri is ugly—she's quite pretty—just that people in politics are driven in a way that's similar to the runaways who make it out to Los Angeles every year, needing so badly to see their name in lights they don't care who they have to suck off. They give themselves completely, so great is their need.

11. At lunch the next day Stefan insists Kerry does not wear a toupee. Google re-

search so far supports Stefan's assumption. Still, do men his age naturally have that much hair? It's suspicious if nothing else.

12. A year later I would decide that I could indeed vote for John Kerry. Because by July 2004, with holy war spreading across the Middle East, Bush had the country in such a mess one no longer had the privilege of splitting hairs. By July 2004 all I wanted was a government that was efficient and honest and a president who would surround himself with advisers willing to offer opinions based on facts as opposed to ideology or religion.

13. The AP will report in an article picked up by a dozen major papers that there were a thousand people in the room. This is ludicrous and false. The room couldn't possibly hold a thousand people.

14. Al Sharpton was quoted in *Slate* magazine saying that the Reverend Jesse Jackson smeared Martin Luther King Jr.'s blood on himself the day that King was shot. I was there the day Jessie Jackson and Al Sharpton made their truce at the National Action Network headquarters, just down the street from the Starbucks in Harlem. I didn't know the story behind the rift at the time. I called Sharpton later to ask him to confirm or deny the report but he never called me back—nobody ever does.

15. I like Carol Moseley Braun. Though if I was to stay with that high-school-kid theme that I kind of leaned on throughout this chapter, I would say Carol Moseley Braun is the honor student who overextended herself in the Polish and Latin clubs and ran for Student Council President. A classic nerd grown likable with age.

16. This turned out to be completely untrue, but there was no way for me to know at the time that I would end up on the campaign for a year of my life and that the election would wreck my relationships and change me in ways I still haven't come to terms with.

II. LET ALL KNOW WHO WOULD ENTER HERE

1. OK, that's a lie, but doesn't it ring true?

2. I met with *Harper's* editor Bill Wasik in New York. Over Chinese food I tried to convince him to let me cover the Iowa caucuses but he didn't seem too hot on the idea. I then sent him an idea to cover the Hawaii caucuses. He liked it but was unable to convince the editorial board at *Harper's*. The same idea was shot down at *Esquire*. In the end, I didn't go to Hawaii, though I would have liked to.

3. John Edwards will refer to himself as an outsider four times during the nationally televised debate.

4. The spin room is a very strange idea. After debates and forums the candidates and their press aides arrive in a room away from the event and tell as many lies as possible. They claim that they have won the debate or that things are going

really well for their campaign. It's totally bizarre because to "spin" is to lie, so the room might just as well be called the lie room.

5. When I called Joe Lieberman's office to find out if this was true Lori Nunan told me she wasn't allowed to talk on record. These are the same people who complain about not getting coverage from the press, people who won't even answer a straight yes-or-no question. If I was a journalist I wouldn't cover these people either—it's too much work.

6. From 2000 to 2002, according to the Democratic Policy Committee, 3.8 million more people joined the uninsured.

7. On November 1, 1993, Hillary Clinton launched an attack against the insurance industry to counter the damage done by the Harry and Louise ads. Her assault called more attention to the Health Insurance Association of America. The HIAA spent almost $50 million on the lobbying effort and produced more than 450,000 contacts with Congress via phone calls, visits, and letters, almost a thousand to every member of the House and Senate.

8. I should state that some of the information in this digression was gleaned from a conversation I had with Jodi Wilgoren of *The New York Times* in the back of a Howard Dean press van. David Redlawsk at the University of Iowa also contributed, as did a brochure quoting Ken Thorpe put out by the Service Employees International Union.

9. Brian, age eight, from Ottumwa, Iowa, has a spinal cord injury between the C2 and C3 vertebrae and supports John Kerry because John Kerry supports stem cell research.

10. Jim was talking about *What It Takes* by Richard Ben Cramer.

11. John Kerry will bungle the Saddam capture badly, first by suggesting on network news that Saddam might have been captured earlier if he was president. When asked at a press avail the next day if that didn't conflict with what he had been saying the days before— *"If you think we'd be at war with Iraq now if I was president you shouldn't vote for me"*—the senator refused to get into specifics. Ironically, most of the focus will land on Dean for his statement that we're not any safer with Saddam behind bars.

12. After the debate, ABC also pulled its reporters from the Sharpton and Braun campaigns.

13. It should be mentioned that in March 2004, *The New York Times Sunday Book Review* finally reviewed my fourth novel, *Happy Baby*. The review ran in the Books in Brief section and Curtis Sittenfeld called *Happy Baby* "Surely the most intelligent and beautiful book ever written about juvenile detention centers, sadomasochism and drugs." Not long after the review in *The New York Times,* foreign rights were sold for *Happy Baby* in Norway.

14. The story behind my year as a search engine consultant would take more pages than I have here. To sum up: it was the boom time in San Francisco, 1998. I started as a temp writing catalogue descriptions for lawn furniture— *We bring the good life to your own backyard*—and two months later was offered

my first and last full-time job. The truth is, though it was my idea to sell search engine optimization and though I priced it and wrote the white papers, and though at one time I had thirty people working for me, I never really knew how it was done.

15. The night before hooking up with Dennis Kucinich, I lost $26 playing 50 cent/one dollar Texas Hold'em at a bar in Iowa City called the Foxhead. I was recognized twice in Iowa City and someone in the Foxhead asked me directly if I would write a poker report on my experience playing there. But I was too embarrassed by the whole thing to commit any of it to paper. The worst hand of the night happened when I paired up a king-jack and got outkicked by a king-ace.

16. Though Braun, Sharpton, and Kucinich are often lumped together the reality is that while Sharpton and Braun have raised a couple of hundred thousand dollars each Kucinich has raised five million which as the zookeepers say, isn't peanuts, and at the minimum puts Kucinich in a league very clearly above the other two "long-shot" candidates, something rarely mentioned in most accounts of this campaign.

17. Michigan threatened to leapfrog Iowa and was told by Terry McAuliffe they would lose half their delegates.

18. The John Kerry press release is available at http://www.johnkerry.com/pressroom/releases/pr_2003_1222d.html.

III. THE EARLY STATE

1. John Kerry came in first in Iowa followed by John Edwards in second.

2. This turned out to be totally untrue for a number of reasons and I have never been able to corroborate the Gephardt/Dean rumor either. The campaigns are filled with rumors. The larger question is, Where do these rumors come from? And are they deliberately meant to throw the media off the trail of something more important?

3. The day before the Iowa primary I met John Hlinko, the guy responsible for drafting Clark. It turns out he's my ex-fiancée's cousin.

4. There is no text reference for note number four in this section. The original footnote, cut by my editor, was a long quote from John Kerry explaining his position on a constitutional amendment barring gay marriage. The feeling on the original note was that it was long and redundant and didn't provide anything that wasn't available in some form or another in other places throughout the text. I'd like to refer people interested in reading the original quote to reference the complete text of the *Milwaukee Journal-Sentinel* debate, which is surely available online somewhere.

5. I asked Bosa about his schedule for the next few days and he told me, "I have a campaign event ever hour of every day. I live here." Bosa called me on the

last day of the convention and encouraged me to hang out with him. It was my idea originally—I thought I should face my fears—but after five days I was burned out and wanted to spend some time with friends, so I decided to head to New York for a couple of days prior to the Iowa caucuses. I told Bosa maybe we could hook up next time but he said it would be too late for the New Hampshire primary, which was true. "You're the only guys that can get the truth out about this stuff. I'm going to beat Bush." Then he started on about some people who had been killed in New York, something associated with organized crime. I couldn't quite make it out as it was during the Clark rally. Bosa said he had film. "When you come back you can stay at my house," he said. "I'll take you up on that," I replied.

6. Before Penna's Web site crashed my computer I searched around and found endorsements from several private companies that have asked Penna to sit on their board. Also listed on the endorsement page was a copy of a note from Verizon customer service wishing Fern Penna luck in his race for the presidency.

7. My father's rebuttal: "Actually, underwear on your head absorbs moisture, so it makes sense." My father initially denied wearing cowboy boots while sunbathing but followed up with me later to say that he probably was wearing cowboy boots.

8. My skepticism of Kucinich being the guy to rid the world of nuclear weapons turned out to be prescient when he gave all of his Iowa non-viables to Edwards and got nothing in return. As much as I like Kucinich in the end he's a sucker.

9. Apparently, it's not a big deal to carry a gun in New Hampshire. As I was checking out of my hotel, I saw a man with a rifle in his hand walk straight across reception and into the convention area. Wesley Clark was still speaking in the auditorium, but before arriving in the auditorium, the man turned right and left through the exit.

10. That would be the last time I would hear Clark give that speech in New Hampshire.

11. This is going to prove a mistake. Many Iowans are offended by the out-of-staters knocking on their doors wearing bright orange hats.

12. I got crushed in my predictions for Iowa.

13. *We Wish to Inform You That Tomorrow We Will Be Killed with Our Families: Stories from Rwanda.*

14. Joe Trippi would quit the Dean campaign on January 29, when Dean decided to hire Al Gore's associate Roy Neel as his campaign manager, demoting Trippi to a position in charge of Internet reachout.

15. I lost that bet as well as a 20 percent over/under on John Kerry. But the worst casualty of my betting turned out to be my relations with the Dean campaign. It started circulating among senior staffers that I was trying to dig up dirt on their campaign, tricking people into betting against their own candidate. The saddest part of this is that I had more faith in their candidate than they did. I was simply trying to make some money.

16. Originally I was certain the other reporter was Vince Morris from the *New York Post,* but when I looked up his picture it wasn't Vince Morris at all but rather a reporter named Bill whom I would become friends with on the Kerry bus driving through Ohio in late April. I had heard from other reporters that a couple of days earlier Vince Morris had challenged a photographer to step outside after the photographer had asked him to move out of the way of the shot. This was mentioned again in an article in *The Des Moines Register,* which might have led to the confusion.

17. Zephyr Teachout is the person in the Dean campaign responsible for the early Meetups and the blog. Though, as Zephyr will be the first to point out, it wasn't long after these things started working for Dean that the other campaigns started doing them as well. Her impact on politics and grassroots in the Democratic party will be felt for a long time even if her candidate loses.

18. This is one of the numbers Joe Trippi floated and then dismissed during an informal chat with reporters in the lounge at the Hotel Fort Des Moines. Note to self: when a campaign manager tells you his candidate is going to poll 18 percent two days before the caucuses, believe him.

19. When the first one went down Edwards stopped his oratory and directed the crowd to get her water and give her room to get out. "Thanks for coming out," he said as she was helped out the door. I don't think he noticed the second one who was kind of behind the stage near the press ropes.

20. It might not have been Jeff Zeleny's steak but it probably was. He had left already, and the steak was in front of his chair. It's possible it was someone else's steak and they had thrown their napkin over it and pushed it in front of the empty chair after Jeff left.

21. This depends on the number of delegates awarded a precinct which is based on previous votes. But what's relevant is that, to receive delegates you have to get 15 percent. Yet to receive half of the delegates, you need 50 percent, and the numbers are often directly at odds.

22. The Japanese cartoon Voltron made its American debut in 1984 and for many Americans it was their first exposure to the cartoon style Anime. Voltron, a human-shaped robot with a flaming sword, was created when five lion-shaped spaceships came together, usually at the end of the episode.

23. This is a debatable point. Nearly twice as many young voters showed up compared with 2000.

24. There are points of agreement between Kucinich and Edwards. Where Edwards is strongest and most specific is on campaign finance reform and putting serious curbs on the power of lobbyists.

25. When I wrote this on the *San Francisco Chronicle* Web site I got the following letter in response:

> *You are pathetic! I've read a couple of your pieces about the campaign and think you are a complete idiot. Why don't you go work for Kerry or one of the other candidates. You think you are being clever but you are not. Your smart ass*

comments do NOTHING to help Governor Dean. They give a misleading ac-
count of the events. If this is such an ordeal for you as it seems to be by your
commentary—Why don't you just go away? Your commentary is worthless and
immature tripe.

Beth M.

(P.S. I was in Iowa too and I worked with the press!)

What Beth didn't seem to grasp was that her reaction essentially proved my point. My theory is that it came from the top, that Howard Dean didn't like the press and this sentiment filtered down into the culture of his campaign.

26. The debate actually turned out to be make-or-break for Wesley Clark who seriously flubbed a question on whether or not he agreed with Michael Moore's comment that Bush was a deserter. His refusal to answer would dog his campaign for weeks.

27. At Edwards' current rate of spending he will run out of money by May. Since he opted in to public financing (Kerry and Dean opted out), he is unable to raise more money until after the Democratic convention. Meaning if he were to win the nomination Bush would have months to pummel him while Edwards would lack the resources to fight back.

28. I was interviewed on Philadelphia's ABC affiliate for its Sunday morning show. I have no idea why they asked me to be on the show or who they thought I was. I wanted to be judicious but when they asked me about Lieberman I said he was done for and I called Al Sharpton a noncandidate. Josh told me I needed to stop doing that, people were going to hate me. And I agreed with him. The TV station didn't invite me back.

29. In actuality, following New Hampshire Dean still had more delegates than anyone else because of pledges from super-delegates. In the end the winner will be one with 50 percent of the delegates, and less than 1 percent of the delegates have been chosen so far. Still, there are ominous signs coming out of the Dean camp: the first is called fund-raising, the second is called Al Gore. The clouds gathering above Burlington appear white but inside are black and filled with coal.

30. In December 2002, Trent Lott told the world that if Strom Thurmond had won his presidential bid in 1948 America would be a better country. Strom had run in 1948 as a segregationist candidate despite having a black daughter who was kept secret until after his death. When Howard Dean made his infamous comment about attracting voters with Confederate flags on their pick-ups people pounced on him for his insensitive remarks. However, since there was no history showing Howard Dean to be a racist the charges did only minor damage. Trent's comment, on the other hand, caused a serious look into his history and ties to white supremist organizations, and it was the close look at this history that forced Trent to resign his post as senate majority leader.

IV. THE LONG-TERM EFFECTS OF OPTIMISM

1. It turns out New England did win. But not by as much as anyone expected. I took a late bet on Carolina a few moments after the kickoff with three and a half points though officially I should have gotten six. Carolina covered for me but just barely. It was the best Super Bowl and certainly the best halftime show I think I've ever seen and it was the first bet I've won since I started covering the 2004 election. The next day the only news to be found was on Janet Jackson's breast. Matt Drudge ran a close-up on her nipple, pierced with a bar and surrounded by a metal sun. I called Josh Bearman who was back in Los Angeles doing set design for a major Hollywood film. "Did you see Janet Jackson's breast?" I asked him. I could hear the director in the background saying, "No darling, you're in England!"

   "You bet your sweet ass I saw Janet's breast. Greatest moment of my life!"

   "I know," I said. "I've liked her ever since she was a fat kid on *Fame*."

   "What were we doing on the Dean bus?" he asked. "We should have been covering the Super Bowl."

   "Forget it," I said. "Getting close to politicians is easy. We'd never survive the NFL screening process."

2. Since the Clark campaign folded John has started a new venture, ActForLove.org, personals for activists. The slogan is "Take Action, Get Action."

3. It's a lot easier to prove someone a liar than an idiot. The fact remains that, aside from weapons of mass destruction–related activities, a major portion of the State of the Union was devoted to steroid use among athletes and a constitutional amendment banning gay marriage. Which makes me think that *evil* is a better word than *idiot*. And it takes solid brass balls to forward this kind of agenda and do the damage he's done.

4. Not his real name or organization. Toni was reassigned the next day, more than a week before the primary.

5. Americans for Jobs, Healthcare, and Progressive Values (AJHPV) was working through a loophole in the campaign finance regulations. These groups, known as 527s, are not supposed to be affiliated with any one candidate and can raise unlimited funds while not disclosing their sources of financing for up to thirty days. The link between AJHPV and John Kerry was furthered on February 10, when it was revealed that fifty thousand dollars had been contributed to AJHPV by the defunct (Robert) Torricelli for Senate Committee. Torricelli has also admitted to raising one hundred thousand dollars for John Kerry and he took part in a meeting the week before with the Democratic front-runner in New York City. John Kerry has denied involvement with AJHPV. Federal Election Commission spokesman Bob Biersack said it was "fuzzy" whether Torricelli's contribution was permissible under FEC rules.

6. All of the Dean supporters were encouraged to come to Iowa to help in the final days before the caucuses. Code name Perfect Storm. They were given bright orange hats and sent out with lists of addresses and little training to knock on doors. But the people didn't like the outsiders canvassing their state. "Dirty hippies from California," one lady told me.

7. The darker story behind Clark's resignation is that Chris Lehane announced the resignation the night before Clark resigned in Little Rock. Lehane had left the John Kerry campaign for Clark, claiming that Kerry lacked the fire to win. But nobody else in the Clark camp was told of the resignation and a conflicting faction led by Wesley Clark's son spent the rest of the night trying to retract the resignation. No one knows for sure whether the general authorized the resignation or not.

8. Meditating on this later I decided that there is no excuse for being a producer for Fox News. A producer or a writer for an organization that intentionally misstates the facts with the explicit intention of making the world a meaner place is not a morally tenable position.

9. In another strange twist to this meaningless tangent three days later a journalist told me they did buy the socks and that Howard Dean seemed very embarrassed by it. I was doing vodka shots with two Russian cameramen from the John Kerry campaign and there were trays of sandwiches laid out from a Kerry event earlier in the day.

10. This is my name for the game. Jodi referred to it as Brilliant Ploy, which is what Howard Dean called the miscommunication that resulted in a statement to withdraw from the race if he lost Wisconsin, followed days later by a retraction of that statement.

11. This is tough to prove with Kerry. At some point he's mentioned every issue. He certainly mentioned the economy. But when you attend a lot of these events you quickly divine where the emphasis is, and that's what it comes down to. Which issues do the candidates go back to again and again in order to define their candidacy. It certainly wasn't the Patriot Act or the No Child Left Behind act, both of which Kerry voted for. Though in July I heard him criticize the lack of funding for the No Child Left Behind act. But it's easy to critique a lack of funds. There's always a lack of funds—there's never enough money to go around.

12. This can go further. Back in December when people were referring to John Kerry's bus as the Death Bus, the dictum I heard most often was that Kerry was the best candidate to beat George Bush. I would always reply that if John Kerry can't beat Howard Dean there's no way he can beat George Bush. The reverse should also apply: the person best suited to run for president will also win the primary. But there's no way to test that theory, since only one person gets to run for president on the Democratic ticket. There's no way to know, for example, if Gary Hart would have made a stronger showing than Walter Mondale or if Bill Bradley would have done better than Al Gore.

13. The rumor about the intern, Alexandra Polier, seems to have come out of the Clark camp. Possibly from Chris Lehane. To rebut the charges, Alexandra held her own news conference in Africa, where she was vacationing with her fiancée.

14. Two days before the primary, a Zogby poll would show Dean gaining steam, with 23 percent of the vote, compared with 19 for John Edwards, but with John Kerry still holding a commanding lead.

15. Ralph Nader will declare his candidacy five days later while talking to Tim Russert on *Meet the Press.* An uproar ensues but there is a general failure to take into account all of the reasons why Ralph Nader will not win many votes this time. The first reason is that he's running as an independent and has no organization behind him. The final reason is all of the guilt felt by people who voted for Ralph Nader in 2000—something that will not be easily forgotten and that was a major part of the Dean candidacy.

V. A PHOENIX FROM THE LANDFILL

1. *Days of Heaven*, the second film by former philosophy professor Terrence Malick was shot entirely during the golden hour.

2. The metaphor here is George Bush's declining credibility rating. Now that it's clear to the nation that we were led to war under false pretenses, people are beginning to question chapters of the Bush résumé that used to be taken at face value. This is fueling a new focus on his tenure in the National Guard, a tenure that showed a considerable lack of selflessness and courage. Though as of yet there is no real attention being paid to how his father, the congressman, got his son out of having to really put his ass on the line in the napalmed rice fields of Vietnam.

3. Several hours before the debate I did meet Angelyne in the dark lobby of the Roosevelt Hotel at the end of the walk of fame and across the street from what used to be Mann's Chinese. She was with her assistant, Rider. She reminded Rider to pull out her chair for her. She kept asking me if I was going to need any photographs for my article but I told her that wasn't necessary. When I asked her how she managed to keep up the plethora of billboards across the city with her image on them she replied cryptically, "Why should I have just one investor?" I wasn't able to get her to go any deeper that that, on anything. She did go off on a brief tangent about how Arnold Schwarzenegger was good luck for her and pointed out the irony that, etymologically, Schwarzenegger was "black," twice, and she had run a "pink" campaign. "Schwarz and Negger, get it?" She asked me if I might be interested in writing for a television show she was working on. "I love discovering new talent. I have this magic ability to open up someone's mind." After about twenty minutes in her company, I was certain that I was in a David Lynch film. The furniture in the hotel was covered in upholstery, as if it hadn't been unpacked

yet. Giant plaster beams surrounded by wood paneling rose into a gothic ceiling. Angelyne was unaware of who the current political candidates were, as she was too busy "creating culture." Nothing she said is worth repeating here except this quote, which makes her seem far more articulate than she actually was, when referring to her own run for governor: "Politics is like making love to somebody you hate but it feels really good. You love it, the speed, the vibe, the intensity, but you know something's wrong."

4. I would find out in the spin room after the debate that things were so bad for Edwards in California that he decided to change his schedule and fly out to Minnesota as soon as legally possible.

5. The race across the desert turned out to be a farce. None of the competitors went any reasonable distance so the prize money was not awarded. Josh decided he would do it himself, on foot. A week later he turned up at a gas station begging for water and took a Greyhound home. The point of the race was to discover the technology to fight wars in a desert in unmanned vehicles. Bearman's weeklong trek did nothing to further the Defense Department's cause.

6. It's been suggested that the relationship between Roger Stone and Al Sharpton is not as strange as people might think. On Stone's part Sharpton is seen as helping the Republican Party. For Sharpton, the Democratic Party was never more than a vehicle to replace his former mentor, Jesse Jackson.

7. Wilhelmina gave me a stick of Carmex. My lip didn't actually split until after I started using her balm and it seemed to me that the more I used the drier my lips became. It was as if using the balm increased the need for the balm. My lips would feel great for a half hour but then would dry up worse than before. It might be psychosomatic.

8. *Sharpton Talks of Conditional Exit*
   by James Rainey, Los Angeles Times, *3/5/04*
   The Rev. Al Sharpton may soon drop his longshot campaign for the presidency if presumptive Democratic nominee John F. Kerry agrees to adopt a more pronounced "urban agenda," sources in Sharpton's camp said Thursday.
   Sharpton confirmed in a telephone interview that representatives of his campaign have talked to the Democratic National Committee and Kerry operatives about how he might "fold into" a campaign to defeat President Bush.
   Nursing a cold at his home in Brooklyn, Sharpton said the discussions with Kerry's campaign had just begun and that he planned to continue his candidacy for the time being. A trip to Florida this weekend was likely. "I don't know if 'discontinue' is the word I would use," said Sharpton, referring to his candidacy.

9. Most notably by insisting that the votes had already been recounted.

10. Most Democrats are still in denial about this crucial point preferring instead to blame Nader first and Republicans second. Which is their own tragedy because until they accept full responsibility they will be unable to learn from their mistakes.

11. A notable exception is the Chicago truck scam story that broke in the *Sun-Times* in January 2004. It was revealed that the city pays forty million dollars a year for dump trucks that do essentially nothing. Most of these trucks are owned by various political leaders and there are ties to organized crime. The mayor has said he is embarrassed and takes full responsibility while also maintaining no knowledge of the scam.

VI. AND I WILL SHOW YOU RUST

1. The president actually abandoned the tariffs before the WTO leveraged sanctions but after the tariffs were declared illegal. The word from people in the know is that it wasn't the WTO that forced Bush's hand, it was the business leaders.

2. In Toomey's office they loaded me down with photostats from *The Wall Street Journal, The New York Times,* and a copy of the March 22 issue of *The National Review,* whose cover story on Toomey is a plea so beautiful and passionate it makes my teeth hurt:

> The National Review, *Cover Story 3/22/04*
>
> *For conservatives who generally support President Bush but are concerned about the Republican party's drift under his stewardship, the Specter-Toomey race and a handful of other primary elections offer the opportunity to make a midcourse correction.*
>
> *This is important for conservatives, because we are in one of our seasons of discontent. Conservatives are always tempted, in such moments, to throw up our hands in disgust. Here and there one hears calls for conservatives to sit out the November elections. The question that the Pennsylvania campaign—and a few others—raise is whether conservatives are prepared to do something constructive about their dissatisfaction.*
>
> *There are two theories that underlie the sit-it-out strategy. The first is that there's no difference between the Republican and Democratic candidates, and it will make no difference who wins. The second is that the Bush Republicans need to be taught a lesson about what happens when they drift from conservative principles.*

3. In Arlen Specter's campaign literature he boasts of "supporting a permanent repeal of the estate tax, which is particularly burdensome for family farms and small family owned companies." In fact, it isn't. A family farm has never been repossessed as a result of the estate tax. The estate tax actually only affects the super wealthy. This is typical Republican posturing about the good they're doing the common man, when they aren't, and goes a long way to explaining why so many poor people vote for Republicans. Many of these poor are uneducated and have no idea they are being lied to, but they get off on the hate.

4. What Arlen Specter actually did was invoke Scottish law to rule "Not Proven," which had the same effect as voting against the impeachment but with a twist of silliness thrown in.

5. The 527s are an outgrowth of the McCain-Feingold campaign finance laws. They are allowed to raise unlimited amounts of cash but are not allowed to be associated with a candidate. So the Club for Growth is not so much for Toomey as against Specter. Of course, it's the same thing. The shady organization I mentioned earlier, Americans for Jobs, Healthcare, and Progressive Values, which ran attack ads against Howard Dean, was also a 527. It came out soon after Dean lost Iowa and New Hampshire that Americans for Jobs, Healthcare, and Progressive Values had ties to Richard Gephardt and John Kerry, but there was no consequences. People figured, what's done is done. It's all very similar to 2000 when groups associated with George Bush sent mailings around South Carolina about John McCain's illegitimate black child. The links to the Bush campaign were later proven conclusively but by then McCain's candidacy was over, and with it any desire to look further into the Bush campaign's fiercely dirty tactics in the Republican primary.

6. The reverse is not necessarily true. The Democrats lost Pennsylvania last time around. Kerry would need to also carry Ohio to have a similar effect. It seems implausible, at least right now, in late April, that Bush could win Pennsylvania and not win Ohio.

7. In 2000 I thought Bill Clinton had sold the liberals down the river by locking up more people than any president before him and not fighting the three-strikes laws or drug-testing regulations. And he did. Yet looking back, Clinton seems a lot more liberal than he did at the time. It has become very fashionable among thirty-year-old liberals like myself to express fondness for Clinton. Clinton was all we ever knew. And as in most first relationships set upon a base of disagreement, resentment, and falling out, you don't how good the other person was until he's gone. In politics, as in romance, you hold out for true love the first time around. Heartbreak teaches you compromise.

8. After his talk Toomey asks me who I'm writing for. When I tell him *The Believer* he says, "I've never heard of that magazine." His face is filled with suspicion. I tell him I'm looking forward to spending a week with him and he nods, looking like he wants to engage me in a fistfight. I use my one question to ask if it was true what he said on CNN yesterday about having only a quarter of Specter's money when one takes into account the contribution from the Club for Growth. He admits that when taking that into account it's closer to, though not quite, half. If the Club for Growth comes through with another million, which many expect them to do, Toomey will easily reach 50 percent of the incumbent's war chest.

9. On this same day three car bombs explode in Basra killing sixty-eight people including twenty-three schoolchildren.

10. I sent John an e-mail asking if he could give me some more information on

the spike in divorce rates following the banning of school prayer. He responded with two articles, one by Tom Geoffrey, the pastor of the Christian Life Fellowship arguing for a national day of prayer. The other was by Scott H. Northrup, published in *Essays in Supernatural Christianity*. When John sent me these "robust articles," he preempted my criticism with this disclaimer: "People who are opposed to the idea of a God who has the power to bless a nation or to withdraw and leave it on its own will likely find many ways to explain away the 'coincidence' of the statistics."

11. It seems only fair to reprint John's entire e-mail on this subject:

    The reason I think cutting taxes, even during a war, is good, is that we are already being taxed too heavily in the first place. With each passing year we are seeing more of our net spendable income be drawn in to a growing quagmire of spending. I personally believe in a free and just society, and further believe that educated and moral individuals are the best money managers.

    If we continue to look to the government to be our "savior," and fund it with almost HALF of what we earn, we are headed for a great disappointment. No, that's too soft; we are headed for a stifling, restrictive, heavy-handed Big Brother society. That's not the America I want to live in.

    Ever speak to anyone who's had to deal with getting health care in other countries (where the heavy-taxed, government-provided system exists)? Ever wonder why the God-starved former Soviet Union is inviting missionaries to proclaim the good news in their public schools? Big government can't replace God, and that's what we are trying to do on an ever-increasing scale. You see, most people are smart enough to see the injustice and poverty and cruelty in the world. They just aren't always willing to look UP for the answers.

    This is an age-old problem: we are all sinners: "all have sinned and fall short of the glory of God," but "every man does what is right in his own eyes," and we want to believe anything but the truth. There IS a God; He is PERFECT and we are NOT, and we have to come back to Him on HIS TERMS.

    Is He MEAN? Does He enjoy seeing us wallow in our own self-destruction? NO! Does He have a PLAN? Does He want us to find our way BACK? YES! "For God so loved the world (including Steve and John), that He gave His only begotten Son, that whoever believes in Him (including Steve and John), shall not perish, but have everlasting life."—John 3:16.

    What do you think of all this stuff? I am wondering if you are sensing God speaking to your heart even now. Would you like to continue corresponding?

    Your friend, (I mean that) John

12. It has been suggested to me that Judith was channeling FDR, which is ironic.

13. Randy Weaver was found guilty of lesser charges.

14. The interviewer, Robert Birnbaum, was talking with me about my novel *Happy Baby*, which is about Theo who was raised in group homes in Illinois, as I was. There are a lot of differences though between my story and Theo's story not least of which is that Theo enters the system at the age of eleven

after his father is shot with a shotgun. The book is dedicated to the State of Illinois.

15. See footnote 4 Chapter four.

16. The tape was released by the Republican National Committee to ABC News and *The New York Times,* which made no mention in their original stories of the source of their information. The argument, of course, is that they have to protect their sources. Still, it would seem relevant to mention at the minimum that the information was received from a group hostile to Senator Kerry. Within two days the tapes origins were public but immediately upon hearing of the tapes Kerry had exclaimed, "God, they're doing the RNC's bidding!" Which turned out to be correct. Stranger still, a month later the story is still alive on Web sites like ABC's Noted Now while the story of George Bush's service in the National Guard has all but disappeared, despite Gary Trudeau's offer of ten thousand dollars in the pages of *Doonesbury* to anyone who can furnish proof that Bush completed his National Guard service. As of this writing that reward is still unclaimed.

17. He also takes credit for going after the boys who stole my shoes but my father has his incidents confused. What actually happened was a kid named Scott McClain kicked me off the back of my bicycle while I was hanging out in front of my friend Albert's house talking with his crazy landlord. I chased Scott and was chased in turn by Scott's older brothers. My father invited some of the guys who did security and other jobs for a building he owned on the south side of Chicago and together we all went to the McClain's house and my father essentially threatened Scott's father and I didn't have any more trouble with the McClain's after that. But my shoes were stolen about two years later when I was living in a group home called McCormick House. I had just bought a new pair of canvas sneakers with my clothing money and I was taking the old North-South train to the 55th-Garfield stop. To make a long story short I was jumped at the 55th station, which is really no place for a white boy anyway, and they took my shoes. They also took my receipt so my next month's clothing money was docked by the home. To the best of my knowledge my father had nothing to do with it.

18. And yet I remember sleeping in a basement the night I turned fourteen. I had broken into the basement with my friends John and Albert and we each had a half pint of vodka to celebrate. John and I both confessed to masturbating that night but Albert remained resolute. The next day I was nearly suspended from eighth grade for reading a *Playboy* interview with John Wayne during math class.

19. Leaving the panhandle through Pennsylvania toward Youngstown, the Kerry bus makes an unannounced stop at the Hotdog Shoppe in Beaver, Pennsylvania. The prophetic sign greeting the candidate is an announcement in Plexiglas letters assembled most likely by a store employee on work study the day before: "Practice Integrity Until You Get It Right."

20. This may prove not to be true. It's certainly true in April but by June the administration's glaring failures in Iraq, coupled with the Abu Ghraib prison scandal, starts to weigh down the presidential approval numbers in a serious way.

21. It's an interesting shift. With some exception I was ignored by most of the press corps prior to April. But by this point they've seen me often enough to know I really am writing a book about the campaign. And as I get to know the press I find any number of decent people among them, about as many percentage-wise as the population at large.

22. The Sheraton Cleveland is one of the more awful hotels of the campaign trail. In the bar/restaurant that is located in the basement, Jodi Wilgoren offered to share a plate of garlic buffalo wings that looked and smelled so foul I was tempted to immediately call the health inspector. Jodi is on the Atkins diet, so she's hungry all the time now. The Sheraton Cleveland was my least favorite hotel of the entire campaign. And that was before they overcharged me an extra night and I was unable to contact anyone willing to reverse the charges.

23. This is mostly unconfirmed. What is true is that we stayed at the Hampton Inn next door to the Original Roadhouse and across the street from a truck stop and a strip club sandwiched between a massage parlor and an adult bookstore. The massage parlor had a sign inside the door offering body shampoos for twenty dollars and half-hour massages for forty dollars. If you looked inside you could see a group of Asian women sitting on the floor in a small, smoke-filled room. Heinekens at the strip club cost $3.25. A female reporter from one of the news weeklies made the comment at the Roadhouse, before ten P.M., that she had never been to a strip club before. James Rainey from the *LA Times* pointed out to her that I used to be a stripper, which is true, but I explained that was over ten years ago. Rainey, who is forty-four and has three children, is often acknowledged as the best-looking reporter on the bus and would probably make a better stripper than I did.

24. At the last minute, the name is changed. The Winning the War on Terror tour is used for the various stops Dick Cheney and other surrogates make the weeks before.

25. Marc Smith is the founder and host of the first poetry slam in the nation which takes place at the Green Mill in Chicago every Sunday night. The winner of the slam is offered a choice between ten dollars cash or six dollars' worth of lottery tickets each valued at a dollar apiece. The lottery tickets are referred to as the Big John Scam and a lot of people take them. In fact, when I won the poetry slam eight years ago, I also elected for the Big John Scam. But then I like to gamble, and it's a six-dollar cover charge at the door anyway. The lottery tickets offer the only chance to really come out ahead. The nation as a whole is following this philosophy as more and more casinos are moved into impoverished communities desperate for tax dollars. Soon the ghettos will be glittering meccas where the compulsive and agitated will return day after day to feed the one-armed bandits. The idea of casinos being

good for the economy is one of those big lies that, once accepted, has the ability change a person's most basic perceptions.

26. When Ted Koppel ran a *Nightline* special called "The Fallen," highlighting and honoring the American soldiers who have been killed in Iraq, Sinclair Broadcast, an ABC affiliate which owns sixty-two television stations across thirty-nine markets refused to air the program. In their own poll 80 percent of their viewers came out against this decision.

VII. THREE POINTS OF VIEW ON GEORGE W. BUSH

1. *The Anatomy of Fascism* by Robert O. Paxton. I originally wrote an entire section comparing the Bush administration to the young Mussolini. But my editor thought it was heavy-handed, and I had to agree. The analogy doesn't work, even when one takes into account that Mussolini was in power sixteen years before he started killing Jews. If Bush *was* a Fascist all of this would be much easier to understand. But history does not repeat itself. History imitates itself, taking what is useful and discarding the rest. And Fascism was always anti-capitalist. More important, the Fascists didn't possess nuclear bombs.

   Politics never makes sense when one thinks about it too hard. Still it's always a good thing to stay well read. If you think through an idea well enough to see that it doesn't work it might make space for a new idea in its place. Would an appropriate term for the Bush politic be Global Nationalism?

2. I realize on this bus trip that I've become very close with members of the media whom I started out distrusting and disliking. Making the exception for Fox News reporters, who can't be forgiven, most journalists are just people, maybe a little more ambitious than average. I find there are a lot of good people among the press corps, Michael Roselli being just one example.

3. In an effort to sell the new Medicare bill the White House released a tape they prepared using actors imitating reporters saying how great the bill was. Many news stations ran the clips as they were without stating where they got the clips or that the "reporters" did not work for the station.

4. In a way, I never really do meet the president. That is, I never shake his hand and I never exchange a word and I don't think he would recognize me or remember my name. But I think there should be a different standard for "meeting" the president. Just as sleeping with someone doesn't necessarily mean having sex, meeting doesn't have to mean shaking hands. I'm within fifteen feet of the president many times. And if the Secret Service wasn't always hovering around, ready to put me in a half nelson if I even look like I'm thinking about bolting past the velvet rope and lunging toward the leader of the free world, then I would certainly "meet" the president many times.

5. It will turn out to be the wrong day for this. Too many crowds, too much control, too organized. The ones who smile all seem like friendly, brainwashed ro-

bots and the ones who cheer, cheer from anger and hatred and deep-seated ugliness. A rally with people you disagree with is no place to connect. I resolve to find myself a Republican to like tomorrow. I'll call Ben Peterson's father, a California Republican, a patent attorney, and a very likable guy. He gave Ben the floor model TV on which we watched the first season of *Survivor* every Thursday. The first season of *Survivor* was a time of great peacefulness for me. Later, the show got boring and formulaic. Ben left the neighborhood to move in with his girlfriend while I was away on the campaign trail.

6. This depends on whom you ask. If you're asking me I'm going to say not true.

7. Dan went back to school and is now a nurse.

8. I was traveling with two friends who were operating a Bondage Booth at the festival and writing an article on Pulse Ultra, a band playing on the second stage. I learned some startling things while on the tour. First, many people told me the second stage was actually pay-for-play. In other words, Atlantic Records had paid to get Pulse Ultra on the bill. When I started to look into this, everybody denied it. The second thing I learned was that Ozzy wets his pants, at least according to the music critic Jim DeRogatis. To hide this he continually dumps water on himself and sprays the first twenty rows with water, which sucked.

9. The 45-foot bus is painted with red and white stripes across a blue body. According to *USA Today* Hemphill Brothers in Nashville customized the bus, with "executive VIP" interiors. The buses have been used by music stars including Britney Spears, Beyoncé, and Cher and lease for $45,000 a week. The press ride behind in regular buses.

10. Here in my notes I write, "What's that supposed to mean?"

11. This was the first precipitous drop in alcohol tolerance associated with the unhealthy life of the campaign trail. Within three weeks I could not drink even two beers without waking up nauseous. My body was crying for something, but what? It may or may not have been related to the amphetamine I had been prescribed after undergoing a series of tests to determine whether or not I had attention deficit disorder.

12. I realize that all this TV talk makes it seem like I watch a lot of television, but I don't. The only show I make any effort to watch on a regular basis is *The Sopranos*. Still, when something is culturally relevant like *Friends* is then I try to watch it. I've never had my own television and most would call me TV illiterate. I'm like that guy in the *Onion* article who never misses an opportunity to tell you he doesn't own a TV. "You watch the news? I read the news."

13. A week later it would be well known that the administration had a much heavier hand in the creation of the conditions inside the prison. According to a memo from, January 2002, written by White House counsel Alberto R. Gonzales and acquired by *Newsweek*: "In my judgment, this new paradigm renders obsolete Geneva's strict limitations on questioning of enemy prisoners and renders quaint some of its provisions."

14. The secretary of defense and the new head of the prison now assert the rules

of the Geneva Convention *do* apply after all. The secretary says that previously he was referring to Afghanistan, not Iraq. He had forgotten to point that out and they are two years and hundreds of pictures too late.

15. I had bought the purple jumper at Urban Outfitters along with a yellow button-up from the Gap for my author photo shoot. My publisher wanted a picture of me smiling and all of my previous author photos had been dark and unhappy and usually I was dressed in a wife-beater with my tattoo showing. I don't know why I didn't have any happy photos. Anyway, the photographer, Greg Martin, didn't like the shirt or the jumper and dressed me instead in his dark shirt and leather jacket, resulting in the picture you see in the back of this book.

16. Freedy's was the center of West Rogers Park, down Pratt from the grammar school and across the street from the Jewish high school where the students were forbidden to eat at Freedy's. The food at Freedy's was legendary, the best hamburgers on the north side of Chicago along with tight-skinned hot dogs and handcut fries.

VIII. SUMMER'S PROMISE

1. On this particular flight, a nonstop from Chicago O'Hare, the bathroom door would get stuck with an old woman locked inside. I was sitting in the last seat on the airplane, right next to the rest room. She was yelling and rattling the door, and everyone was looking back at me like I had something to do with it.

   "Take it easy," I told her. "I'm calling the stewardess." But it took the stewardess a while to come for some reason, and the lady in the rest room kept kicking at the door, as if that was going to help. I tried to focus on my work and the small bag of pretzels on the tray table next to me. When the stewardess finally arrived she unhinged the latch from the outside.

   "Don't touch the door," the stewardess said, but the woman trapped inside wouldn't listen. Twenty minutes later the woman was finally out. This was not enough of a lesson for the next old woman, who entered the bathroom and locked the door and was also unable to get out. This time I refused to call the stewardess.

2. The response Laura sent me was exactly the one I expected: upbeat, mildly apologetic. "Sorry it took so long to get back to you," etc. In my original request for clarification, I asked Democracy for America to reimburse my expenses. In her reply Laura Gross made no mention of this, probably assuming I was just making a joke. I wrote Laura one more time, saying I would still like to interview Dean in Boston. This time she didn't bother to respond at all.

3. Several days before the caucus, I put five dollars on Howard Dean to take 30 percent. Jeanie bet against her candidate, and when I mentioned it in my Web

log, Matt Drudge featured the bet on his Web site under the headline "Dean Staffer Bets Against Own Candidate." What Drudge had failed to notice was, further down in that same column, I referred to him as a first-rate scumbag. Also, Jeanie had made a good bet based on insider information, which is what you're supposed to do. At any rate, the campaign freaked and word went out that I was looking for dirt. Which wasn't actually true. After all, I was the one betting *for* their candidate.

4. Nothing came together during this time, and I flew around the country like a deranged bat. Lewis and I stayed with State Senator Ethan "Scooby" Strimling, a progressive Democrat in Portland, Maine. Then I went back to San Francisco, where Lemony Snicket and Tobias Wolff denounced George Bush. I had a reading in Los Angeles and I saw Josh Bearman there. He pointed out that there wasn't a lot of point in coming all the way to Los Angeles to do a reading when only six friends showed up, plus a couple of stragglers. I had walked the Sunset Strip to get there and my face was covered in dirt. It was hard to argue with Josh's logic, so instead I asked, "What's the point of being Josh Bearman?" Josh decided that would be the title of his next book. I flew from Los Angeles into Louisiana. I started to get depressed. Every time I opened a newspaper, Dick Cheney told another lie. I realized I was flying all over the country for no good reason. So I moved in with Chad Prather, a dermatologist in New Orleans, for a couple of days and I called Michelle Orange in New York City. She told me that my problem with relationships was that I put the cart before the horse. Chad's apartment is right across the street from the Café du Monde and from his rooftop you can see the entire French Quarter, including the oldest apartment complex in the country. You have to take an elevator to get to his place, and the elevator opens directly into his apartment. I was lying flat on the couch when Michelle told me what my problem was. I agreed with her at first but later, surrounded by the noise of Bourbon Street at three A.M., I decided she was wrong. It was time to go back home and regroup, if only for a couple of days. Things were moving too fast; I wasn't getting any sleep.

5. In May I began organizing and hosting a monthly fund-raiser for Moveon.org featuring Bay Area authors, musicians, and theater groups. At the end of the event, they gave me the cash that I was supposed to deposit and then send as a personal check. After the second event, the responsibility for the money was given to one of the other organizers.

6. Nader's press secretary, Kevin, is right. The hatred of Nader stems from the Left and more than he knows, I think. Three different people, all well-known writers nominated for many awards, have asked me to kill Ralph Nader if I get close enough. Nobody asked me to kill George Bush, even after I said I would get within ten feet of the president. When I point out that liberals hate Ralph Nader more than they hate George Bush, people always laugh first and then deny it. But it's true.

7. Gary McLendon, *The Democrat and Chronicle*, Rochester, New York, May 22, 2004, reports that:

> The May 1 accident was the fifth time since 1999 that a patron has fallen from a ride made by Intamin. In all five cases, the T-bar lap restraint was called into question. Four of the accidents were fatal. The nonfatal occurred in May 1999, when a Cattaraugus County man was thrown from the Superman coaster at Darien Lake and escaped with minor injuries.

8. I stayed with David in October 2000, during the Nader campaign. It was late and I'd been in a van for many hours. Early in the morning his wife, Natalie, arrived from western Texas. She was wearing a see-through white outfit and spoke with an accent that was both British and Venezuelan. While David lectured us that morning on the evils of capitalism and the state's rigged electoral process, I focused on Natalie and wrote out my fantasy of her. But a sheet of my notebook got torn and I didn't notice it still sitting on the couch as we got up to leave a little while later. This act precipitated my final turn as a Green, which came two months later, after the election. Cobb and Natalie arrived in San Francisco and invited me to a party at the house of Green Senate candidate Medea Benjamin. Medea was the big name in San Francisco politics that year. At the party Cobb confronted me with the knowledge that he had found the page from my diary. Natalie was in the other room with a plastic cup of wine in her hand. People were celebrating the election of a Green candidate to the San Francisco school board. David said he was flattered I was attracted to his wife, but the whole thing made me uncomfortable. I went into the kitchen, where Medea was busy washing dishes. Medea told me she had read my dispatches from the campaign and she thought they were sexist. I realized I didn't know anybody and I didn't belong. I'm not a joiner. I left without saying good-bye and changed my e-mail address.

9. The reasoning behind this is fairly specious. Of course most people, especially Republicans, are going to say they would prefer open debates. If another question was asked, "Should John Kerry and George Bush have a right to a debate between themselves?" most people would probably agree with that as well. It's all in how you ask the question. In 2000 Patrick Buchanan, who was polling beneath Ralph Nader, offered to debate Nader. Major media outlets agreed to sponsor the debate. But Nader said he would only take part in debates that included Gore and Bush. Both were polling above Nader. The least popular candidate in a debate always has the most to gain.

10. Two other candidates were also part of the debate, and in fairness I should mention them and their positions, but I've decided not to.

11. In 1976 Camejo ran on the Socialist Workers Party ticket. People in the convention told me that Camejo still spoke like a Socialist.

12. Later, in Seattle, I'll get a phone call from one of the Greens who has left the party to work for Nader. She'll tell me that the Greens and the Nader people

have worked out a system so everything should be OK. But then my phone loses reception and I don't hear the rest of what she has to say.

13. I only heard this from Camejo. I haven't independently verified the story. But it certainly stands up to the Cheney standard of evidence when making a decision to invade another country. "That's never been proven and it's never been refuted," Cheney said when questioned about a meeting between Mohammed Atta and a senior Iraqi official in the Czech Republic. The 9/11 Commission had refuted the meeting days earlier.

14. I went to lunch with Bernie Sanders in the Congressional Office Building a couple weeks later. He explained how Republicans are using wedge issues like guns and marriage to fool poor white voters. In 2000 he was sympathetic to Ralph Nader even though he ultimately supported Al Gore. But this time, he told me, he was doing everything he could for John Kerry and said, in regards to third party candidates like himself and Ralph Nader, "Anybody with common sense understands you can't have a rigid approach to that [third parties]. Not if it means reelecting the most reactionary president in the history of modern America. That's absurd." The day after we met, the House approved an amendment written by Sanders prohibiting the federal government's Export-Import Bank from approving subsidized loan assistance to corporate expatriates—U.S. companies who "moved" their headquarters offshore to avoid U.S. taxes. The bill passed overwhelmingly with two-thirds of the vote.

15. Nader accepted support but not money. Nader only accepts campaign contributions from individuals.

16. On the Nader Web site there's a particularly strange letter to Michael Moore titled, *Hey Michael Where Were Your Friends*, imploring him to return to his true friends and castigating him for not sending Nader and others a personal invitation to a screening of *Fahrenheit 9/11*. The letter finishes with this paragraph: "Your old friends remain committed to blazing paths for a just society and world. As they helped you years ago, they can help you now. They are also trim and take care of themselves. Girth they avoid. The more you let them see you, the less they will see of you. That could be their greatest gift to Moore the Second—the gift of health. What say you?"

Following the letter, Nader continued to talk about Moore's weight with *The Washington Post*. "He's over three hundred pounds. He's like a giant beach ball." Michael Moore's publicist called the whole thing "sad."

17. Following the speech and the fund-raising, Nader took questions from the audience. Two queues formed on either side of the auditorium. But rather than ask questions, most of the participants just offered their praise. Several of them read from prepared remarks, statements of why they support Ralph Nader, using words and phrases like *thereby* and *do solemnly declare*.

IX. THE RISING CURTAIN

1. In the end it seems Kucinich's campaign didn't amount to anything. I saw the first cracks in Iowa, where Edwards tricked Kucinich out of his nonviables. For a while Kucinich was saying that none of the candidates was going to have enough delegates to win the nomination on the first ballot and so the nomination would be decided by the convention. It didn't turn out that way. Once Kerry sewed up the nomination, Kucinich started saying the purpose of his candidacy was to influence the Platform Committee. But when the Kucinich delegates tried to place language in the platform referring to Iraq as an illegal war, the Kerry delegates turned them down and the Kucinich camp folded like a house of cards.

2. On Friday afternoon Josh and I went to meet with Professor Thomas Patterson, author of *The Vanishing Voter*, at his office in the John F. Kennedy School of Government. He pointed out with charts and polls that the stories in the media were mostly irrelevant. "I'll give you two examples," he said. "One of the big issues during the primaries was whether Kerry threw away his medals or his ribbons. That probably tells you nothing about what a President Kerry would be like. Same-sex marriage is another example. It's a great press issue. It has very little to do with the federal government. If John Kerry gets elected I don't know how far down the ladder that issue is going to be, but it's going to be pretty far down."

   Patterson thought it was horrendous that the networks were only showing three hours of live convention coverage. He argued that politicians should be given more time to speak on network news. "It used to be that in a story about a politician the politician would do half of the talking. Now the newsperson does six times as much speaking as the politician."

3. At the beginning of the convention a photographer friend writes to me from Iraq:

   > Still slaving away in Baghdad. It looks like I'm going to miss the elections al-together. Apparently I'm supposed to make sure this bureau can run with just Iraqis once I'm gone. I'm not the boss here, but somehow it's become my re-sponsibility anyway. The whole thing is pretty neo-colonial, and kind of freaks me out. You know, the Western company relying on whitey to make sure the lo-cals don't squander all the money on tribal bullshit. That's exactly what's hap-pening, but no real way to avoid it either. That's just the way business is done. It's been a cultural exchange, I can tell you that. So the bombings continue un-abated, despite the fact that they aren't reported much. There's absolutely no physical way elections can happen here in January, but everyone is busy pre-tending they can't see that train wreck coming, so nobody wants to publish re-ports of it for now. This place is so fucked, it can get a little dispiriting.

4. At the blogger party on Wednesday night Jay Rosen said to me, "If I hear the word *scripted* one more time I'm going to scream. You ever tell somebody their wedding sucked because everything was so scripted?"

5. On July 19 *The New Republic* broke the story that the White House was pressuring Pakistan to capture a major Al Qaeda operative during the Democratic Convention. Several days before John Kerry's acceptance speech the Pakistanis captured Ahmed Khalfan Ghailani, a Tanzanian Al Qaeda operative associated with the 1998 bombings in Kenya and Tanzania. They wait until just hours before John Kerry's acceptance speech to make the announcement (paraphrased from *The New Republic Online*).

Acknowledgments

I'd like to thank the following people for giving me places to stay while on the campaign trail:

California: Geoff Brock, Tom Kealey, Tina Gerhardt, David Roderick, John Lundgren, Ben Peterson, Karina Arambula, Christine and Catharine Fox, Andrew Miller, Joshua Bearman, Thomas McNeeley, Sheryl McGraff
District of Columbia: Natasha Choi, Brian Sutherland
Florida: Larry and Janet Davis
Illinois: Christine Bell
Iowa: Sarah Rogers, Michelle Falkoff, Jennifer Kelly
Louisiana: Chad Prather, Andrew and Dawn Black
Maine: Senator Ethan "Scooby" Strimling
Maryland: Padma Viswanathan
Massachusetts: Silvia Kuo and Brian Knight, Kathleen Geary
New Hampshire: Dave Eggers
New York: George Loew, Tom Bissell
Oregon: Pete Rock, Ella Vining
Vermont: Lewis Rickel
Washington: Ryan Boudinot

I'd also like to thank the following people in the following order who didn't put me up, though some of them offered: Joshua Kendall, Frances Coady, Amber Qureshi, Tanya Farrell, Emily

Haile, Katherine Monaghan, Andrew Foster Altschul, Jessica Partch, Julia Caitlin Craven, Anthony Ha, Karan Mahajan, Alicia Erian, Jamie Berger, Andrew Leland, and Ted Weinstein. I would also like to thank Dave Eggers, who provided the initial opportunity for what would become this book.

Portions of this book previously appeared, in different form, in *The Believer*. Considerably smaller excerpts were published in *SFGate.com*, *McSweeneys.net*, the *San Francisco Chronicle*, *The Sun Magazine*, and *The Village Voice*.

Credits for the Photographs